Michael Field's Revisionary Poetics

Nineteenth-Century and Neo-Victorian Cultures
Series editors: Ruth Heholt and Joanne Ella Parsons

Editorial Board
Rosario Arias, University of Malaga, Spain
Katherine Bowers, University of British Columbia, Canada
Jessica Cox, Brunel University, UK
Laura Eastlake, Edge Hill University, UK
Kate Hext, University of Exeter, UK
Elizabeth Ho, University of Hong Kong, Hong Kong
Tara MacDonald, University of Idaho, USA
Charlotte Mathieson, University of Surrey, UK
Royce Mahawatte, Central Saint Martins, University of the Arts London, UK
John Miller, University of Sheffield, UK
Grace Moore, University of Otago, New Zealand
Antonija Primorac, University of Rijeka, Croatia

Recent books in the series
Domestic Architecture, Literature and the Sexual Imaginary in Europe, 1850–1930
Aina Marti

Assessing Intelligence: The Bildungsroman and the Politics of Human Potential in England, 1860–1910
Sara Lyons

The Idler's Club: Humour and Mass Readership from Jerome K. Jerome to P. G. Wodehouse
Laura Fiss

Michael Field's Revisionary Poetics
Jill Ehnenn

Forthcoming
Lost and Revenant Children 1850–1940
Tatiana Kontou

Olive Schreiner and the Politics of Print Culture, 1883–1920
Clare Gill

Literary Illusions: Performance Magic and Victorian Literature
Christopher Pittard

Pastoral in Early-Victorian Fiction: Environment and Modernity
Mark Frost

Spectral Embodiments of Child Death in the Long Nineteenth Century
Jen Baker

Women's Activism in the Transatlantic Consumers' Leagues, 1885–1920
Flore Janssen

Life Writing and the Nineteenth-Century Market
Sean Grass

British Writers, Popular Literature and New Media Innovation, 1820–45
Alexis Easley

Oscar Wilde's Aesthetic Plagiarisms
Sandra Leonard

The Provincial Fiction of Mitford, Gaskell and Eliot
Kevin A. Morrison

Michael Field's Revisionary Poetics

Jill R. Ehnenn

EDINBURGH
University Press

Edinburgh University Press is one of the leading university presses in the UK. We publish academic books and journals in our selected subject areas across the humanities and social sciences, combining cutting-edge scholarship with high editorial and production values to produce academic works of lasting importance. For more information visit our website: edinburghuniversitypress.com

© Jill Ehnenn 2023, 2024

Edinburgh University Press Ltd
13 Infirmary Street, Edinburgh, EH1 1LT

First published in hardback by Edinburgh University Press 2023

Typeset in 11/13pt Sabon
by Cheshire Typesetting Ltd, Cuddington, Cheshire

A CIP record for this book is available from the British Library

ISBN 978 1 4744 4839 0 (hardback)
ISBN 978 1 4744 4840 6 (paperback)
ISBN 978 1 4744 4841 3 (webready PDF)
ISBN 978 1 4744 4842 0 (epub)

The right of Jill Ehnenn to be identified as the author of this work has been asserted in accordance with the Copyright, Designs and Patents Act 1988, and the Copyright and Related Rights Regulations 2003 (SI No. 2498).

Contents

List of Figures   vi
Acknowledgments   viii
Series Preface   xi

Making All Things New: An Introduction   1

1. Rewriting History: The Early Plays and *Long Ago*   48
2. Ekphrastic Poetics in and after *Sight and Song*   88
3. "Come and sing": Elizabethan Temper, Eco-entanglement, and Lyric in *Underneath the Bough*   133
4. "Our dead": Michael Field and the Elegiac Tradition   169
5. Becoming Catholic, Desiring Disability: Michael Field's Devotional Verse   207

Writing a Life: A Conclusion and a Provocation   232

Bibliography   248
Index   267

Figures

I.1 Bramblebough insignia (c. 1888) from *Sight and Song* title page (1892). Courtesy of the Mark Samuels Lasner Collection, University of Delaware Library, Museums and Press.   9

I.2 Photograph of Michael Field, 1891, Hugo Engler studio, Dresden. Likely copied and placed in an older Bromhead Studio (Bristol) mount dated c. 1884–9. Courtesy of the Mark Samuels Lasner Collection, University of Delaware Library, Museums and Press.   11

I.3 Thyrsus and rings logo from *Underneath the Bough* cover (1893). Designed by Selwyn Image. Courtesy of the Mark Samuels Lasner Collection, University of Delaware Library, Museums and Press.   20

1.1 *Fair Rosamund* (1863). Edward Burne-Jones. Gouache. Private Collection. Courtesy of the Maas Gallery.   60

1.2 Poem XLV from *Long Ago* (1889). Courtesy of the Mark Samuels Lasner Collection, University of Delaware Library, Museums and Press.   80

1.3 *Long Ago* cover (1889). Courtesy of the Mark Samuels Lasner Collection, University of Delaware Library, Museums and Press.   86

1.4 *Long Ago* frontispiece (1889). Courtesy of the Mark Samuels Lasner Collection, University of Delaware Library, Museums and Press.   86

2.1 *St. Catherine of Alexandria* (1510/11). Attributed in 1891 to Bartolomeo Veneto. Oil on poplar. Courtesy of the Städel Museum, Frankfurt am Main.   102

List of Figures   vii

2.2 *Narcissus at the Fountain* (1510/11). Altobello Meloni. Oil on poplar. Courtesy of the Städel Museum, Frankfurt am Main.   102
2.3 *The Wedding of Ariadne and Bacchus* (1578). Jacopo Tintoretto. Oil on canvas. Courtesy of the Sala dell'Anticollegio, Palazzo Ducale, Venice.   109
2.4 *Kneeling Leda and the Swan* (1505/10). Leonardo da Vinci. Pen and brown ink over black chalk. Courtesy of the Museum Boijmans Van Beuningen, Rotterdam.   114
2.5 *Circe and Her Lovers in a Landscape* (c. 1525). Dosso Dossi. Oil on paper. Courtesy of the National Gallery, Washington, DC.   118
2.6 *Portrait of Composer Adrian Willaert at the Spinet* (c. 1550–90). Jacopo Tintoretto. Courtesy of the Colonna Gallery, Rome.   121
2.7 Pendant (three views): *Pegasus Drinking from the Fountain of Hippocrene* (1901). Carlo and Arthur Giuliano and Charles de Sousy Ricketts. Gold, enameled in royal blue, green, red, and white, and set with four cut garnets, a cabochon garnet, two large pearls, one small pearl, and a baroque pearl. Courtesy of the Fitzwilliam Museum, Cambridge.   125
2.8 Sketch of Charles Ricketts. Pencil on paper. Courtesy of the Bodleian Library, Oxford. MS. Eng. misc. c. 654/3 fol. 27r.   131
6.1 *Works and Days: The Diary of Michael Field.* Journal entry dated February 28, 1893. Hand of Katharine Bradley (top) and Edith Cooper (bottom). Courtesy of the British Library, London. MSS Add. 46781. folio 22r.   237

Acknowledgments

Writing this book during an administrative gig, four years of political tumult, and a global pandemic gave much-needed creative purpose and pleasurable intellectual focus to my days, even when writing was difficult, which of course it often is. I could not have completed it without the sustained help and support of family, friends, and colleagues near and far.

For generous and generative feedback on chapter drafts at various stages (including earlier and related article incarnations) I am incredibly grateful to Joseph Bristow, Kimberly Cox, Carolyn Dever, Dennis Denisoff, Gail Hamner, Nathan K. Hensley, Martha Stoddard Holmes, Linda K. Hughes, Randy Johnson, Beth Newman, Sarah Parker, Marion Thain, Ana Parejo Vadillo, Heather Bozant Witcher, and the reviewers at Edinburgh University Press. For brilliant answers to often random research questions, I owe a huge debt of gratitude to Sharon Bickle, Stephen Calloway, Julie Codell, Paul Delaney, Carl Eby, Dino Felluga, Kate Flint, Dustin Friedman, Pamela Gilbert, Amy Huseby, Michael Hurley, Joshua King, Mark Samuels Lasner, Michelle Lee, Diana Maltz, Kristin Mahoney, Fiona Mann, Ruth McAdams, Alex Murray, Fred Roden, Jason Rudy, Talia Schaffer, Margaret Stetz, and Paul van Cappelleveen. And for camaraderie, support, and conversations that resulted in insights and improvements large and small, I am thankful for my fellow travelers at Appalachian State University: Joseph Bathanti, Sushmita Chatterjee, Tina Groover, Alison Gulley, Elaine O'Quinn, David Orvis, Susan Staub, and Jennifer Wilson. Writing is, indeed, a collaborative endeavor.

Michelle Houston and Susannah Butler at Edinburgh University

Press get their own paragraph for their incredible patience and guidance. Thank you for believing in this book.

My work on this project has been eased by the skilled assistance of librarians Greta Browning and Breanna Crumpton at Appalachian; numerous archivists and staff at the Bodleian, the British Library, and the National Library of Scotland; Helena Ritchie at the Fitzwilliam Museum; Stephan Dahme at Klassik Stiftung Weimar, and Stefania Girometti and Bastian Eclercy at the Städel Museum, Frankfurt am Main.

For financial support for travel to archives, thanks to the Department of English, the College of Arts and Sciences, and the University Research Council at Appalachian State University. Thanks also to my graduate research assistants Hannah Chaney and Sophia Donadio.

Extracts from unpublished Michael Field papers appear with permission of The British Library, The Bodleian Library, and The National Library of Scotland, and with the very kind permission and support of the literary executors of The Michael Field Estate: Leonie Sturge-Moore and Charmian O'Neil. For permission to reproduce images I am especially grateful to the Mark Samuels Lasner Collection, University of Delaware Library, Museums and Press. Acknowledgment for images is also due to The Maas Gallery, London; The Städel Museum, Frankfurt am Main; Sala dell'Anticollegio, Palazzo Ducale, Venice; Museum Boijmans Van Beuningen, Rotterdam; National Gallery, Washington, DC; Colonna Gallery, Rome; The Fitzwilliam Museum, Cambridge; The Bodleian Library, Oxford; and The British Library, London.

A portion of the introduction was originally published in a section of "'Our Brains Struck Fire Each from Each': Disidentification, Difference, and Desire in the Collaborative Aesthetics of Michael Field" which appeared in *Economies of Desire at the Victorian Fin de Siècle: Libidinal Lives* (Routledge, 2016. pp.180–204). It is reprinted here with permission from Routledge. Chapter 2's discussion of Saint Katherine reprints, with some revision, a section of "On Art Objects and Women's Words: Ekphrasis in Vernon Lee (1887), Graham R. Tomson (1889), and Michael Field (1892)" which can be found in *BRANCH: Britain, Representation, and Nineteenth-Century History* under a Creative Commons license. Chapter 4 is a revised and expanded version of "'Dragging at Memory's Fetter': Michael Field's Personal Elegies, Victorian Mourning, and the Problem of Whym Chow" (*The Michaelian* 1,

June 2009) and appears here with permission from Rivendale Press. A version of Chapter 5 was originally published as "'Thy body maketh a solemn song': Desire and Disability in Michael Field's 'Catholic Poems'" in *Michael Field, Decadent Moderns* (Ohio UP, 2019. pp. 188–209). It is reprinted here in a revised and expanded version with permission from Ohio University Press.

To my parents and other family members, especially Kenny, Rory, and Sheila, you are a consistent and loving source of warm support and inspiration, for which I am truly grateful. To Sam and Frodo, my feline companions, you came into my home and heart during the last third of this project and have filled my writing space with immeasurable light and joy. And finally, to Kim, my beloved partner in all things, thank you for being with me every step of the way and for reading every word. You make me a better writer, a better thinker, and a better person. You give me hope; and you help me make all things new.

Series Preface

Nineteenth-Century and Neo-Victorian Cultures
Series Editors: Ruth Heholt and Joanne Ella Parsons

This interdisciplinary series provides space for full and detailed scholarly discussions on nineteenth-century and Neo-Victorian cultures. Drawing on radical and cutting-edge research, volumes explore and challenge existing discourses, as well as providing an engaging reassessment of the time period. The series encourages debates about decolonising nineteenth-century cultures, histories, and scholarship, as well as raising questions about diversities. Encompassing art, literature, history, performance, theatre studies, film and TV studies, medical and the wider humanities, *Nineteenth Century and Neo-Victorian Cultures* is dedicated to publishing pioneering research that focuses on the Victorian era in its broadest and most diverse sense.

Dedicated to the memories of
José Fumero (1924–2016) and
Rosemary Horowitz (1952–2021).

In their unique ways they each lived for art . . .
. . . and loved retelling a good story.

Making All Things New: An Introduction

> Immature poets imitate; mature poets steal; bad poets deface what they take, and good poets make it into something better, or at least something different.
> —T.S. Eliot, *The Sacred Wood* (1920)

All authors try to do something new: to tell a new story, or tell an old one in a new way. This book is about two late nineteenth-century female co-authors who were passionate about rewriting old histories and stories and who did so with extraordinary innovation—what we might call revisionary poetics. Indeed, for aunt and niece Katharine Harris Bradley (1846–1914) and Edith Emma Cooper (1862–1913), who called themselves "Poets and lovers" and who wrote as Michael Field,[1] the revisionary poetics of repurposing old stories, histories, and traditional literary forms was nothing short of high art.

In 1892, Bradley wrote the following in a letter to her beloved life and writing partner: "To see things for oneself, to speak of them as they really are to oneself, to face life with unbiased eyes as the men who began literature did—this is the longing of the modern world."[2] Here, echoing a Paterian aestheticism as she also expresses affinity for "the men who began literature," Bradley

---

[1] Throughout the book, I'll use Michael Field when referring to published work and Bradley and Cooper or their respective nicknames Michael and Henry when referring to biographical events. Generally, but not always, I will use plural pronouns and verbs in sentences that contain the plural name, Michael Field.
[2] Archive of "Michael Field." MS Eng lett d 120. Oxford, Bodleian Libraries. Subsequent references to this collection will be footnoted by shelfmark.

articulates both a fascination for the past and a keen sympathy with the affect of the modern world. Indeed, for collaborative authors and female aesthetes whose *oeuvre* is so clearly inspired by figures and literary forms from the past, both Bradley and Cooper devote considerable energy in their diaries and letters, both of their own volition and at the urging of their friends, to the modern and the new. In their diaries and letters we learn that even while admiring many of Michael Field's adaptations of figures and texts from the past, their friend, art critic Bernard Berenson, repeatedly advised them to "Be Contemporaneous;"[3] and when in 1888 their work was not received as warmly as they wished, Robert Browning counseled them to "wait fifty years."[4] For every published treatment of figures such as Sappho, Mary Queen of Scots, La Gioconda, Callirrhoë, and Canute the Great, and for every reworking of the Sapphic fragment, Elizabethan and Jacobean verse drama, paintings by Grand Masters, Renaissance lyric, elegy, or devotional verse, in Michael Field's more private writings we can also find the co-authors repeatedly expressing sentiments such as "I do not yet realize where modernity is taking me,"[5] and "We must make all things new."[6]

Michael Field's Revisionary Poetics asks: How does experimentation with literary form and genre help Michael Field navigate the paradox of looking backward in order to achieve their stated goal to be contemporaneous and to make all things new? How do the coauthors' anachronisms and formal literary innovations function in the context of being homoerotically-inclined, female authors and Aesthetes dealing with both the exciting and the dis-

---

[3] *Works and Days: The Unpublished Journals of Michael Field*. MSS Add. 46781, July 12, 1893. (KB). fol. 47v. The British Library, London. Throughout, I'll use shelfmarks in footnotes to reference quotes from the unpublished diaries, indicating the hand of the scribe as either KB or EC. I'll use in-text citations with the abbreviation WD before the page number to refer to quotes from the diary that can be found in T. Sturge Moore's edition of *Works and Days, from the Journal of Michael Field*.

[4] *Works and Days*. MSS Add. 46777, 1888–9. (KB). fol. 5r. The British Library.

[5] *Works and Days*. MSS Add. 46781, December 31, 1893. (EC). fol. 104r. The British Library.

[6] The co-authors repeat variations on this sentiment over the years, including a letter KB to EC, August 31, 1882 (in Bickle, *Fowl* 64); after Tennyson's funeral, *Works and Days*, MSS Add. 46780, October 12, 1892. (KB). fol. 140r; and after Whym Chow's death, *Works and Days*, MSS Add. 46795, January 1906. (EC). fol. 20v.

tressing aspects of late-Victorian modernity? Through an interdisciplinary approach that considers Michael Field's passionate and sometimes eccentric diaries, verse, and drama in context of their influences (both historical and contemporary), my aim in this book is to provide new analyses of both familiar and undertheorized selections from their works with particular attention to the phenomenology and form of their revisionary poetics; to provoke thought about Michael Field's *fin de siècle* milieu; and to more firmly situate the co-authors as important bridge figures between Victorian and modernist styles and thought. At the same time, I also invite current literary critics and students, like Michael Field themselves, to innovatively and perhaps anachronistically engage the past in order to make sense of the present.

Here I employ a threefold method, braiding together historical, phenomenological, and formalist concerns in my interrogation of Michael Field's revisionary poetics. Over a decade has passed since the first monograph on Michael Field was published: Marion Thain's *'Michael Field', Poetry, Aestheticism, and the Fin de Siècle* (2007). Thain's work complicates earlier scholarship focused mostly on the fact of Michael Field's lesbianism and dual-authorship. She identifies "paradox as the paradigm underlying Michael Field poetry" (16) and examines the temporal paradoxes driving each of Field's major poetic works in order to demonstrate how, for the co-authors, "the dialectics of life are turned into art" (17). A wealth of Michael Field criticism has followed, including two important collections by Margaret Stetz and Cheryl Wilson (2007) and Sarah Parker and Ana Parejo Vadillo (2019) and Carolyn Dever's full-length study of Field's joint diary (2022); this scholarship has successfully moved Michael Field out of the margins and firmly into the canon of Victorian literary study. My intent in *Michael Field's Revisionary Poetics* is to complicate and deepen our knowledge of the quirky, prolific, and innovative co-authors, not only by building on previous scholarly interventions but also by capitalizing, when opportune, upon the rich theoretical developments that have emerged in the academy subsequent to Thain's foundational work. New developments and debates regarding historicism and presentism, queer subjectivities, queer ecologies, and queer temporality, phenomenology and the affective turn, New Formalism, and disability studies usefully inform the work I do here, which coalesces in the following triad of claims as its thesis: (1) Michael Field's *oeuvre* can be read as a series of ambitious experiments with literary traditions and forms; (2) their revisionary poetics are shaped by a Dionysian eros and queer-feminist sensibility that complicates their otherwise Paterian aesthetics and Hegelian view of history; and (3) we can observe, in their varied formal and historical experiments, an affective orientation toward and phenomenological engagement with the unknowable and unutterable that, among other things, also reflects their status as embodied female, homoerotically inclined *fin de siècle* subjects.

I've organized each chapter of this book around Michael Field's revisionary engagement with a specific literary-historical form: a concept, device, or genre. I do so with attention to the fact that Michael Field's formal interests emerged chronologically, yet they tended to hold on to and revisit forms and genres even after their initial project on that form was completed: for instance, they wrote closet drama and elegies throughout their career, *Long Ago* is not the only project invoking the fragment, they continued to produce ekphrases after *Sight and Song*, etc. Before I further explain the complex methodological foundations that frame my study and before I outline the specific premises of each chapter, the next two sections will provide context: first, a substantial chronological review of Michael Field's life and works; and then, a biographically inflected accounting of Bradley and Cooper as queer female aesthetes writing within and against the male-centered movements of Aestheticism and Decadence.

"Our united life"

On October 27, 1846, Katharine Harris Bradley was born into a family of prosperous tobacco manufacturers living near Birmingham. Her parents, James Bradley and Emma Harris, were members of an intellectual and political family and Bradley's early years, although unmarked by formal education, indicate an early love of the classics and writing poetry.[7] In 1861, Bradley, then fifteen, with her widowed mother, moved to Kenilworth to live

---

[7] Mary Sturgeon's *Michael Field*, Emma Donoghue's *We Are Michael Field*, Marion Thain's *Michael Field and Poetic Identity, with a Biography*, Sharon Bickle's *The Fowl and the Pussycat: Love letters of Michael Field, 1879–1909*, and Carolyn Dever's *Chains of Love and Beauty: The Diary of Michael Field*, each offer rich detail of Bradley's and Cooper's lives.

with Bradley's elder sister Emma (Lissie) and her new husband, James Cooper. Edith Emma Cooper was born there on January 12, 1862, and as Marion Thain observes, "Katharine became to Edith everything one woman can be to another: mother, aunt, sister, friend, and eventually, lover" (Thain, *Poetry* 3). When in 1865 Lissie became largely bedridden after the birth of her second daughter, Amy, Bradley helped to run the extended Bradley-Cooper household. In 1867 they moved to Newton Leys, "an old farmhouse property known as Parwich Leys set in the beautiful countryside near Tissington" (in Treby 28). In 1868, during her mother's last months, Bradley began a diary, a practice that she'd keep only spottily until 1888, when Cooper and Bradley would begin to faithfully compose the double-voiced journal, *Works and Days*, from which scholars and historians now can glean so much about their lives and their literary and cultural milieu. Mrs. Bradley died in May 1868 and by October Bradley was studying at the College de France in Paris. There, the 22-year-old developed "a passionate attachment" to sculptor and stained glass artist Alfred Gérente, who was the brother of a friend and twenty-five years her senior (in Treby 28). Gérente was the first in a long line of father-figure/mentors for Bradley, and her grief over his sudden death in late 1868 culminated in a notebook of poems characterized by the wild passions that would later become a distinguishing mark for both Bradley and Cooper. Despite Bradley's later writings about her intellectual, romantic, and physical admiration of various men throughout her life, it seems that Gérente was the only male that she ever seriously considered a love-object.

Upon her return to England and the Bradley-Cooper household, Bradley continued and young Cooper began writing both verse and drama. Lissie was a creative and intellectual influence upon Katharine, Edith, and Amy. The family moved back near Birmingham, to Solihull in 1873; and the next year Bradley documented that she went up "emptyheaded" to Newnham College, Cambridge (Treby 28). There, as part of the first small cohort of female students, Bradley met the first female lecturer in economics at Cambridge, Mary Paley Marshall, who referred to Bradley as "The Newnham poet" (Bickle, *Fowl* xvii). As she continued to develop her intellectual, aesthetic, and political interests amid the female homosocial world of Newnham, Bradley studied both modern and ancient literatures, notably Greek. In 1875, at the age of twenty-nine and likely influenced by *Aurora Leigh*, Bradley published her first verse collection *The New Minnesinger* under the name Arran Leigh and circulated it to all the men of letters she could think of. The family moved to Ivythorpe, Freshford, near Bath in 1876. It is around this time that Cooper dubbed Bradley with the nicknames "Sim" and "AWF" for "All Wise Fowl"—both references to the simiorg of Persian mythology. Cooper's nickname was "P.P." or "Persian Puss." Also around this time, Bradley became a devotee of John Ruskin, seeking his mentorship and joining his Guild of St. George. However, the productivity of the relationship was short-lived; and as Thain demonstrates at length, their correspondence in 1877 and 1878 provides a picture of Ruskin's escalating attacks upon Bradley's literary ambitions, largely on the basis of her sex. He advised her against dreaming and reading books, and urged her to curb her "moribund intellectual tendency." Bradley records particularly devastating excerpts from Ruskin's letters: "you thought yourself very clever and are astonished that I think nothing of your poetry—and less than nothing of your power of thought (*WD* 158); but ultimately gives up on him, concluding, "There is to me a speckled silliness in Ruskin's dealings with women" (*WD* 115).

In 1879, when the family moved to Stoke Bishop near Bristol, Bradley, now thirty-three, and Cooper, seventeen, began to attend University College, where they would take classes over the next five years. There, according to biographer Mary Sturgeon, they championed "Higher Education and Women's Rights and Anti-Vivisection ... and aesthetic dress" (20). Cooper took a first in philosophy, Bradley continued with Greek; they visited art galleries and avidly read Swinburne, Pater, Morris, and D. G. Rossetti; they joined the debating society and were enthusiastic participants in a circle of women committed to social reform. Friends describe Bradley here and throughout her life as hearty and robust: "emphatic, splendid and adventurous in talk, quick in wit" (Rothenstein ix). Cooper possessed a more ethereal beauty: delicate in health, more reserved in conversation, and more spiritual and intellectual in her manner. In 1881, under the pseudonyms Arran and Isla Leigh, Bradley and Cooper published their first joint play, *Bellerophôn*, which Wendy Bashant reads as "a pledge of the principles of the aesthetic movement" and "a sharp critique" of Ruskin's essay *The Queen of the Air* (74–5). Their contemporary, Professor Edward Dowden, described the work: "in one word, FIRE!" (in Treby 29). These were busy years in which their letters indicate an awakening sense of one another as both romantic and artistic partners: they wrote love poetry to one another, referred to one another as "man and wife," and conceived of and began to bring to fruition several early plays and poems. They continued their efforts to place themselves more centrally among the established and rising stars of the English literary world; they hosted and attended literary soirees; and notably, in 1883 after Cooper published an appreciative essay on Robert Browning's "Jocoseria" in *Modern Thought*, they began a correspondence with him that would develop into a deep friendship and mentorship.

In 1884, soon after moving to Stoke Green, Bristol, "Michael Field" made "his" literary debut with the verse plays *Callirrhoë* and *Fair Rosamund*, both to great acclaim. Over the next two years the coauthors added J. A. Symonds, George Meredith, Mark Andre Raffalovich, Algernon Swinburne, Arthur Symons, John Miller Gray, A. Mary F. Robinson, and Havelock Ellis to their list of correspondents, and met Browning in person for the first time at the home of the influential author and philanthropist Anna Swannick, who, like Bradley and Cooper, was a translator of German and Greek. Michael Field soon published the verse dramas *The Father's Tragedy/William Rufus/Loyalty or Love?* followed by verse in *The Spectator* and, in 1886, verse in *The Contemporary Review* and the dramatic work *Brutus Ultor*. They were thrilled when Browning told them their work was "indubitable poetic genius," (WD 2) and that he had announced at a dinner party that "there is a new poet." But they also worried that he had inadvertently revealed that Michael Field was not a man. "I beg you to set the critics on a wrong track," they wrote to Browning:

> We each know that you mean good to us: and are persuaded you thought that by "our secret" we meant the dual authorship. The revelation of that would indeed be utter ruin to us; but the report of lady authorship will dwarf and enfeeble our work at every turn ... We have much to say that the world will not tolerate from a woman's lips. (*WD* 6)

In 1886, they visited Scotland, touring Edinburgh with John Miller Gray. In 1887 two more historical verse dramas were published: *Canute the Great* and *The Cup of Water*.

In 1888 Bradley, Cooper, and the extended family moved to Blackboro' Lodge, Reigate, and, likely referring to the bramblebough woodcut insignia that, a "symbol of our united life,"[8] graced the front matter of many of their early published works (see Fig. I.1), they wrote "we hope boldly to transform the name into Blackberry" (in Treby 31). The following year would be one marked by both triumph and tragedy. *Long Ago* was published, to much praise. In its revision of Sappho's fragments, Michael Field's *Long Ago* had been greatly influenced by H. T. Wharton's *Sappho, Memoir, Text, Select Renderings and a Literal Translation* (1884), which made the homoeroticism of Sappho's work perceptible to the general reader for the first time. But in August 1889 Cooper's mother finally died; and following another trip to Edinburgh to continue their research on Mary Queen of Scots, in December Robert Browning "goes evergreen to God" (in Treby 31). Bradley and Cooper deeply felt the loss of these two beloved and influential figures but nevertheless continued juggling several poetic and dramatic works in progress. By now, their circle of correspondents had expanded to include Vernon Lee and A. W. Ward, and they met Herbert Spencer, Selwyn Image, Herbert Horne, and W. M. Rossetti.

Over the years, Bradley and Cooper had often traveled to visit friends and mentors; they had taken short seaside holidays, made research trips to explore various historical sites, and frequently ventured to London for plays, lectures, galleries, concerts, and the British Library. But the death of Lissie Cooper gave the co-authors, especially Cooper, a greater sense of freedom that permitted the couple to travel to the Continent and for longer periods of time. In 1890 they toured Paris, Italy, and Switzerland; meeting art historian and critic Bernard Berenson for the first time, focusing deeply on learning about art history from him and taking detailed notes on the paintings that would become the "picture-poems" of *Sight and Song*. In the same year, *The Tragic Mary*, a protofeminist, highly sympathetic, and somewhat homoerotic portrayal of Mary Queen of Scots was published with a celebrated cover design by Selwyn Image. Upon their return to England, Edith's father James moved the family to Durdans, where they created a "House Beautiful" and lived in relative seclusion for the next nine years. Surrounded by wallpaper and carpets from Morris & Co., custom furniture, Etruscan pottery, Jacobean brasses and a

---

[8] For more on the bramblebough, see Ehnenn "Our Brains" and Thomas "Vegetable Love."

SIGHT AND SONG WRITTEN
BY MICHAEL FIELD

ELKIN MATHEWS
AND JOHN LANE
AT THE SIGN OF
THE BODLEY HEAD
IN VIGO STREET
LONDON 1892

Fig. I.1 Bramblebough insignia (c. 1888) from *Sight and Song* title page (1892). Courtesy of the Mark Samuels Lasner Collection, University of Delaware Library, Museums and Press.

"Bacchic library," they devoted themselves to their life and work together, against the world as "Poets and Lovers." Yet despite their self-imposed isolation, the Reigate, Surrey location continued to provide easy access to London, where among intellectual and other cultural pleasures, they attended lectures by Berenson and Walter Pater and industriously continued to expand their network of literary acquaintances. In London they met George Moore and Oscar Wilde at the popular salon of Louise Chandler Moulton, the American poet and critic who had written a glowing review of *The Tragic Mary* for the *Boston Sunday Herald*. Ivor Treby notes that when the 1891 census records "James R. Cooper, widower, and his family living with two servants," Bradley and Cooper are each listed as "Dramatist Author" (in Treby 32). No doubt they informed the census taker of their professions with much gusto and pride.

A visit to Dresden to see galleries and the opera in the summer of 1891 resulted in both Bradley and Cooper being hospitalized with scarlet fever. There, Cooper's hair was cut boyishly short (see Fig. I.2), which resulted in the permanent nickname, "Henry," and she resisted the erotic advances of a female nurse. From her description of the event, it is clear that "Henry" was familiar with what the nurse wanted, but she kindly but firmly declined, eventually recovering from her illness and returning to Bradley's arms. They returned to England via a gallery trip to Frankfurt and began corresponding with the artist-couple Charles Ricketts and Charles Shannon, who had reached out in praise of *The Tragic Mary*. The ekphrastic collection *Sight and Song* was published in 1892 and was widely admired; according to *The Academy*, it was "the most Keatsian thing since Keats" (Donoghue 69). That summer they embarked upon what would become a painful holiday to Paris with Berenson and Mary Costelloe, taking art lessons from Berenson, and participating in a pattern of love-hate interactions that would persist for many years to come. Both Cooper and Bradley passionately admired Berenson, who was soon to enter into long-lasting affair with Costelloe. They returned to England to write, "We hate him, we hate him" (in Treby 32).

Stephania was published in late 1892; according to Michelle Lee, their retelling of the deposed Roman empress departs from Decadent representations of the courtesan, adopts Symbolist tenets in its structure, and in so doing, critiques "English Art in decay and in need of resuscitation through women's choices, resilience,

Fig. I.2 Photograph of Michael Field, 1891, Hugo Engler studio, Dresden. Likely copied and placed in an older Bromhead Studio (Bristol) mount dated c. 1884–9. Courtesy of the Mark Samuels Lasner Collection, University of Delaware Library, Museums and Press.

and intrepidity" (127). A round of apologetically negative reviews indicate that *Stephania* marked the beginning of "a downward spiral" for Michael Field's success as dramatists (Lee 137). The following year they begin a correspondence with decadent poet, John (Dorian) Gray, about his collection of verse, *Silverpoints* (1893). Bradley began using an old nickname "Michael" with increasing frequency; soon most of their circle referred to the co-authors as Michael and Henry, or collectively, "The Michaels." They again met up with Berenson and Costelloe during an extended trip to Paris and Italy. *Underneath the Bough* (1893), a verse collection inspired by Renaissance lyric and Omar Khayyám was published, as was the play *A Question of Memory* (1893), the only drama in their *oeuvre* on a contemporary subject. The latter was performed at The Independent Theatre, with disastrous results. Despite their relative success as poets Bradley and Cooper also yearned for fame as dramatists and were increasingly dispirited that their ongoing efforts in verse drama never earned the accolades enjoyed by their earlier plays. Nevertheless, as aesthetes and creative souls, their blossoming friendship with Ricketts and Shannon, whom they called "The Artists" and "The Painters," provided much solace; they recognized a deep kinship with the artist-couple, writing in 1894 "we have walked into a friendship as deep as mowing-grass" and "Ricketts adores Shannon as I adore Henry" (in Treby 33).

The long-lasting friendship with "The Painters," especially in its early years, also stands in contrast to Michael Field's ongoing tumultuous personal and professional relationship with Berenson. *Works and Days* reveals how Cooper struggled over the years to balance her love for both Berenson and Bradley, especially in light of that fact that Berenson, who considered Cooper a kind of intellectual handmaiden, had a paralyzing effect on her writing, in contrast to Bradley who nurtured and facilitated it.[9] Meanwhile Bradley attempted to give Cooper the space to explore her (unrequited) passion for Berenson while managing her own jealousy and insecurities. Both Bradley and Cooper yearned for Berenson's advice and praise; yet bristled mightily when he repeatedly proved

---

[9] In October 1894, Cooper writes of Berenson, "[he]e would like me to be his Maenad; he has no intention of serving me (*Works and Days*, MSS Add. 46782. 93r, 93v. The British Library). For more on Edith and Bernard see Vicinus, "Faun Love"; Ehnenn, "Our Brains"; Dever, *Chains of Love and Beauty*.

to be more cutting than constructive in his criticism. One might suspect that, despite the pain Berenson frequently caused them, Bradley and Cooper, ever pursuant of living with Dionysian passion, fed off the turmoil and personal drama.

During the next two decades, Michael Field continued to publish closet drama (mostly tragedy), much of it featuring gorgeous Art Nouveau covers, illuminations, and other decorative elements by Ricketts and Shannon, who also created sculpture, jewelry, a fan, and other gifts for them over the years. The latter verse dramas are: *Atillia, My Atilla!* (1895), a revision of *Fair Rosamund* (1897), *The World at Auction* (1898), *Anna Ruina* (1899), the masque *Noontide Branches* (1899), *The Race of Leaves* (1901), *Julia Domna* (1903), *Borgia* (1905), *Queen Mariamne* (1908), *The Tragedy of Pardon*, and, *Dian, A Fantasy* (1911), and *The Accuser, Tristan De Léonois, A Messiah* (1911). None were particularly well received although it is important to note that *Borgia*, which was published anonymously, along with the subsequent plays which were published by "the author of *Borgia*," fared much better with the critics than those by Michael Field, by then widely known to be two women. The gendered dynamic of this fact was indeed noted by Bradley and Cooper (Thain, *Poetic* 10). More plays were published posthumously under the name Michael Field: *Deidre* (1918), a revision of *A Question of Memory* (1918), *Ras Byzance* (1918), and *In the Name of Time* (1919).[10]

In 1897, as Emma Donoghue chronicles, "for the first time their quiet family life became a public tragedy, in what the papers called 'The Zermatt Mystery'" (94). As they had done the two summers prior, James Cooper and his younger daughter Amy went on a mountaineering trip in the Alps, but this one was to end with James's disappearance. His frantic daughters and sister-in-law enlisted the help of the Secret Police and the devoted assistance of an Alpine climber, Edward Whymper, but the women eventually returned from the Continent with the mystery still unsolved. James's body was found four months later at the bottom of a forty-foot precipice. Donoghue describes how Bradley and Cooper

---

[10] All these later plays, along with various essays that appeared in *The Contemporary Review* and other journals, deserve much more attention than they have so far been given by literary critics; but it is well beyond of the scope of this project, which will only examine a selection of the early dramas in Chapter 1, to address them here.

returned to Switzerland for the funeral, retraced James's steps, and "at the summit, they exchanged rings, feeling more wedded than ever because of their loss" (95). A few months later, in January of 1898, a golden-red chow puppy arrived from the Sturges (friends from Bristol) for Cooper as a birthday present. She and Bradley named the dog Whym Chow after Edward Whymper; and their passionate devotion to Whym, who become a sort of familiar for Michael as well as a symbol for their shared love, grew to far exceed their love for any dog they had previously welcomed into their family.

Ricketts and Shannon convinced Bradley and Cooper to become their neighbors in 1899 and "The Poets" moved to Richmond, where "The Painters" had moved a year before. They leased 1 Paragon on the Thames, the first home that belonged, from the start, only to them; and decorated "our married home" in an updated Aesthetic style with delicate eighteenth-century satinwood furniture, gold and silver Japanese wallpaper, Hiroshige prints, sculpture by Ricketts, and lithographs by Shannon. In the following years, they often visited with the Sturge Moores, Ricketts and Shannon (who helped them with their "Roman Trilogy") and they met Yeats. Frequent ill-health prevented further travel to the Continent, though they continued to take trips more locally, notably to the New Forest and multiple stays at Rottingdean. Berenson, who by now had married Mary Costelloe, was again a welcome but frequently irritating presence in their home, as well as *Silverpoints* poet John Dorian Gray, who was now a Catholic priest.

Tragedy struck again in January 1906 when Whym Chow developed a brain disease. As guns were not permitted in Richmond, Bradley took the beloved Whym to Twickenham so she could put him out of his misery by the bullet, "as a gentleman."[11] He was buried in the garden at Paragon in an elaborate funeral and over the subsequent months the Michaels poured out their grief in poetry and in the pages of their shared journal, much to the irritation of The Painters, especially Ricketts, with whom Bradley began to spat. In December they declared their interest in becoming Catholic and during the following year their lives became filled with visits and letters from Father John Gray, Catholic chemist

---

[11] *Works and Days*. MSS Add. 46795, January 28, 1906. (EC). fol 18r. The British Library.

and politician Emily Fortey, and two new priests who become friends, confessors, and spiritual mentors: Gerald Fitzgibbon, who they called Gosscannon, and Vincent McNabb. Cooper converted in April, 1907. Her sister Amy, who had married Professor of Experiential Physics and Engineering John Ryan in 1899 and had moved to Ireland, converted in May, as did Bradley. Early in 1908 Michael Field published *Wild Honey from Various Thyme*, their longest and most complex verse collection, with poems written over the past decades. *Wild Honey* celebrates each other, Whym Chow, Ricketts and other friends, both pagan and Catholic sentiments, and "The Longer Allegiance"—an elegiac section that documents their passage through the grief of losing James in his tragic mountain accident.

Bradley and Cooper's final years were greatly influenced by illness and by their ever-increasing engagement with Catholic ritual and theology, especially their interest in the Spanish mystics St. John of the Cross and St. Teresa of Ávila. In 1910 Amy died of influenza at the age of forty-six, and Cooper suffered hysterical blindness for over a month in her grief. Michael Field continued to publish closet drama while they experimented with writing three books of devotional verse: *Poems of Adoration* (1912, written mostly by Cooper), *Mystic Trees* (1913, written mostly by Bradley), and the posthumous *The Wattlefold* (1930), edited by Emily Fortey. Cooper was diagnosed with terminal cancer in early 1911 but refused morphine so she could remain clear-headed and continue to write. She viewed her pain as bringing her closer to God and, "When the pain is very bad, Michael takes me in her arms, & the vital warmth of her being is of such power the pain goes to sleep" (in Donoghue 134). Bradley nursed Cooper devotedly over the next three years; her letters and verse from this time indicate how very great a physical and emotional toll it took upon her. Bradley herself developed breast cancer in June 1913, telling only Father McNabb and refusing a potentially remedial operation. Cooper died December 13, 1913, a month before she would have been fifty-two. Bradley would follow nine months later; but before she died she managed to publish two more books of verse by Michael Field: *Whym Chow: Flame of Love* (1914) as a loving tribute to Whym and Henry; and *Dedicated: An Early Work of Michael Field* (1914), which, with the pagan flavor of the co-authors' earlier work, featured many poems written between 1899 and 1902. Bradley continued to write in *Works and Days* during her pain-filled last months; the diary documents frequent communication with Tommy Sturge Moore—who was to become her executor—her confessors, ongoing visits with the Berensons, Ricketts and Shannon, and trips to church: "I motor to Mass past bracken, heather, & firs. I am a Maenad."[12] Katharine Bradley finally died September 26, 1914, a month shy of sixty-eight, two months after the outbreak of World War I.

Michael Field published nine books of verse; Ivor Treby catalogues 1,725 published and unpublished poems.[13] Bradley and Cooper—as Michael Field, Arran and Isla Leigh, and under the guise of anonymity—also published thirty-two dramatic works and many essays; they left full-length drafts for eight more plays, notes for at least twenty more projects, and the joint diary *Works and Days*, which in twenty-nine large white notebooks runs continuously from 1888 to 1914.[14] Notably, Michael Field appears in Edmund Stedman's *Anthology of Victorian Poetry 1837–1895*, which did much to define the term "Victorian" as well as the characteristics of verse associated with the period. As the brief biography just provided and as the rest of this book will show, for all Bradley and Cooper's often eccentric and innovative ideas, in some ways Michael Field was not atypically Victorian. Their life and work often reflects the interests, styles, and biases of their era; and their ideas are in conversation with many well-known Victorians. Even their interest in the past, writ large, does not set them apart from their contemporaries: their interest in the Renaissance and in creating medievalisms places them in the company of mid-Victorian voices such as Tennyson, both Brownings, FitzGerald, and the Pre-Raphaelites, among others; and many *fin de siècle* Aesthetes and Decadents shared their fascination with ancient Greece and Rome. Indeed, since their initial "rediscovery" in the late 1970s by lesbian literary historians, Michael Field has increasingly become less and less a marginal figure for nineteenth-century studies, and work on them has

---

[12] KB letter to John Gray, July 30, 1914 (qtd in Treby 53).

[13] For a very useful and complete if somewhat eccentrically arranged catalogue of primary material related to Michael Field, including the letters held in Bodleian and elsewhere, see Ivor Treby's *The Michael Field Catalogue, A Book of Lists*. His commentary is often odd and decidedly anti-feminist, but his bibliographic notes are meticulous.

[14] There is an international collaborative digital transcription project of the diary currently underway, housed at Dartmouth.

become quite varied and more theoretically complex, contributing much to our knowledge about nineteenth-century England, particularly about aesthetics, gender, and queer subjectivities in the period.

It is well known that modernist writers and authors frequently claimed that they despised the overwrought work of the Victorians, especially the Aesthetes. Interestingly, however, growing recognition of Michael Field's specific contributions to late Victorian thought—and their role as Aesthetes—has been facilitated by interlocutors who assert that the Aesthetic and Decadent movements with which Michael Field are associated not only put a flourish on the end of the nineteenth century, but also had a complex and formative relationship to the innovations of twentieth-century modernism. Accordingly, at least in part, my aim in *Michael Field's Revisionary Poetics*, like the aim of the co-authors themselves, is to consider their work in dialogue with those who came after the Victorian period even as their work repurposed what came before it. How do we situate Michael Field's work in relation to the concerns of the modernists who followed—and how do we read Michael Field in relation to our own concerns? Thus I conclude this biographical section and with the words of the co-authors' first biographer, Mary Sturgeon:

> The weeks of Michael's passing witnessed the passing of the age to which she belonged, for they were those in which the Great War began. It is clear that Michael Field, in the noble unity of her life and work, represented something that was finest in the dying era; and yet she was, in certain respects, aloof from the Victorian Age, and in advance of it. (59)

Michael Field, Aestheticism, and Decadent poetics

Michael Field's Revisionary Poetics situates the co-authors as homoerotically inclined female Aesthetes writing within, and to some extent against, a male Aesthetic Movement. Certainly, in many ways, Michael Field's life and work epitomizes Walter Pater's art for art's sake credo in *Studies in the History of the Renaissance* (1873): to seek impressions; to value the pursuit of beauty and aesthetic truths over artistic products that merely reinforced accepted moralities and conventions; and to center questions of one's own subjectivity and pleasure in visual and sensual experience. Further, as Richard Dellamora, Joseph Bristow, Stefano Evangelista, and Dustin Friedman among many others have noted, from its inception, Aestheticism—in its objects, philosophical and sensual concerns, and styles—was a vehicle for recognizing and expressing male homoerotic desire—for recognizing and expressing queer subjectivities. As ambitious, homoerotically inclined women of the period, Bradley and Cooper felt many affinities, personally and professionally, with male Aesthetes such as Pater, Ricketts and Shannon, Symonds, and Wilde.

Such affinities with their male contemporaries coexist, in the work of Michael Field, with some (but not all) of the characteristics that Kathy Psomiades, Talia Schaffer, and others have identified as a female aestheticism, that is, women's ways of negotiating the heteropatriarchal realities and challenges of the nineteenth century and of aesthetic traditions. For instance, Michael Field's work recognizes the aesthetic value of domestic and other objects as well as those perceived as "high art"; it emphasizes, and where necessary creates, alternative literary and aesthetic histories and genealogies; and it "takes into account desire between women as well as between men" (Schaffer and Psomiades 11). Indeed, the feminist literary historians who first "rediscovered" Michael Field were drawn to the fact that Bradley and Cooper's life writing and their published writing as Michael Field reveal a homoerotically inclined propensity to celebrate women's beauty, their keen sense of a distinctly female affiliation with nature,[15] and what we would today call queer and feminist critiques of patriarchy. Yet ironically, Bradley and Cooper included few women among their intellectual intimates. Ultimately, as Julia Saville points out, Bradley and Cooper attempted to place themselves at a remove from the "feminine affect or Victorian slush" traditionally associated with Victorian poetesses (179) and instead, more firmly in conversation with their male contemporaries associated with Aestheticism and Decadence.[16]

---

[15] Chapter 3 explores Michael Field's complicated use of nature, which sometimes employs, but often departs from, male decadent tropes of the evil, decaying femme fatale.

[16] Both Tricia Lootens and Yopie Prins also write of the poetess being a trope, an empty figure: "to sign Poetess is, then, to practice signature as a form of erasure: it is to sign 'Nobody'" (Lootens 3–4), certainly a reason for Bradley and Cooper to distance themselves from Poetesses and to self-fashion Michael Field, "A Poet."

Making All Things New: An Introduction 19

To that end, *Michael Field's Revisionary Poetics* proceeds with recognition that "decadence and aestheticism have always stood in uneasy relation to Victorian Studies," and despite their many points of overlap they "are two distinct phenomena, with distinct characteristics and emphases" (Evangelista, *British Aestheticism* 106).[17] When I say *poetics*, I gesture not only to prosody and meter, but also to "a multiplicity of forms of cultural production that exert significant pressure at the fin-de-siècle" (Hall and Murray ix). Yet I also place particular emphasis on the root of poetics in the Greek *poiein*—to make, to form, to transform. My position in this project is that Michael Field's poetics, like the poetics of other Aesthetic and Decadent contemporaries, contribute to a stylistic bridge between Victorian, Decadent and modernist poetics;[18] but their transforming queer, feminist, and artistic relationship to those impulses and styles is more, or at least differently, fraught than many of their contemporaries, and thus requires more analysis than they hitherto have been given.

Such further analysis can be facilitated by considering Michael Field's own emblem commissioned from Selwyn Image in the early 1890s: the Dionysian thyrsus, interlaced with rings (see Fig. I.3). Functioning as metonym for their personal and professional union, the symbol graced the cover of *Underneath the Bough* and interior pages of other Michael Field texts. It appeared on stationary, was used in initial correspondence with new acquaintances, and was stamped on their luggage. The logo combines eternally united wedding rings with the staff of Dionysus, symbolic of ecstatic abandon, sacred rites and fertility; it also is reminiscent of the ankh, the cross and the chi-rho, with all their attendant evocations of resurrection. A telling reference to the image appears in 1896, when after a wonderful day outdoors with Cooper, Bradley finds the sign of the cross insufficient to express their worshipful, creative joy in each other and in Nature. She rhapsodizes, "What better than our own sign—the inwoven rings and the thyrsus—in token

---

[17] See also the essays in Hall and Murray's *Decadent Poetics*.
[18] For further reading on the influence of *fin de siècle* literary forms upon modernism, see Meisel, *The Absent Father* and *The Myth of the Modern*; McGrath, *The Sensible Spirit*; Weir, *Decadence and the Making of Modernism*; Sherry, *Modernism and the Reinvention of Decadence*; and Mahoney, *Literature and the Politics of Post-Victorian Decadence*, among others.

Fig I.3 Thyrsus and rings logo from *Underneath the Bough* cover (1893). Designed by Selwyn Image. Courtesy of the Mark Samuels Lasner Collection, University of Delaware Library, Museums and Press.

of our worship and praise and bliss."[19] Thus, as the co-authors do elsewhere in words, Michael Field's visual proxy combines both pagan and Christian tradition in a skillful disidentificatory appropriation that enables Bradley and Cooper to represent themselves precisely at the site where two powerful and potentially limiting narratives of femininity converge.[20] Personified as Bacchic maenads but also bound in a sacred union—a marriage that is not subject to the patriarchal conventions of heterosexual marriage—they are dangerous women creating through the brain if not through the body, yet celebrating both. Instead of allowing traditional narratives to compromise them, Bradley and Cooper's ringed thyrsus is a queer visual text that makes concrete what they most desire: passionate eternal union as "Poets and lovers," in and through the name of Michael Field and the immortality of "his" poetry.

Michael Field's thyrsus, chosen with such deliberation, casts a judgmental shadow as Cooper reacts to a friend's wedding:

> [The bride] stands like a willing victim, but a victim to the first Great Illusion. I feel as though I am assisting at some rite of an old world. The Illusion is strong as the Earth, but the worship paired to it must have new forms or new freedom if it is to be living as the power it celebrates. Then comes all the deformation of love by cake, champagne, stupid hopes, emphasis of the new condition. Ugh! But the cake is excellent.[21]

---

[19] *Works and Days*. MSS Add. 46785, [May 5]1896. (KB). fol. 63r. The British Library. It is important to note that while MF's thyrsus functions as a useful metonym for their Dionysian passion, especially vis-à-vis their attitude toward *fin de siècle* Decadence, the centrality of Dionysian passion to Bradley and Cooper's *raison d'être* predates the thyrsus emblem by over a decade. Stefano Evangelista notes "Michael Field's poetry of the 1890s should be retrospectively recognized as Nietzschean in all the radical implications of this term" (*British Aestheticism* 123). While that statement is certainly correct, Chapter 1 will demonstrate Michael Field's Dionysian impulses can be traced to the earliest years of the 1880s, if not earlier.

[20] See José Esteban Muñoz (*Disidentification*) on queer disidentification. Sometimes implicit, sometimes explicit, much of the work of my study will be to suggest an overlap between adaptation (presenting the same material but with a difference) and queer disidentification (doing something one is traditionally excluded from, but in an unexpected way).

[21] *Works and Days*. MSS Add. 46780, April 20, 1892. (EC). fol. 76v. The British Library.

The next day, perhaps inspired by all that conventional marriage does *not* represent to them, they pledge themselves to one another in their own way. Cooper writes, "My love and I go to the Station that I may see her off to Dover. We swear with the bright world round us that we will remain Poets and Lovers whatever may happen to hinder or deflect our lives."[22] On the train Bradley penned their now most anthologized poem, "It was deep April," which was first published in the thyrsus-decorated *Underneath the Bough* (1893):

> It was deep April, and the morn
> > Shakespere was born;
> The world was on us, pressing sore;
> My Love and I took hands and swore
> > Against the world to be
> Poets and lovers evermore,
> To laugh and dream on Lethe's shore
> To sing to Charon in his boat,
> Heartening the timid souls afloat;
> Of judgment never to take heed,
> But to those fast-locked souls to speed,
> Who never from Apollo fled
> Who spent no hour among the dead;
> > Continually
> > With them to dwell,
> Indifferent to heaven and hell. (Field, *UTB* 79)

In this context, this poem does not merely pledge female marriage, brave and impassioned and beautiful though that pledge may be. It is an innovative manifesto for survival that discloses a deep-seated and inseparable desire for both authorship and interpersonal communion; yet the poem also demonstrates an uncanny anticipation that they must be/become a Foucauldian author-function, "Michael Field," in order to fulfill their dreams of fame *and* of living passionately in their worship of one other and of art.[23] And so "It was deep April" appeals to multiple sources for

---

[22] *Works and Days.* MSS Add. 46780, n.d.1892. (EC). fol. 78r. The British Library.

[23] In "What is an Author?" Foucault argues that the author, or person who has done the writing, is not the same as (and is less important than) the author-function, or set of beliefs, ideas, and value that comes out of associating a particular text with a particular name.

legitimacy: the national bard, Greek mythology, and the institution of marriage. "My Love and I" are placed in a creative space at mid-spring, but also a liminal one—between life and death, heaven and hell—aware that their resolve in their project and their alliance is as unyielding as the judgment they will undoubtedly face. Read as queer disidentification, what becomes most remarkable about this lyric is its resignification of contradiction. It engages the speakers' mixed emotions and the world's ambivalent responses, thereby functioning like the thyrsus in the above example where Bradley chooses "our own sign" over the cross. In its mix of wistful nostalgia, passionate commitment ceremony, and artistic self-promotion, Michael Field sings of the desire to have what they want and be what they feel they are, despite the world's hostility, and yet be joyful. The voice is playful yet determined—fully aware they are courting the dangers of earthly reprobation—yet more worried about the damnation of literary oblivion. Under the sign of the rings and the thyrsus, the vital authority rests within. It is no wedding license but rather documents a new rite: a joint performance of self-(re)creation. And just as Michael Field's thyrsus helps us understand their negotiation of conventional ideas about femininity, marriage, and creativity, it also helps us understand their negotiation of Aestheticism and Decadence.

Bradley and Cooper's fraught relationship to Decadence, its French forbears and its *fin de siècle* British inheritors, is complex. They despised Zola's *Nana* (1880), yet admired Verlaine and Baudelaire, who are mentioned in *Works and Days* and are the subject of several lyrics. They were also very fond of Arthur Symons, who in "The Decadent Movement in Literature" (1893) defends and characterizes the movement as "an intense self-consciousness, a restless curiosity in research, an oversubtlizing refinement upon refinement, a spiritual and moral perversity" and "a desperate endeavor to give sensation, to flash the impression of the moment, to preserve the very heat and motion of life" (135, 138). Yet they were so offended by the *Yellow Book*, they refused to publish in it and returned their copy:

> We have been almost blinded by the glare of hell ... One felt as one does when ... a wholly lost woman stands flaming on the pavement with the ghastly laugh of the ribald crowd in the air round ... the book is full of cleverness such as one expects to find in those who dwell below light and hope and love and aspiration. The best one can say of

any tale or of any illustration is that it is clever—the worst one can say is that it is damnable.[24]

This is a far cry from how Symons describes Verlaine's decadence: "[The] poetry of sensation, of evocation which paints as well as sings. To fix the last shade, the quintessence of things; to fix it fleetingly; to be a disembodied voice, and yet the voice of a human soul" (140–1). But it does echo the way Symons speaks of "the literature of a civilization grown over luxurious, over-inquiring, too languid for the relief of action, too uncertain for any emphasis in opinion or in conduct. It reflects all the moods, all the manner of a sophisticated society; its very artificiality is a way of being true to nature" (136). These observations raise questions about Michael Field's claim to revile decadence, and how we should situate them today in conversations about the similarities and differences between Aestheticism and Decadence, as well as we should read Michael Field's revisionary work vis-à-vis Decadent poetics.

Michael Field's verse sometimes, but not always, employs form and/or content in the same manner that contemporaneous male-authored poetry does. As Chapter 1 in particular demonstrates, from the earliest work in the 1880s onward, Bradley and Cooper certainly engage decadent tropes—much of their work is replete with fervor, death, corruption and decay, desire, and despair; and is situated within gorgeous, exotic, and richly textured visual scenes. Some of their verse negotiates traditional representations of sexually aggressive women as well as ambivalent narratives of poetic autonomy. Nevertheless, unlike female poets such as Graham R. Tomson, Bradley and Cooper do not feminize decadence (to use Linda K. Hughes's most useful phrase) in the way that perhaps they could be said to feminize aestheticism. Instead, it is at a vague and permeable boundary between aestheticism and decadence that Michael Field pursued their literary goals and articulated their own queer poetics.[25] It is my assertion that because the co-authors were not willing to compromise their fierce

---

[24] *Works and Days*. MSS Add. 46783, April 7, 1894. (EC). fols 37v, 38r. The British Library.

[25] I use the phrase queer poetics in order to evoke the broad range of ways that Michael Field's life and work departs from heteropatriarchal norms, such as expressing anti-heteronormative desires, employing the not anticipated and the strange, and often queering the temporal.

dedication to the impassioned Dionysian impulse signified by the thyrsus, their poetic rendering of the Paterian impression could not accommodate the fascination of (some) Decadents with morbidity born of ennui.[26]

Chris White, Stefano Evangelista, and T. D. Olverson have examined Michael Field's ongoing exploration of erotic Hellenism, with Olverson suggesting that the co-authors "replicate Swinburne's literary and philosophical premise, that it is the poet's (moral) duty to record one's passion for life and its potentially tragic cost" (*Women Writers* 124). Indeed, as the following meditation on Dionysian resurrection stories illustrates, Bradley and Cooper found ways to connect their early pagan rapture for the Bacchanal with their interest in Christian tradition and ritual, but only within a framework that insists upon intense engagement:

> It is sometimes said that shortly after his burial [Dionysus] rose from the dead and ascended up to Heaven or that Zeus raised him up as he lay mortally wounded or that Zeus swallowed the heart of Dionysus. It appears that a general doctrine of resurrection or at least of immortality was inculcated on his worshippers for Plutarch. The women of Elis hailed [Dionysus] as the Bull. They sang, "Come here Dionysus, to thy holy temple by the sea; dance with the graces to thy holy temple, rushing with thy bull's foot, O goodly bull, O goodly bull." Therefore, in tearing live bulls and calves the Maenads were killing the god, eating his flesh, drinking his blood.[27]

This over-abundant and gory passage certainly does not shy from excess. However, it is motivated by a zest for sensation, not decadent poetics of languor. Indeed, in 1892 Bradley and Cooper assert, "ennui [is] made impossible by the multitude of thoughts and hopes. Ennui is the plague of life, punishing us when we refuse to be about our father's business—which is, we must always remember that we should have life, and have it more abundantly."[28] Ennui is, in other words, contrary to the "light and hope and love

---

[26] An important exception is the style and thinking of what Denisoff terms eco-decadence, which I discuss in relation to *Underneath the Bough* in Chapter 3.
[27] *Works and Days*. MSS Add. 46789, n.d.1900. (EC). fol. 103r. The British Library.
[28] *Works and Days*. MSS Add. 46780, August 20, 1892. (KB). fol. 136r. The British Library.

and aspiration" that Bradley and Cooper sought, but found sorely lacking, in the *Yellow Book*. In contrast:

> At home in the evening Sim and I went over the larger fragments of Otho.[29] Our brains struck fire each from each—we conceived his final exit, his farewell to Death, his joyous acceptance of everlasting anguish that is quick with life. We both felt it was the even of our resurrection as artists—as George Moore writes "To create soul is to accomplish the work of God."[30]

In this thrilling moment of collaborative jouissance, the Promethean and Judeo-Christian impulse coexist, and artistic agency is reborn. Ennui, that constant companion of the decadent aesthete, has no place in Michael Field's world.

The above consideration of Dionysian resurrection has significant implications for how Michael Field's characteristic engagement with both sacred and profane, made manifest in their pagan/Christian disidentification with the ringed thyrsus, plays out in their post-conversion devotional poetry, a topic partially explored in Chapter 5. It also begins to explain their rejection of the *Yellow Book* and of Thomas Hardy:

> *Jude the Obscure* (obscene) I could not read. Offal was thrown in my face. I turned away forever from the thrower. Hardy appears to me to be in Hell, not on Earth. He has no pulse for life—he blasphemes what he has never experienced. I felt this when I met him; he seemed less than an echimus, alive in the limitless seas—he was echimite—the mere petrifaction. The "still, sad music of humanity" played under the low roof of his pessimism becomes disgraceful noise. He is the Scribe of the Tragedy of Science-neither an Artist of Apollo nor of Dionysus.[31]

Here, Michael Field, with characteristic indignation, complicates Oscar Wilde's stance that "[t]he artist can express everything" (*Dorian Gray* 4). Within Bradley and Cooper's poetics, things are rarely if ever perverse in themselves; but Aesthetic or Decadent,

---

[29] Bradley and Cooper's working title for *Stephania* (1892).
[30] *Works and Days*. MSS Add. 46779, Easter Saturday [March 28] 1891. (EC). fol. 27r. The British Library.
[31] *Works and Days*. MSS Add. 46784 (November, 1895). (EC). fol. 25r. The British Library.

representation without authentic and spontaneous intensity of experience becomes contrived, sterile, and blasphemous. Without a "pulse for life," there is no Paterian gemlike flame. Without a place for the Dionysian passion of the thyrsus, expression is not art.

Method

The approach I take in this study is threefold, weaving together historical, phenomenological, and formal concerns in my interrogation of Michael Field's revisionary poetics.

The uses of history

When we think of Michael Field's revisionary poetics, we are, of course, thinking of re-vision as seeing history—things, events, stories, people—again, and differently. Seeing things from a different point of view. And when we think of seeing again, and differently, we consider perhaps that the viewer *needs* to see again because the way things hitherto have been seen, or told, or used before is no longer working. Perhaps the old way of seeing excludes this new kind of thinker or has never included the (perhaps minoritarian) perspective of such thinkers. History—and its narratives and artifacts—needs to be thought and used anew, because claims to objectivity and truth have failed, or at least are incomplete. A change is needed. Histories and cultural artifacts need to be adapted to new contexts and put to new uses.

One way to begin to examine Michael Field's literary adaptations of history is to remember that they emerged both alongside and as part of a broader phenomenon of nineteenth-century replication. Granted, postmodern theory, especially the work of New Historicism, postcolonialism, feminism, and queer theory, suggests that the urge to destabilize history and narrative in this way is a particularly postmodern phenomenon, and perhaps it is. *Particularly* postmodern; but not *specifically* so; as prominent theorist of postmodernism, Linda Hutcheon, observes in *A Theory of Adaptation* (2006), adaptations are not new to our time. The nineteenth-century world provided multiple models through which people like Bradley and Cooper might imagine adaptations of literature and history: discourses such as Darwinian adaptation, resurrection, reform, and translation, among others. To that end, Julie Codell and Linda K. Hughes's collection of essays, *Replication in the Long Nineteenth Century* (2018) considers the pervasive variety of re-makings, replicas and reproduction during the period. They place their interdisciplinary examples within the framework of what Mieke Bal calls a traveling concept: "As a traveling concept 'replica' can embrace multiple meanings and intersubjective knowledge ... while maintaining some specificity of historical meaning. Ambiguity and indeterminacy are thus to be expected" (Codell and Hughes 5). As the contributors to that collection trace the life of diverse phenomena—newspapers, sciences, species, workers, archeological casts, art reproductions, new literary editions, typescripts, copies, forgeries, and imitations, among others—Codell and Hughes argue, "we believe that what became an industry of replicas reveals the fundamental cultural beliefs of the nineteenth-century ... Replicas, as forms of reception, epitomized the late 19th century marginalist economic theories of Alfred Marshall, in which value was determined by consumption and desire rather than by production, as in the labor theory of classical economics" (13). Thus, replications create relationships and networks, and are made possible by and require new technologies. Codell and Hughes conclude: "the history of nineteenth-century replication also suggests that replications expand creativity, political and ethical awareness, and shared access to increased knowledge" (292). In the chapters that follow, many of these themes will re-emerge.

Next, I want to establish specifically philosophical and literary frames for understanding Michael Field's adaptations of history, because in addition to the nineteenth-century discourses of replication I have briefly listed above, Michael Field drew inspiration for their revisionary projects from two philosophers they studied intensely: Hegel and Nietzsche. Here it is quite important to note, as William Shuter and Dustin Friedman do, that like most Victorians, Michael Field's understandings of Hegel's views on history and art would have been mediated by two influential contemporaries: G. H. Lewes and Walter Pater. In a review of Hegel's *Aesthetics* (1835) in *The British and Foreign Review* (1842), Lewes explains Hegel's notion that the purpose of history is only understood retrospectively. Lewes calls particular attention to Hegel's treatment of anachronism, quoting the German philosopher with an example regarding drama: "the public has a right to demand a certain national revision and alteration to suit their taste. In this respect even the most excellent require revision" (Hegel, in Lewes 48). As I discuss at length in Chapter 1, Michael Field's use of anachronism echoes Lewes's sentiments here about revision.

Even more than Lewes, it is "Pater's" Hegel, as articulated in his essay on Winckelmann, various lectures, in personal conversation, and channeled in *Marius the Epicurean* (1885), that would have made a constructive impression upon Michael Field—a Hegel read through Heraclitus and through the spirit of the Oxford Hegelians, especially Plato scholar Benjamin Jowett. In *Plato and Platonism* (1893) Pater synthesizes his particular understanding of Hegel both with Heraclitus and with Victorian discourses of replication, change, and development:

> The entire modern theory of "development," in all its various phases, proved or unprovable—what is it but old Heracliteanism awake once more in a new world, and grown to full proportions? ... It is the burden of Hegel on the one hand, to whom nature, and art, and polity, and philosophy, aye, and religion too, each in its long historic series, are but so many conscious movements in the secular process of the eternal mind; and on the other hand of Darwin and Darwinism, for which "type" itself properly is not but is only always becoming. (13–14)

While Hegel's aims in his theories of history are quite teleological and universalist; Pater's use of Hegel throughout his career is perhaps a bit less so and is certainly more subjective, as is Pater's take on Heraclitean flux. Pater's Hegelian query about history at the conclusion of *Greek Studies* (1895): "What is there in this phase of ancient religion for us, at the present day?" (151) seems an echo of the question that drives his preface to *Studies in the History of the Renaissance* (1873), "What is this song or picture, this engaging personality presented in life or in a book, to me?" (viii). The conclusion to that work, of course, begins with an epigraph from Heraclitus: "All things are in motion and nothing at rest" (207). We can see in both Pater's questions quoted above, what Carolyn Williams identifies, for Pater, as three simultaneously diachronic and synchronic concerns: (1) how the artist might "maintain the historical specificity of [similar types of cultural artifacts] while also asserting their generalized value and their relations to one another over time"; (2) how the artist might achieve both aesthetic and historical value, "absolutely unique yet also the representative of his age"; and (3) how a type expresses concrete historical identity while also expressing something beyond itself (127, 138). Michael Field's work also reflects these Paterian concerns, as the following chapters show.

But Michael Field's philosophy of history is even more complex. When they finally read Nietzsche in the 1890s, Bradley and Cooper's long-held Dionysian ideals, combined with their Hegelian-Paterian view of history, made them conclude that they had already been for some time quite Nietzschean. Nietzsche, who calls Hegel "monstrous" in *Untimely Meditations* (1874) nevertheless writes, "The genuine historian must possess the power to remint the universally known into something never heard of before" (94). Michael Field had already been using a similarly "untimely" approach for over a decade, with their revisionary adaptations of Sappho, the Early English figures of their early closet dramas, and the ekphrases of *Sight and Song* demonstrating what Pater calls "the impress there of the writer's own temper and personality" (*The Renaissance* 172). And if we push Michael Field's untimeliness into our time and into dialogue with Mieke Bal, we can recognize that, in their hands, figures and forms from art and history do indeed manifest as traveling concepts that "can embrace multiple meanings and intersubjective knowledge ... while maintaining some specificity of historical meaning" (Codell and Hughes 25). They are reshaped, adapted, transformed.

In Michael Field's hands, such a transforming view of history also has provocative implications for conceptualizing the role of the self—especially an aesthetic and erotic self—within history. As Dustin Friedman compellingly theorizes in *Before Queer Theory: Victorian Aestheticism and the Self* (2019), Pater's concept of the artistic process—and the development of an autonomous artistic subject—involves a Hegelian dialectic through which a destructive but transforming force, *Negativität*, "inaugurates new patterns of thought that push against dialectical stalemates" and by which "consciousness undergoes meaningful transformations" (Friedman 40, 38). According to Friedman, for Pater and other homoerotically inclined aesthetes including Michael Field, this Hegelian negativity also manifests as an erotic negativity that results in a "radically queer-affirming discourse" (7); "the writings of the aesthetes ... show that it is possible to imagine a sexually nonnormative subject who gains some measure of genuine self-determination through engagement with art" (20). Thus Friedman argues for Aestheticism as one of queer theory's hitherto unacknowledged ancestors, a position I fully endorse as I examine the Michael Field's queer-feminist adaptations of history and art.

Albeit without an explicitly Hegelian framework, other literary critics of the queer nineteenth century including Richard Dellamora, Linda Dowling, Stefano Evangelista, and Kevin Ohi have also written about homosexual desire being displaced on the past, which Ohi calls "queer belatedness" (27). And indeed, more contemporary feminist and queer authors as diverse as Adrienne Rich, Mary Daly, Gloria Anzaldúa, Audre Lorde, Jean Rhys, Judith Butler, and others have long shown us the power of reclamation, while others, including Elizabeth Freeman, Jack Halberstam, and Lynne Huffer, have written extensively about queer time. Of particular relevance throughout my project is Heather Love's work on the queer structure of feeling that she terms "feeling backward," a relation with that past that negotiates histories of injuries and a longing for community; and José Esteban Muñoz on the utopian potential of negative affect for "enacting a mode of critical possibility" and the notion of queer hope as "a backward glance that enacts a future vision" (Muñoz, *Cruising Utopia* 4). Such work has been and continues to be valuable when examining the work of Michael Field, since Michael Field's revisions reclaim, adopt, and adapt old stories and forms for new times and transformed purposes. As this study unfolds, I will be highlighting Michael Field's affinities with these and other queer-feminist methods regarding reclamation and temporality.

I close this first of my three methods sections by returning to the adaptation theory generated in our own postmodern moment, as much of it resonates productively with the texts I analyze in the chapters to come. What can adaptation theory bring to our thinking about Michael Field's uses of history—to our thinking about their revisionary experiments both in content and form? This is a question that immediately must be qualified by Thomas Leitch's observation that the first fallacy of adaptation theory is that there is no single adaptation theory; nevertheless, there are five recurring areas of concern within adaptation studies that I wish to gloss here, as they will usefully contribute to the theoretical tapestry I am weaving to facilitate this book's inquiry.

First, adaptation theory teaches us that adaptations never occur in a vacuum—adaptations are always responding to something in the environment. And among other features of such responses, some adaptations reify and others trouble the notion of progress; some evoke and others dismiss a sense of nostalgia. *Michael Field's Revisionary Poetics* will, where possible, call attention to the historical specificities that inform Michael Field's texts, especially when their adaptations can be read, as so many adaptations are, as implicit or explicit political acts.

Second, as Julie Sanders notes, adaptations and appropriations are phenomena with much overlap; but it is useful to distinguish between these two terms. Sanders writes that "an adaptation most often signals a relationship with an informing text either through its title or through more embedded references," while an "appropriation frequently effects a more decisive journey away from the informing text into wholly new cultural product and domain, often through the actions of interpolation and critique as much as through the movement from one genre to others" (35). These are fraught distinctions for the work of Michael Field. Many of their revisions may signal a source text through their titles and might seem like adaptations in their attempt to replicate a certain spirit even while commenting, usually from a queer-feminist perspective, upon that source text; but at the same time Michael Field may switch the genre and/or experiment with form, or create a heroine from a minor or underappreciated character in a manner that Sanders might define more properly as an appropriation. In what follows I use the terms adaptation and appropriation where they are useful to calling attention to these distinctions, but otherwise I employ other terms, such as version, reclamation, or revision to describe Michael Field's experiments with well-known persons, narratives, and forms.

Third, is a cluster of issues related to intertextuality, and the value of an intertext vis-à-vis concepts like originality and fidelity. Much adaptation theory dispels Walter's Benjamin's "aura," that is, counters the notion that "source texts" are necessarily more original or creative than adaptations. Leitch, Hutcheon, John Glavin, Robert Stam, and others similarly caution against positing fidelity as the most appropriate criterion for analyzing or judging adaptations. These ideas converge in definitions for adaptation as being fundamentally palimpsestic; such as Hutcheon's observations that adaptations are "derivations that are not derivative"; and "repetition without replication" (96, 7). Such ideas culminate in the recognition that all adaptations are intertexts and imply that greater attention should be paid to the intertextuality of *all* texts; with some (though not all) theorists suggesting that there is perhaps something to be gained in considering intertexuality, writ large, as a form of adaptation. Michael Field, who wrote ". . . The rest / of our life must be a palimpsest" in a lyric published in *Wild Honey from Various Thyme* anticipates many of these postmodern claims about adaptation as intertextuality. I'll return to this poem in this book's conclusion. For now, I merely note that although previous analyses by Virginia Blain and others have read this poem's figure of the palimpsest as metonym for ongoing intersubjectivity in the queer co-authors' lives (a reading I agree with), we can also observe in "A Palimpsest" intertextual echoes of Heraclitus, Hegel, Pater, and Nietzsche, and thus we can read it as lyrical shorthand for the historical methods that shape their adaptations and other revisionary poetics.

Fourth, in its treatment of adaptations' intermedial transposition—that is, shifts in genre and medium—adaptation theorists wrestle with claims like literary texts are verbal, films visual; novels deal with concepts, film percepts; and claims about how genre and medium affect showing vs telling, *fabula* vs *sjuzet*, the consumer's capacity for immersion, etc. These kinds of issues resonate with recent thinking about the affordances of form, which I address later in this introduction. Like the matter of adaptation vs appropriation, Michael Field's work does not take a unified or consistent stance on matters of transcoding, form, and the related aesthetic concept of synaesthesia; but these are nevertheless of tremendous interest to my project.

Finally, adaptations are also sometimes considered translations; for instance, Sanders considers translations studies to be an "important cognate" of adaptation studies, finding that for translation as for other adaptations, "the concept of strict fidelity is unhelpful" (9). Paraphrasing Susan Basnett on translation, Sanders states, "Translation too is a form of rewriting, a transformative act of adaptation and variation in which the notion of what constitutes the 'original' is increasingly unclear" (201). As Fehrle and Schmitt write in "Adaptation as Translation":

> the work of the translator is by no means restricted to finding semiotic equivalents. In order to convey the meaning of a text in another language and to a culturally different audience, the translator will have to build a bridge between cultures that is not exclusively restricted to

the linguistic sphere. The translator as transposer between different languages frequently encounters cases in which the target language does not have the proper semiotic equivalents necessary to convey the meaning of the source text. (3)

Thus, as Sanders asserts, "All adapters are translators, then, and all translators are creative writers of a sort" (9).[32]

While all the concepts from adaptation studies I've enumerated above are relevant to Michael Field's revisionary poetics, it is the overlap between the task of the translator and task of the adapter that interests me most for the purposes of this project. Well over a decade ago, I first started thinking about Michael Field's revisions through their ekphrastic readings of the Grand Masters in *Sight and Song*, which is a text with a preface that specifically invokes translation: "The aim of this little volume is, as far as may be, to translate into verse what the lines and colours of certain chosen pictures sing in themselves" (*SS* v).[33] What strikes me now when thinking about Michael Field's revisions/adaptations through the lens of translation is how their view of the flux and untimeliness of history, as traced through Heraclitus, Hegel, Pater, and Nietzsche, intersects in provocative ways with how Michael Field engage the ultimate unknowability of translation. I am interested in how the discourses of translation negotiate the refusals, and indeed the impossibility, of fidelity to a so-called original, along with the lived experience and affect associated with such creative refusals. This is, in part, the subject of the next section.

Phenomenology

A phenomenological approach is grounded in realizing that "our body is our general means of having a world" and that "thought is a relationship with oneself and with the world as well as a relationship with the other (Merleau-Ponty *Phenomenology* 147; *Visible* 145). In other words, phenomenological approaches turn

---

[32] The view of translation as adaptation has only a bit in common with Walter Benjamin's "The Task of the Translator," which places much more emphasis on the inherent virtue of the original and the inherent virtue (although admitted difficulty of) fidelity. I will engage Benjamin's important essay at greater length in Chapter 2.

[33] See Ana Parejo Vadillo, "Transparent Translations" for a strong analysis of *Sight and Song* using Benjamin's notion of translation.

to experience as lived in order to think about the structures that give these experiences meaning and to question our assumptions about experience and "ordinary" life. In choosing to focus on the phenomenology of Michael Field's experiments with history and form, I am, at least in part, thinking about affect and motivation as Bradley and Cooper revised particular figures and forms in the ways they did. I am also interested in Bradley and Cooper as queer co-authors involved in the embodied act of writing—specifically the embodied act of writing with one another, about art and about the past, in verse. Throughout *Michael Field's Revisionary Poetics* I will be thinking about how Michael Field's creative process could be said to anticipate two ideas later associated with the works of Maurice Merleau-Ponty: Merleau-Ponty's own notion of *l'engrenage*—a "gearing into and taking up" of the other, the past, the unknown; and Sara Ahmed's queer phenomenological approach to orientation. And I will be thinking about how these two phenomenological frames are particularly useful for queer and feminist scholarship on Michael Field.

At the close of the previous section, I began to consider Michael Field's revisionary poetics as involving a creative process akin to translation—one specifically in which one's relationship to the object being re-created or translated involves a significant element of engaging the unknown. Although Walter Benjamin's "Task of the Translator" is often considered the Ur-text for theorizing translation, and although that essay certainly does admit the inevitable difficulty of translation, Benjamin nevertheless asserts too persistent an investment in the inherent superiority of the original and the desirability (if the impossibility) of fidelity to that original to be wholly useful in the context of adaptation and queer feminist revision. Benjamin is also focused on the "what" of translation and the material product, while I seek a method that accounts for the lived experience—including the process of perception and the affect—of the embodied authors producing the creative re-vision. What was the experience of adaptation and appropriation like for Michael Field? And how did that experience give shape to the texts they created?

Phenomenology, especially the work of Merleau-Ponty, provides a useful method for my concerns, since, as Jonathan Gilmore explains in "Between Philosophy and Art," "for Merleau-Ponty, art, artist, and artist's life are interdependent; each explains the other and the others explain each in turn" (293). Like Pater,

Michael Field, and Nietzsche, Merleau-Ponty's work contains echoes of Hegel, for whom history is a process of becoming, as discussed in the previous section. For Merleau-Ponty, the embodied subject also is always in a process of becoming, and in a reciprocal relationship with the environment, which for Merleau-Ponty includes everything one perceives around one—human and non-human—including history, the arts, language, and all aspects of the self. Notably, as William A. Cohen observes in *Embodied: Victorian Literature and the Senses* (2009), Victorian literature across genres and across the period, similarly "argues for the materiality of self and soul, mobilizing the senses to gain access to these entities" (16). Thus, while my study of Michael Field will certainly be in direct conversation with contemporary Foucauldian scholarship that helps us understand how *discourse* inscribes identities categories upon bodies within historical and sociopolitical contexts, I am also very interested in what Cohen describes as "a focus, by contrast, on the interior, subjective experience of self and sensation [which] can yield an account of the ways in which such politics come to be *felt* internally (16).[34]

As this study will show, Michael Field's uses of historical figures and forms echo Heraclitus and Hegel while also prefiguring Merleau-Ponty. In the affect as well as the expression of Michael Field's revisionary poetics we find ideas akin to Merleau-Ponty's assertions that "The subject is simultaneously creating [*naturant*] and created [*naturé*], and simultaneously infinite and finite" (*Phenomenology* 383) and "the world is always already constituted, but also never completely constituted. In the first relation we are solicited, in the second we are open to an infinity of possibilities. Yet the analysis remains abstract, for we exist in both ways *simultaneously*" (*Phenomenology* 480). Such views have important implications for theorizing creativity; for Merleau Ponty, "the work of the artist is an intention that creates its own instruments and its own means of expression" (*Phenomenology* 471). In other words, "Merleau-Ponty shows how creativity testifies to the constitutive embeddedness of subjectivity in the world and to the essential function of our relationship with others in the formation of meaning" (Summa 117). Even as one's perception of the world

---

[34] Foucauldian notions of discourse are often taken to be at odds with phenomenology, but as recent work by Cressida Heyes has demonstrated, there is much to be gained by thinking through the effects of discourse and affect, together.

is shaped by one's horizons of meaning, creativity opens new horizons of meaning. For Michael Field, perceiving history and historical artifacts through ideas like Pater's subjective impressions and Nietzschean untimeliness results in creative engagement with the (historical, literary, artistic) world that accounts for their own lived experience of becoming as nineteenth-century, female, queer subjects—and as becoming-authors. And that creative engagement also opens new horizons of interpretation.

To reiterate the ideas of Nietzsche that spoke to them so powerfully, Michael Field's revisionary poetics are invested in reshaping "the universally known into something never heard of before" (Nietzsche, *Untimely Meditations* 94). Especially in light of Bradley and Cooper's commitment to living with Dionysian passion, I want to press upon this point to ask about this process of revising histories, figures, and forms in an evolving context in which sense is protean as well. Affectively speaking, *what is that experience like?* Here again, Merleau-Ponty has language for the kind of sense experience we find in the work of Michael Field.

At important moments throughout his works Merleau-Ponty employs the noun *l'engrenage*, "the gearing into and taking up," and the verb *engrener*, "to gear into." Here Merleau-Ponty refers to something evocative of the coming together of teeth on gears, a trying to find a fit, a chain of events, or an intertwining; and his translator Donald Landes observes that "Merleau-Ponty draws upon the figurative aspect of this image such that 'the fit' is something to be accomplished by the act, not something pre-determined by the shape of the gears and teeth" (*Phenomenology* 496, 47n). Thus *l'engrenage* can be used to describe the paradoxical experience of encountering an other in a context, often across time and/or space, where "sense is not solid and fixed, but fluid and evolving" (Landes, "Translation" 1). To provide just one example, in *The Phenomenology of Perception* Merleau-Ponty writes:

> Just as the other person's perspective affects the world for me, the spatial domain of each sense is, for the other senses, an absolute unknowable and limits their spatiality accordingly ... for us the unity of space can only be found where the sensory domains **gear into each other**. (231, my emphasis)

In pondering *l'engrenage* in the context of translation, Landes emphasizes that *l'engrenage*—this gearing into—always involves the sense of not knowing. For example, in the above quote, the experience of intersubjectivity involves a certain unknowability. In the case of translation, one will never know if one's version—translation—of the text captures the complete sense of the original. One wonders if it is correct—but one does the translation anyway.

There are several key points to be emphasized about the experience of *l'engrenage* that are relevant to Michael Field. First, approaching adaptation / appropriation / translation as *l'engrenage* highlights the illusory nature of the stable original—ontologically it does not even exist—because the reader (not being the writer) cannot inhabit the true sense that was the writer's mind. Thus, although one is compelled to look and feel backward, that enterprise is really a shot in the dark, although one does it anyway. Second, the new version is going to be different from the original in ways that are perhaps unexpected or surprising; difference is the truth of repetition and necessitates a gearing into the unknown. Finally, there is a sense of transtemporal community:

> to translate is to construct a bridge, inviting new performances from a radically new network of reading and speaking bodies that will inevitably reshape this trajectory of sense ... The art of translation is the attempt to bridge difference through open invitations to reperformances. (Landes, "Translation" 5)

These phenomenological elements of *l'engrenage* can be usefully discerned in Michael Field's revisions, as the following chapters show.

In *Queer Phenomenology: Orientation, Objects, Others* (2006), Sara Ahmed outlines a queer and feminist phenomenology that also proves useful for my analyses of Michael Field. Following Merleau-Ponty, Ahmed considers the subject not merely as an object in the world, but as a point of view in the world, with specific emphasis on questions of how lived experiences are oriented and re-oriented, for female and queer subjects. Ahmed writes:

> Orientation shapes not only how we inhabit space, but how we apprehend this world of shared inhabitants as well as who "or what" we direct our energy and attention toward. A queer phenomenology, perhaps, might start by redirecting our attention toward different

objects, those that are "less proximate: or even those that deviate or are deviant." (3)

For Ahmed, gender and compulsory heterosexuality orient one both in space, toward certain types of others, but also in time, toward certain kinds of life trajectories—a line or path that one is expected to follow. In making such a claim, Ahmed invokes Judith Butler's theories of performativity and citationality: "So we walk on the path as it is before us, but it is only before us as an effect of being walked upon. A paradox of the footprint emerges. Lines are both created by being followed and are followed by being created" (Ahmed 16). Michael Field's revisionary poetics, as the subsequent chapters demonstrate, frequently engage such paradoxes, commenting upon them, attempting to retrace the steps of previous narratives, writing over the story, often narrating a new path. Furthermore, even as Michael Field's varied uses of history and forms-in-flux sometimes result in positive expressions of community and empowerment, in other instances we will see, as Ahmed also notes, that "[b]ecoming a member of . . . a community, then, might also mean following this direction, which could be described as the political requirement that we turn some ways and not others" (15). In other words, at times for Michael Field their gearing into the past—and the present—and the future—instead conveys a queer, feminist sense of disorientation, frustration, and critique.

L'engrenage and orientation are, phenomenologically speaking, key methods and characteristics of the texts I examine in *Michael Field's Revisionary Poetics*. We can observe differing formal strategies for each of Bradley and Cooper's revisionary projects—historical closet dramas and expansions of Greek fragments, ekphrasis, experimentation with lyric, elegiac, and devotional poetic forms,[35] and their diary—but despite their varied inspirations for each project and the differing formal characteristics of their diverse revisionary endeavors, each can nonetheless be said to possess characteristics of a gearing into and taking up of the other which is often a willful engagement with the unknown. As the co-authors encounter and engage objects, figures, narratives, and forms, I will be placing the affective elements of those encounters in conversation with historical and literary matters.

---

[35] For an extended formalist approach to Michael Field's *oeuvre*, see Richardson.

Thus the chapters that follow examine the affective orientation and *l'engrenage* of the co-authors as they are overcome by passion and deal with unknowability (Chapter 1); reflect upon haptic encounters with art (Chapter 2); document and celebrate shared sensual/erotic experience with one another in nature (Chapter 3); mourn (Chapter 4); and experience physical pain in the dual context of disease and spiritual growth (Chapter 5). As each chapter explores Michael Field's experiments in depth, I will demonstrate how each project, in its own way, exemplifies an engagement with and orientation toward the not-knowing that is also, phenomenologically speaking, *l'engrenage*.

Form, affordance

"What form is best for poems?"[36] This is the question posed by the eponymous heroine of Elizabeth Barrett Browning's *Aurora Leigh* (1856), who then dares to rethink tradition by questioning the necessity of five acts for a drama. In their own approach to poetics, Michael Field, who admired Barrett Browning, demonstrate that they shared her heroine's ambitions. In taking the spirit of Aurora Leigh's questions to heart, Bradley and Cooper paid no heed to critics like W. E. Aytoun who decried the verse novel's philosophical questions about writing, and who scoffed that "the tendency to experiment" was "simply a token of a morbid craving for originality" (qtd in Martin 38). Instead, as Ana Vadillo observes: "Michael Field was an artificial poetic construct and in that artificiality rested their originality, for it enabled the poets to think of poetry and language in radical ways" ("Poets of Style" 239).

Indeed, from their earliest published work, Michael Field's works are experiments with form: such as their expansion of Sappho's fragments in *Long Ago* and their ekphrastic experiments with the picture poems of *Sight and Song*. The latter collection opens with one of their most famous short verses, which I reproduce here in its entirety in order to demonstrate how the subject of this particular experiment eschews language for dance:

> He dances on a toe
> As light as Mercury's :
> *Sweet herald, give thy message!* No,

---

[36] Elizabeth Barrett Browning, *Aurora Leigh*, Book V, l. 223.

He dances on; the world is his,
The sunshine and his wingy hat;
    His eyes are round
    Beneath the brim :
To merely dance where he is found
    Is fate to him
  And he was born for that.

    He dances in a cloak
    Of vermeil and of blue :
Gay youngster, underneath the oak,
Come, laugh and love ! In vain we woo ;
He is a human butterfly ;—
    No soul, no kiss,
    No glance nor joy !
Though old enough for manhood's bliss,
    He is a boy,
  Who dances and must die. (Field, *SS* 1)

Inspired by Watteau's oil painting, *L'Indifferent* (1717), Michael Field's "sweet herald" refuses to give his "message." He ignores the conversation in the italicized phrases, along with the (heteronormative) social conventions such conversations facilitate. "To merely dance" is his sole *raison d'être*. Elsewhere, I have commented upon the gender politics of this poem,[37] but here I am interested in how it plays with philosophical and aesthetic questions: How does a two-dimensional painting—and how does language—convey movement? How can language translate the embodied sensations that the viewer experiences while looking at a painting, and how can language communicate those sensations to the reader? Michael Field's questions are difficult ones, but as they engage—as they "gear into" —these questions and Watteau's painting, the boy in motion—the embodied performance of the dance itself—seems to be the answer. Michael Field's poem performs a moment of complete absorption—complete flow—for both the dancer and the spectator/author/reader. Nothing else matters as "the world is his," subsumed into wherever he finds himself dancing. Vision and words both are, and collapse into, the dance.

[37] See Ehnenn, "Looking Strategically."

A similar example appears in a song from *Callirrhoë*, one that later reappears as a stand-alone lyric poem in *Underneath the Bough*:

> I DANCE and dance! Another faun,
> A black one, dances on the lawn.
> He moves with me, and when I lift
> My heels his feet directly shift:
> I can't outdance him though I try;
> He dances nimbler than I.
> I toss my head, and so does he;
> What tricks he dares to play on me!
> I touch the ivy in my hair;
> Ivy he has and finger there.
> The spiteful thing to mock me so!
> I will outdance him! Ho, ho, ho! (Field, *Call.* 108–9)

This lyric, like the previous one, attempts the difficult task of representing movement in words. As the speaker, a faun, dances with his shadow, the poem provides a lively rhythm and some detail about this dance: there are lifted heels, tossed heads, and touching the ivy in one's hair. Yet these concrete aspects of the dance alternate with more vague descriptions that have to do with energy: the reader can only imagine what might be going on in the moments when the speaker proclaims, "I dance and dance" and that his shadow "plays tricks" on him. What movement has been executed that the speaker concedes, "he dances nimbler than I"? This amusing song performs an ongoing effort to pursue an elusive task—to outdance the shadow; yet it simultaneously models the more general process of thinking about elusive questions: How to represent motion in words? To what extent is one's shadow oneself? One grasps the answer to the question—like catching a glimpse of one's shadow—and then the issue becomes vague once more. Yet like the dancer who becomes more and more determined to "outdance" his shadow as he sings, the process of considering such difficult tasks becomes an all-absorbing end in itself. This lyric about the determined faun and his shadow also suggests the simultaneously goal-driven yet playful lovers behind the dual Michael Field persona itself. Especially since the journal documents many instances of the poets' woodland dancing and frolicking, once might imagine Bradley and Cooper playing at their own version of "me and my shadow," performatively engaging questions of self and other.

These and Michael Field's other invocations of dancing, of movement, remind us that writing is not a still endeavor. Writing moves the writer and the reader. It moves us in terms of feeling, emotion; and it also moves us through time in important ways, both literally and figuratively. Literally, time passes when we write or read; indeed, often time seems to fly when a one is in the flow of engaging a text by reading or thinking or writing. For Michael Field, writing is the movement of ideas between two people who, at least publicly, claim to think and act as one. And, figuratively (or perhaps literally) writing and reading moved them (and moves us) backward and forward in time. But how does this happen? *What are the steps?* While the philosophical and phenomenological frameworks of the previous two sections provide some answers, this section recasts the question to specifically ask: How does the author employ form to ensure that certain things happen in the text? And what else might happen for the reader—in the world—as a result? To arrive at some answers to these questions, let us consider Michael Field's revisionary poetics in context of recent theories about form and affordances.

As Caroline Levine has shown, forms contain affordances, a term she borrows from design theory and defines as the potential uses or actions latent in materials or their designs (*Forms* 6). Forms *form*, they *do things*. Literary forms don't just reflect, they "trouble and remake political relations" (Levine, "Strategic Formalism" 656). In *Michael Field's Revisionary Poetics*, I don't focus solely upon large scale forms like "unity" or "network" as Levine does in *Forms*, but I do bring her provocatively useful perspectives to a variety of forms more commonly thought of as literary device or as genre. Large or small in scale, each form has affordances, a potentiality that does not change regardless of the topic the form is employed to describe. Levine urges us to think about what forms are capable of doing, "what potentialities lie latent" and observes that forms can be "picked up and moved to new contexts ... But as they move, forms bring their limited range of affordances with them" (*Forms* 6, 7). Since forms travel, we can observe how Michael Field's experiments with form take advantage of certain affordances while using the forms to do new personal and cultural work.

In this book I not only will be asking of Michael Field: How does thinking something new allow us to do something new? but also: How does *doing* something new allow one to *think* something new? In *Forms of Empire*, Nathan K. Hensley aptly identifies form as "technologies of mediation": he writes, "form marks for me the capacity of literary ensembles to set ideas into motion in ways particular to their suite of affordance—ways that, by definition, other modes of presentation cannot" (18). Hensley urges us to read in ways that we think about how texts "reconfigure their moments, rather than reflecting them, reproducing them, engaging them" and thus to "imagine Victorian objects as particular kinds of subjects: dynamic agents of thought, speakers from the grave, commenting on their historical conditions of emergence" (20). This kind of thinking is particularly apropos to Michael Field, who deliberately experimented with various literary forms in order to look both back and forward, reconfiguring their objects in the process of so doing. In their writing we see the root of poetics—*poiein*—to make or transform, at work.

Revisionary poetics do not necessarily change the affordance of a form, but bring to light different potentialities—perhaps potentialities also always latent in that form—perhaps potentialities that signify differently once in a different context. As Meredith Martin observes:

> women poets used their poetic forms to transform convention and to push the boundaries of what was expected of them ... manipulating and expanding the possibilities of each genre's themes and meters ... [they] used meters to manipulate the emotional tenor of their poems but also manipulated the emotional tenor of their poems to call attention to the performance of meter. (Martin, "Prosody" 32)

As *Michael Field's Revisionary Poetics* examines Michael Field's experiments with forms and their affordances, we will see how these experiments do things both for the individual (in this case, queer, female) author and more broadly. Since no form operates in isolation, attending to the affordances of form opens up a generalizable understanding of political power (Levine, *Forms* 7). As forms travel to new contexts they rub up against other forms and how they are organized vis-à-vis one another (and thus how power operates) may change, allowing some affordances to be more prominently active /observable than others (Levine, *Forms* 7). For female writers like Michael Field, according to Vadillo, "formal experimentation was an attempt at generating questions about the independence of art, an issue particularly important for women, who saw in the notion of art for art's sake a form of social and political revolution" (Vadillo, "Poets of Style" 230). As I consider how form may be deployed as reinscription or as intervention, I am interested also in how experimenting with form involves engaging the unknown—and this is where my reading of history and form in the revisionary poetics of Michael Field also necessitates space for phenomenology, and the recognition of their *l'engrenage* and its cultural work.

Michael Field's revisionary poetics

Michael Field's Revisionary Poetics unfolds roughly chronologically, examining the co-authors' varied literary experiments in chapters organized by form or genre. Chapter 1, "Rewriting History" addresses the revisionary histories and poetics of the co-authors' earliest verse dramas (1884–7) and their book of verse after Sappho's fragments, *Long Ago* (1889). In so doing, Chapter 1 sets the stage for my approach to Michael Field's adaptations of subject and form throughout *Michael Field's Revisionary Poetics*. Here, in addition to comparing Michael Field's early adaptations to their classical and early English precursors, I trace the affordances and *l'engrenage* of their uses of anachronism, violent rhetoric, and of tragedy in some of their early closet dramas and of the fragmented Sapphic lyric in *Long Ago*. The approach to understanding Michael Field's uses (and abuses) of history and form that I develop in this first chapter then becomes a thread that weaves throughout the rest of my study.

Chapter 2 examines Michael Field's ekphrastic poetics in and after *Sight and Song*. The chapter begins by positing the ekphrastic verse collection, *Sight and Song* (1892), as a series of resistant readings that critique Victorian ideologies regarding sex, gender, and aesthetics from what today would be called queer and feminist perspectives. Through a synaesthetic strategy that emphasizes the haptic as well as the visual, Michael Field rewrites the histories of the figures depicted, the Western tradition of art history, and the history of the (female) spectator. Through the *l'engrenage* and orientation of their queer feminist revisionary poetics, their ekphrases perform metaleptic leaps that test the boundaries of and reveal the gaps between existing discourses on art, and suggest other possibilities for reading and being in the world. Chapter 2 then moves beyond *Sight and Song* to identify Michael Field's continued deployment of ekphrasis in their later collections and closes by gesturing to the rise of modernist ekphrases that, to varying degrees, resonated with their verse.

Chapter 3 is "'Come and sing': Elizabethan Temper, Eco-entanglement, and Lyric in *Underneath the Bough*." *Underneath the Bough*'s title is taken from Edward FitzGerald's popular 1859 adaptation of *The Rubáiyát of Omar Khayyám*; this chapter analyzes *Underneath the Bough*'s relationship to Khayyám alongside Michael Field's other lyric inspiration at this time: Renaissance songbooks. In *Underneath the Bough*, historical figures, archaic language, and references to the animate and inanimate natural world permit the lyric speaker to express the great emotion associated with their varied passionate entanglements. For Michael Field, nature is universal (and thus somewhat objective in its transhistoricism); but their appropriation of and experimentation with specifically Elizabethan lyric modes render all experience—including ineffable experience and experience in Nature—accessible for a uniquely subjective state of heightened emotion and aesthetic impression. Ultimately, this chapter considers how Michael Field's ecodecadence both overlaps with and departs from Decadence and from nineteenth-century (and our own) discourses about the environment.

Chapter 4, "'Our dead': Michael Field and the Elegiac Tradition" asks: How do Michael Field's elegiac texts fit into the rich literary tradition of elegy? and: How does Michael Field's writing about grief compare to other Victorian representations of death, loss, and mourning? Through analysis of their early elegiac verse, the "Longer Allegiance" cycle from *Wild Honey from Various Thyme* (1908), and *Whym Chow: Flame of Love* (1914), Chapter 4 argues that the co-authors' paradoxical gearing into and taking up of death and mourning manifests a complex relation to masculine tradition and patriarchal norms: rejecting elegiac tradition to some extent in favor of continued modes of eco-entanglement, yet also continuing to employ the Dionysian and Decadent tropes also used by those homoerotically inclined male Aesthetes who were their contemporaries. Michael Field's later, queer erotics of mourning their beloved dog, Whym Chow, like their earlier elegiac texts and rituals, reside within existing elegiac traditions; but also move beyond them through active mourning strategies also found in modernist, and later, thought. Thus, Chapter 4 demonstrates how Michael Field provides exceptional and important examples of Victorian elegy, examples that both shed light upon and complicate their era's literary elegiac forms and other practices of grief.

Chapter 5, "Becoming Catholic, Desiring Disability: Michael Field's Devotional Verse," demonstrates how Bradley and Cooper sought to become "Catholic poets" in *Poems of Adoration* (1912) and *Mystic Trees* (1913) by appropriating the formal, including metric, conventions of Victorian devotional poetics while also maintaining many of the Aesthetic, queer characteristics of their earlier work. In terms of meter, these queer characteristics manifest themselves in shifting, ambiguous metrics that resonate with today's thinking about queer temporality. In order to support my claims, this chapter examines nineteenth-century writing on devotional form and Anglo-Catholic theology as well as the co-authors' correspondence with their Catholic friends and mentors. By drawing upon recent insights from disability studies, as well as my own previous claims that Michael Field's ongoing re-visionary projects possess qualities we today call both queer and feminist, I show how Michael Field's Catholic verses engage the ineffable and the unknown as they articulate spiritual and homoerotic love and desire specifically in context of being, seeing, and desiring an embodied (female) subject in pain.

"Writing a Life: A Conclusion and a Provocation" wraps up my consideration of Michael Field's revisionary poetics with Michael Field's *Works and Days: The Journal of Michael Field*, thinking about Bradley and Cooper's thirty-year journal in context of queer feminist self-fashioning and the affordances of the nineteenth-century journal as a form. I begin by recalling Robert Browning's efforts to console Bradley and Cooper, saying that the world was not ready for their genius, and they should "Wait fifty years." I also ask what might be gained by juxtaposing Michael Field's sense of themselves as subjects with Victorian fictional autobiographies. This return to the diaries will shift our focus to theories of the archive and to Michael Field's readers, not just fifty years on, but now. What innovations and revisions might scholars and students, captivated by the self-proclaimed "Poets and Lovers," engage in today? Where might Michael Field lead *us* in fifty or more years?

I

Rewriting History:
The Early Plays and *Long Ago*

> The one duty we owe history is to rewrite it.
> —Oscar Wilde, *The Critic as Artist* (1891)

> Dare now to be tragic men, for ye shall be redeemed!
> —Friedrich Nietzsche, *The Birth of Tragedy* (1872)

In the preface to their first published closet drama, *Callirrhoë* (1884), Michael Field proclaims, "this poem pleads guilty to anachronism" (xi). Indeed, much of their life's work features anachronistic content and form. This chapter addresses the revisionary histories and poetics of Michael Field's earliest verse dramas and their book of poems after Sappho's fragments, *Long Ago* (1889), with the goal of more precisely understanding Michael Field's method for producing anachronistic literature. How and why did Bradley and Cooper consume the past in order to heed their friends' urging to "Be Contemporaneous"? How does experimentation with traditional literary forms and genres help Michael Field navigate the paradox of looking backward in order to achieve their stated goal: "We must be modern"?

Here I trace the affordances of anachronism, extravagant tragedy, violently passionate rhetoric, and the form/genre of the closet drama in *Callirrhoë* (1884), *Fair Rosamund* (1884), and *Canute the Great* (1887), and examine these early dramatic adaptations alongside their classical and early English referents. Then I turn to *Long Ago* (1889), a collection of verse that expands Sappho's fragments, in order to reflect upon the affordances of the fragment and to suggest that the fragment facilitates *Long Ago*'s overarching theme of transformation. With a nod to some twenty-first-century thinking about queer temporality, queer affect, and presentism, this chapter examines Michael Field's looking and feeling both backward and forward, demonstrates how their manner of doing so capitalizes on the affordances of their chosen forms, and explores how their revisionary poetics manifest phenomenological characteristics associated with Merleau-Ponty's *l'engrenage*, that is, gearing into and taking up the unknown, which is also consistent with Bradley and Cooper's Hegelian-Paterian views of history and Dionysian eros. The chapter's consideration of anachronism, fragment, *l'engrenage*, and queer-feminist orientation in their early work will then function as a frame by which to read the rest of Michael Field's *oeuvre*, and my subsequent chapters.

Pleading guilty to anachronism

Michael Field's prefaces, taken together, stake out strong theoretical positions on the closet drama, articulating, in particular, their ideas about historical verse drama. The 1884 preface to *Callirrhoë* opens: "Before the bar of Time, this poem pleads guilty to anachronism" (xi). The preface then asserts that, because the classical tale of Callirrhoë has never been rewritten, the author is "permitted a latitude of treatment, unstraitened by the fear of presumption. Greek men and women are approached, not from the centre of nationality, but from the circumference of humanity" (xi–xii). Michael Field then justifies this universalist impulse—their disregard of cultural and historical specificity—by invoking Shakespeare and reminding the reader: "All the world's a stage" (xii).

Michael Field's *Callirrhoë* begins when Coresus, the priest of a cult of Dionysus newly settled in the region of Calydon, bids his chief maenad to help him convert new maenads, in particular the virtuous maiden Callirrhoë, whom he loves. Callirrhoë, whose erotic inclinations appear more homoerotic than otherwise, is secretly intrigued by the thought of becoming a maenad, and she longs for a life outside of her domestic existence caring for her father and brother. Nevertheless, her dutiful loyalty to her family makes her refuse Coresus. In anger, he curses Calydon with a plague, which, as it turns out, can only be vanquished by Callirrhoë's death or the death of someone in her stead. Ultimately, Coresus sacrifices himself for Callirrhoë, who, moved by the day's events, declares herself a maenad and that she loves him, and then fatally stabs herself with the sacrificial knife. At the end of the play (which features many more tragic deaths, including that of a childlike faun devoted to Coresus) Callirrhoë has convinced the town's doctor to become the new Priest of Dionysus, and the once reluctant townspeople of Calydon, also inspired by the sacrifices of Coresus and Callirrhoë, have become believers in Dionysus as well.

Traditionally, Renaissance and Romantic closet drama afforded writers, especially women writers, with "outlets for dramatizing their political and cultural concerns … sexual imagination … and delving into "forbidden" territory (Burroughs 9, 11). Indeed, Ana Parejo Vadillo writes that *Callirrhoë* and Michael Field's other history plays "ventriloquize the past in order to comment upon contemporary issues" ("Outmoded Dramas" 241), a point with which I and many other critics agree. Readers of *Callirrhoë* such as Yopie Prins assert that "in the Greek maenad [Victorian women] found an imaginary alternative to the Victorian spinster … Pater performs the conversion of Classical learning into a queer philology that appealed to women interested in turning Greek eros to their own purposes" ("Greek Maenads" 46–7). Similarly, T. D. Olverson notes that Victorian Hellenism permits Michael Field to "subversively celebrate same-sex sexual pleasure" ("Libidinous" 760). From the fervor of Anaitis, the chief maenad, to the blatant erotic and homoerotic desires of multiple female characters, to the title character's longing for more than patriarchal custom prescribes, to her eventual defiant suicide, Callirrhoë and the maenads certainly can be read as the embodiment of feminine rebellion—sexual and otherwise—both in the past and in the present.

For Sharon Bickle, however, Michael Field's adaptation of the story of Callirrhoë is not, in fact, anachronistic. She describes the co-authors' careful use of the Greek as "strategic ventriloquizing" and states that, after the failures of their first play, *Bellerophôn*,[1] "the accuracy with which the Greek source materials is applied [in *Callirrhoë*] struck many of their early readers as consistent with a male way of knowing" ("Victorian Mænads" 5). Bickle thus concludes that Michael Field's statement that "this poem pleads guilty to anachronism" is "disingenuous" (6). On the one hand, I agree that in *Callirrhoë* and elsewhere, Michael Field strategically adopt a stance akin to that of the male aesthetes they admired, both to

---

[1] Published as Arran and Isla Leigh.

legitimate their work and to distance themselves from what Julia Saville has termed the "feminine affect or Victorian slush" traditionally associated with Victorian poetesses (179). But to dismiss their confessions of anachronism as "disingenuous" is, I think, to overlook the important affective dimensions of their Paterian-inflected engagement with Heraclitean, Hegelian, and Nietzschean ideas of history—their philosophical stance toward history that I began to describe in the introduction. In order to more fully explain Bradley and Cooper's theories about verse drama and their uses and abuses of history—including their feminist and queer appropriations of maenadic and other unruly energies and their "masculine" aesthetic style—let us consider *Callirrhoë*'s preface alongside the prefaces to the closet dramas that follow.

Taken together, Michael Field's prefaces clearly communicate a defense of a poetics that resonates strongly with the Greek root of poet—*poiein*—to make, to form, and especially to transform. The year after the publication of *Callirrhoë* and *Fair Rosamund*, Michael Field declare in their preface to *William Rufus* (1885):

> In the matter of accuracy, this play is not to be regarded as a study of the Past. While the author has felt the sacredness of touching dead character, of which he has striven to bear witness that would not make him ashamed should he hereafter be brought face to face with the personages whose moods and thoughts he has sought to penetrate and reproduce, he has not scrupled to modify or compress events at his pleasure, holding that the dramatists, in face of chronology, may declare with the impudence of Petruccio, "It shall be what o'clock I say it is." (126)

Granted, while it is not uncommon for authors, especially women authors, to make self-deprecating statements in order to legitimate their work, such is not the tone in these and their other prefaces. Like many male-authored defenses of poetry, Michael Field's prefaces are assertive and self-assured, rather than apologetic; thus, I read their assertions literally. Even as we know from their diaries and letters that Bradley and Cooper immersed themselves in rigorous historical study, the prefaces indicate that we should not be surprised when, ultimately, their adaptations stray from historical facts and transform the existing narratives about Callirrhoë, Rosamund Clifford, Mary Queen of Scots, and countless other figures. To that end, in 1882 Bradley (then thirty-five) echoes the biblical authority of both *Isaiah* and *Revelation* in a letter to Cooper (then twenty) when she justifies their dialectical engagement with history by proclaiming, "The motto for the dramatist should be 'Behold I make all things new'" (Bickle, *Fowl* 64).

For example, Bradley and Cooper's source text for *Callirrhoë*, *Description of Greece* by Pausanias, begins the tale like this:

> ... among the Calydonians who became priests of the god was Coresus, who more than any other man suffered cruel wrongs because of love. He was in love with Callirrhoë, a maiden. But the love of Coresus for Callirrhoë was equalled by the maiden's hatred of him. (7.21.1)

Michael Field's version tells a different and much more complex story – one with nuanced gender politics and a keen awareness of the importance of woman's agency. Their *Callirrhoë* makes clear that Coresus' love (as in so many classical and medieval tales) is a product of his gazing upon Callirrhoë from a distance and his fancies about her character and desires. Coresus tells Anaitis, "I caught her face tempestuous with delight" (Field 17) and he concludes she would make a perfect maenad, "Even thus / will that still girl feel the entrancing awe / of the great mysteries" (18). Note how Callirrhoë is "still" and passive as Coresus fantasizes how she will respond when she joins him as his maenad. He imagines her "entranced," and how she will become an instrument in his hands: "Were thou lute to love / There were a new song of the heaven and earth" (32). When Callirrhoë expresses skepticism, Coresus becomes condescending and invokes her gender: "I have been foolish frighting thee with things / Too wonderful for a soul-snooded girl" (32). Though these lines at first seem to indicate that he realizes *he* has made a tactical error, the two alliterative pairs mirror each other such that "foolish and fright[ened]" also seem to apply in his mind to the "soul-snooded" Callirrhoë. He then changes his approach and tries more personal, romantic seduction:

> Think but of me, no veiled divinity,
> Coresus, a mere man a suppliant
> Clasping your knees in his extremity;
> Craving the alms of your great love ... (32–3)

For Michael Field, Coresus' interest in Callirrhoë is both personal and "professional," but clearly, the bottom line is that he has decided he will seduce her, and he won't take no for an answer: Coresus admits, "Withal so ravenous at heart, he scarce / Can bide the time of his petitioning" (33).

But Michael Field's Callirrhoë is more complex and autonomous than either Pausanias or Coresus give her credit for. For instance, although young, she knows that love exists in multiple forms. After her bosom friend and soon to be sister-in-law Nephele confesses that Coresus seduced her into spending the night in a maenadic ritual, Callirrhoë sings: "Eros does not always smite / With cruel and shining dart," (21). That kind of passion "rends the unhappy heart"; Callirrhoë describes such love as "its living fountain drained / Too oft, and overmuch" (22). In contrast, sometimes when Eros strikes he will "Sweep the shaft's feathered end:— / And friendship rises, without pain, / Where the white plumes descend" (22). Both forms of passionate love are erotic and compelling, but the latter—like Nephele's love for Callirrhoë's brother Emathion, as well as the homoerotic love Callirrhoë seems to share with Nephele—is mutual rather than unidirectional.

Callirrhoë's knowledge about the varied faces of eros causes her to feel conflicted. On the one hand, she wants more than domestic existence, and is in fact drawn to the passionate maenadic life:

"Can it be meant," I often ask myself
"Callirrhoë that thou shouldst simply spin,
Be borne of torches to the bridal bed,
Still a babe's hunger, and then simply die,
Or wither at the distaff who hast felt
A longing for the hills and ecstasy?" (25)

Accordingly, when Callirrhoë meets Coresus, she is tantalized by his descriptions of the feelings she will feel and the life she will live if she agrees to become his maenad. But on the other hand, she is not quite convinced: when Coresus urges "be beside yourself / If a god violate your shrinking soul, / Suffer sublimely," Callirrhoë holds fast to her belief that, "Yet I hold it true, Divinity oft comes with quiet foot" (32–3). Callirrhoë wants to live passionately, but without completely sacrificing agency; importantly, some of the choice she wishes to preserve includes her ability to continue to fulfill her duty to her beloved family. Thus we see Callirrhoë articulating concerns about losing herself completely to the Bacchic impulse: she worries "That he provokes men to unnatural deeds /

And once stirred frenzied mother as a fell / Tigress to murder her deluded son" (32). She is unwilling to lose herself—to sacrifice her priorities about the people she loves—and so she resists Coresus' offer:

> My dear father's peace
> I will not wreck, . . .
> . . . .
> . . . It cannot be
> that any but a mocking messenger
> Can come in Heaven's name to set the child
> Against the parent. (33)

In Michael Field's *Callirrhoë*, the conflict between Coresus and Callirrhoë about the role of eroticized passion is a space where the co-authors can theorize about three different, albeit related, kinds of passion that Bradley and Cooper themselves shared within their own relationship as Poet-Lovers: vocational passion, spiritual passion, and romantic passion. All three kinds of love can be characterized by intense eros; all three can come upon one like a fiery dart or a slow burn; and all three can either bolster or destroy one's sense of self and one's autonomy. Michael Field's reclamation of Pausanias demonstrates how a woman might respond to a man whose love emerges from his objectifying ideas about her and his plans for her, rather than being actually about her and her own complex desires. Their Coresus bids Callirrhoë, "Tell me about yourself!" (30); but instead of truly listening to her responses, Michael Field shows how he taunts her, calling her "an apathetic slave of the commonplace" (33). The extended discussion on the nature of eros in Act 1, scene 3 celebrates the intensity of his passion on the one hand—and the reader is supposed to admire this intensity in all its forms. But Coresus' lack of respect for Callirrhoë's views prevents the relationship he wants. In rewriting how Pausanias represents the relationship between Coresus and Callirhoë, Michael Field amplifies the details and provides Callirhoë's perspective. They transform the narrative, making clear that she wants to live passionately, but on her own terms. Thus, in the words of *William Rufus*'s preface the following year, in their version of the tale "It is what o'clock [we] say it is."

While Michael Field do not hesitate to take liberties as they rewrite the plots and persons of past tales and events, what they *do* seem to be interested in portraying with great accuracy is *feeling*—both the feelings they imagine for their subjects and their own. The preface to *The Father's Tragedy*, a closet drama that precedes *William Rufus* in the same 1885 three-play volume, informs the reader that the author has long "felt an intimation that he was consecrated and condemned to hold up the mirror of ideal presentation to the actual pity and terror of . . . history" (3). As the preface continues, it is clear that what the authors intend to portray ideally, as if in a mirror, is *feeling*:

> If it be thought . . . that the author is stern in showing Misery her own feature, Weakness her own image, and Hunger his own form and pressure in the glass of this drama, his best defense is the self-suggested epitaph of the man who is its protagonist [Robert III of Scotland]: —
>
> > Hic jacet Pessimus Rex et Misserimus
> > Hominum in Universo Regno. (3–4)[2]

With their emphasis on "pity", "terror", and "Misery," here Michael Field articulates an intellectual and phenomenological orientation toward accuracy of feeling rather than content, a position described in today's adaptation studies as privileging fidelity to tone over fidelity to content. If Michael Field's early work anticipates Pater's Hegelian query about history: "What is there in this phase of ancient religion for us, at the present day" (*Greek Studies* 154), the answer seems to be that the persons and events they replicate are what we now identify as "traveling concepts" that "embrace multiple meanings and intersubjective knowledge . . . while maintaining some specificity of historical meaning" (Codell and Hughes 5). But always, for Michael Field, the thread that connects present to past—even if it has not been recognized before by (male) historians—is feeling.

To see Michael Field's particular interest in feeling at work in *Callirrhoë*, let us return to Pausanias' *Description of Greece*:

> When everything had been prepared for the sacrifice according to the oracle from Dodona, the maiden was led like a victim to the altar. Coresus stood ready to sacrifice, when, his resentment giving way to love, he slew himself in place of Callirrhoë. He thus proved in deed that

---

[2] Here lies the worst of kings and most miserable of men.

his love was more genuine than that of any other man we know. When Callirrhoë saw Coresus lying dead, the maiden repented. Overcome by pity for Coresus, and by shame at her conduct towards him, she cut her throat at the spring in Calydon not far from the harbor, and later generations call the spring Callirrhoë after her. (7.21.4–5)

In contrast, Michael Field's version of the legend depicts these events as driven by tremendously complex emotions, and they alter the content in order to portray Callirrhoë's feelings—as they imagine them—as accurately as possible. When Coresus lifts the curse by sacrificing himself instead of Callirrhoë, she is moved: "Now he hears no more; I may a little praise him" (106). But as Michael Field's appropriation draws to a close, Callirrhoë is not driven by the pity, shame, or repentance that Pausanias describes. She is inspired by his "holy death" (107): an unselfish passion she never observed in Coresus when he was alive. She also sees evidence that he loved her; and these realizations transform her emotions and actions in complex ways. In a characteristic Michaelian mix of the pagan and the Christian, Callirrhoë's actions directly after Coresus' death turn him into a kind of a Christ figure and she becomes reborn a maenad though his body and blood, extolling, "I looked down on these and drank thy love. I am a maenad; I must have love's wine" (107). She is further thrilled when she overhears Machaon confirm that Coresus died to save her and says,

> I never loved him, *never*
> ....
> ... I confess;
> With this addition, that I love him now
> With woman's rapture, when the man she loves
> Is god for adoration. (124)

Of course, in being inspired by Coresus' passion now that he is dead, in contrast to when he first tried to seduce her, she can become a maenad of her own compulsion, not his. She intends to die a maenad and she finally feels the sublime feelings she has longed for, but on her terms.

Callirrhoë is further inspired—her emotions and actions transformed—when she learns that the faun whom Coresus loved killed himself because he did not feel life was worth living now that Coresus was dead. Contra Pausanias; it's not shame, pity, or repentance that motivates Callirrhoë here, but the realization that:

> Who dwell but with themselves grow impotent:
> They have no Past; the Past is what hath been
> Other than now; the Future is a guest
> Comes not to them
> Who will admit no novel influence.
> Such can but iterate themselves. It needs
> Heaven to transmute our days to yesterdays,
> And touch our morrows with the mystery
> Of hope; when men remembered and desired,
> Straightway they worshipped. (127)

For Callirrhoë, the past is indeed "Other than now"—her beloved Nephele is dead of the plague, she has seen another, less objectifying side of Coresus (who is also dead), and she has been inspired by the faun. These intense events enable her to transform—to "iterate [herself]" much as Michael Field rewrites her—such that she herself can finally perform an act of true eros. Her act of passionate sacrifice is one in which she will join both the faun and Coresus (128); but it is also an act calculated to benefit her community—to convince them, through her sacrifice, to also embrace the new cult of Dionysus.

Because it is read rather than performed, the closet drama as a form affords expectations about telling, rather than showing. Michael Field takes advantage of that expectation, using both dramatic monologue and dialogue for Callirrhoë to describe her feelings directly to the reader, so that both her feelings and actions may be understood. The co-authors' version fills in the gaps not articulated by Pausanias; in imagining more (and different) details for these events, Michael Field makes the feelings of the characters—including the female characters—come alive with much greater nuance. As the preface to *William Rufus* details, such imagining puts the co-authors in a position both "consecrated and condemned" because, to use Merleau-Ponty's term, it necessitates *l'engrenage*. The process of "holding up the mirror of ideal presentation" when remaking Pausanias' brief narrative into a longer and more detailed verse drama is, phenomenologically speaking, a creative act that involves a taking up and gearing into the unknown.

In asserting their dedication to the accurate portrayal of feeling, Bradley and Cooper, as women writers who want to be known as Poets and Dramatists, not Poetesses,[3] enter into precarious territory. Isobel Armstrong notes that nineteenth-century women's poetry was presumed to partake of an affective mode associated with words like "cloying, feminine, female, sentiment, lesson, emotional gush" (*Victorian Poetry* 320); these are the sorts of characteristics that Michael Field did not want applied to themselves or their verse or verse drama. Yet, at the same time, even masculine discourses on the topic identified feeling as the defining factor for poetry. J. S. Mill, for instance, writes, "What *is* poetry, but the thoughts and words in which emotion spontaneously embodies itself?" ("Thoughts" 123). Bradley and Cooper's awareness of how the aesthetics of intense feeling create a catch-22 for them as female authors is exemplified by a now well-known letter they wrote to Robert Browning when they feared he had revealed they were not one man, but two women. There they assert that "We must be free as dramatists to work in the open air of nature—exposed to her vicissitudes, witnessing her terrors: we cannot be stifled in drawing room conventionalities" (*WD* 6). Here we see Bradley and Cooper echoing both Hegel and Schlegel on unacted drama: where Greek drama traditionally embodies communal values, "dramatic poetry conjoins both the external world of objectivity and subjectivity" and is "born out of the need to give full expression to the variegated subjectivity of the author" (Wang xvii, xix). In other words, Michael Field insists upon their right to fully capitalize on the affordances of the closet drama to accommodate that which polite society considers rebellious and/or unutterable. Like Callirrhoë, they don't want to conform to male dictates.

Michael Field's powerful representation of Queen Elinor's jealousy in their adaptation of *Fair Rosamund*, published in 1884 in the same volume as *Callirrhoë*, provides another example of the co-authors' commitment to the accurate representation on intense emotion, regardless of social approbation. When King Henry taunts Queen Elinor with the fact that he never loved her, exclaiming "I embraced your lands / Not you" (Field, *FR* 157), his betrayed wife lashes out with seething hatred more aligned with Lady Macbeth or Rosa Dartle than the angel in the house:

---

[3] See Prins, Lootens, Saville.

Plantagenet, you wronged yourself
As you had made the day and night your foe,
And roused
The violated seasons to confer
Each his particular catastrophe
Of death or pestilence—*Embraced my lands!*
I'll shatter you
As Nature shatters—you, as impotent
As the uprooted tree to lash the earth
That flings its griping roots out to the air.
And plants its burgeoning summits in the soil. (FR 157–8)

Notably, this vivid portrait of vengeful jealousy makes clear that Elinor's reaction—however intense—is a logical, natural response to her husband's betrayal.

The Victorian fascination with medievalisms resulted in many renditions of Rosamund, King Henry, and Queen Elinor: ballads, Swinburne's *Rosamond* (1860), Tennyson's *Becket* (1884), and many paintings. Michael Field's version, first conceived in 1883 when Bradley was thirty-six and Cooper twenty-one, was likely motivated in part by a Burne-Jones watercolor that Bradley admired while visiting Ruskin in 1882 (Bickle, *Fowl* 56). (See Fig. 1.1). While many other paintings depict the moment of confrontation between Elinor and Rosamund, the Burne-Jones that Bradley viewed at Brantwood features Rosamund alone in her bower, dressed simply, engaged in the quotidian task of drawing water from her famed well. In this painting, she is surrounded by flowers—mostly red—contrasted by two white roses that burst from the trellis behind her. The white roses—one at her eye level as she works the well's pulley and the other nestled with an illuminated devotional book—draw the eye across the visual field in a diagonal that includes her pensive, fair face, thereby emphasizing her purity and the purity of her love for Henry, despite her role as his mistress. Indeed, *Fair Rosamund*'s opening Chorus claims:

She whom our first Plantagenet loved too well
Loved, and for whom he built the marble maze
Was no rich crimson beauty of old line
As fabled in proud histories and lays;
No Clifford, as 'tis boasted; but in fine,
A girl o' the country, delicately made

Fig. 1.1 Fair Rosamund (1863). Edward Burne-Jones. Gouache. Private Collection. Courtesy of the Maas Gallery.

Of blushes and simplicity and pure,
Free ardour, of her sweetness unafraid;
For *Rosa Mundi*-of this truth be sure—
Was nature's Rose, not man's: as ye shall see
In this sad tale of Lovers' destiny. (137)

Here we see that once again, Michael Field transforms historical detail in order to deeply examine "free ardour"—in other words, feeling.

I suggest we consider Michael Field's *Fair Rosamund* primarily as three case studies in emotion: how a king and a "girl o' the country" each respond to being in love; and how a betrayed woman might respond to her husband's adultery with such a girl. All three emotional responses are characterized by intensity; and importantly, Michael Field's pen renders them as natural, understandable outcomes of their characters' lived experiences. The play's epigraph, taken from Wordsworth's "Three years she grew in sun and shower", reads:

. . . A lovelier flower
On earth was never seen[4]
This Child I to myself will take;
She shall be mine, and I will make
A Lady of my own
Thus Nature said. (*FR* 136)

By situating Rosamund as a product of Nature, especially through one of Wordsworth's Lucy poems, Michael Field orients the reader's attention away from the context of adultery and toward the context of authentic, natural feeling. King Henry recalls how, surrounded by the palest of cherry blossoms, he kissed Rosamund's white hand, "and her upturned face grew white / To swooning, and the breath stood at her lips" (142); then, because of Rosamund's spontaneous, pure love, "I longed to be a soul from Holy Land / With shrift won at the Holy Sepulchre / To touch her flesh made me a penitent" (142). The reader then learns that the transformation King Henry experiences in his heart and soul occurs because Rosamund loves him for his sake rather than his position, "I've never known / Such homage, only sullen tolerance /

---

[4] Wordsworth's word here is sown, not seen.

And dark-featured hate" (143). Indeed, in a letter dated December 13, 1887, Bradley's friend Dora Leppington reflects at length upon "the complexities of the question" of marriage and concludes, "that [ideal] love, the full spiritual passion, is the one thing that ennobles the physical relation of marriage, *whether under the sanction of the law, and solemnization of the church; or not*. [. . .] This I read as part of the motive of Fair Rosamund too and it seems to me the true doctrine on the subject."[5]

If we return to Elinor's "embraced my lands" speech, we see a similar emphasis on nature and authentic feeling: the spurned queen justifies her threats of vengeance by accusing Henry of setting himself against the seasons and against both day and night. The consequence of setting oneself against nature in this way, she portends, is one he cannot escape and that will leave him gasping for sustenance like an uprooted tree that fruitlessly "plants its burgeoning summits in the soil" (158). From Elinor's perspective, he, like the inverted tree, has turned everything upside down; and as everyone knows from legend, she will have her revenge.

Michael Field's dedication to the accurate portrayal of feeling—even extreme passion and tragic, unlikeable characters—often explains their formal choices as authors, a concept I will return to frequently as this book unfolds. For instance, despite ongoing opposition from critics for doing so, Michael Field wrote verse drama in the style of the Elizabethans and Jacobeans because they believed that particular style is best suited to the expression of emotion. In an 1885 letter, Bradley urges Cooper:

> Do not desert Shakespeare and the Elizabethans. Those with the sobering influence of the great Greek dramatists, . . . are the only Masters for us. Every dramatic writer must be full of his Shakespeare . . . We Must give up the tricks the externalities, the archaisms,—to copy these is imitation, but we must seek to study and touch life as he—Shakespeare studied and touched it, and our speech must always be utterly different from ordinary speech; because ordinary speech is not transfigured by emotion, and the ordinary speech of an Age like ours is base with the exceeding Vulgarity of Materialism. (August 28, Bickle, *Fowl* 149)

---

[5] Letter from Dora Leppington to Katharine Bradley, MSS Add. 45851. fols. 119v–120r. The British Library. I have added italics for emphasis.

This letter responds to William Archer's negative review[6] of *The Father's Tragedy* and *William Rufus* which accuses them of "imitation" and "affected archaisms" irrelevant to "the modern world." For Archer, Michael Field's "fatal error ... as a writer of dialogue consists in his unlagging adherence to the theory that poetical personages must speak a jargon as unlike as possible to ordinary human speech" (20). But for Michael Field, "pleading guilty to anachronism" privileges feeling over content; their creative process of writing is invested in the ways in which people become "transfigured by emotion"; and putting these principles to paper—whether to show the effect of the Bacchic dance upon Nephele, of the faun's death upon Callirrhoë, the effect of love upon fair Rosamund and King Henry, or jealousy upon Queen Elinor, etc.—is best accomplished, at least to their mind, in what they perceived to be the style of the Elizabethans.

As I argued in the introduction, to be "transfigured by emotion" is, for Michael Field, both a necessary precondition for art and a key element of their fierce personal dedication to the Dionysian thyrsus and all it represents. Indeed, many scholars have described Michael Field's celebration of Dionysian passion in their drama, verse, and life writing. As Olverson observes, the plays, in their engagement with both historical and contemporary (in this case Swinburnian) treatment of the maenad and maenad-like figures, convey "it is the poet's (moral) duty to record one's passion for life and its potentially tragic cost" (*Women Writers* 124). Many scholars have also noted how Field's work resonates with Pater's call for the aesthete to occupy themselves with intense, "flame-like," "devouring," impressions of all kinds; in other words, the ideas Pater describes in the essays on the Renaissance with which Michael Field would have been familiar with in the 1880s, and also his later *Greek Studies*, notably "The Bacchanals of Euripides."

As Ana Parejo Vadillo and others argue, in Michael Field's devotion to the Bacchanalian impulse, the co-authors express not only strong affinities with Pater, but importantly, an anticipation of Nietzsche, particularly *The Birth of Tragedy*. In 1895 Bradley and Cooper eventually read Nietzsche with great zest and appreciation; in 1896 Cooper proclaims in the joint diary, "We have met in Nietzsche's works a real Bacchic voice crying in the

---

[6] Archer was translator of Ibsen and advocate for realist drama; he was quite disdainful of contemporary verse drama in general.

wilderness."[7] They were likely drawn to passages in Nietzsche like the following:

> [B]elieve with me in Dionysian life and in the re-birth of tragedy. The time of the Socratic man is past: crown yourselves with ivy, take in your hands the thyrsus, and do not marvel if tigers and panthers lie down fawning at your feet. Dare now to be tragic men, for ye are to be redeemed! Ye are to accompany the Dionysian festive procession from India to Greece! Equip yourselves for severe conflict, but believe in the wonders of your god! (Nietzsche, *Birth of Tragedy* 157)

But as I also noted in the introduction, even before Bradley and Cooper read Nietzsche (and even before they met Bernard Berenson, who falsely presented many of Nietzsche's ideas to them as his own)[8] the co-authors were already incorporating into their early plays Dionysian ideals that would soon be recognized as sharing affinities with Nietzsche. Thus, while Stefano Evangelista writes, "Michael Field's poetry of the early 1890s should be retrospectively recognised as Nietzschean in all the radical implications of this term" (*British Aestheticism* 123), Michael Field's closet dramas of the early 1880s, with characters who love and live with ecstasy, wonder, and tragic, unfettered passion, especially when read in context of their prefaces, should be recognized as an even earlier incarnation of these Nietzschean affinities.

The uses of anachronism in Michael Field's work—especially their adaptations of the past and prefaces to those adaptations that extravagantly convey Dionysian enthusiasm—raise additional questions about Michael Field's revisionary poetics. *How did Michael Field arrive at their interpretations of history? What does their affective process when dealing with history reveal about their ideas about aesthetics, about themselves as artists, and their creative choices?* I address these questions in the next section as I compare their process of thinking and feeling with some twenty-first-century thinking about presentism and queer affect.

---

[7] *Works and Days*. MSS Add. 46785, December 31, 1896. (EC). fol. 196r. The British Library.

[8] The 1895 diary is peppered with the Fields' tremendous outrage and betrayal over Berenson's misrepresentation of Nietzsche's ideas as his own. Cooper's New Year's Eve entry asserts, "His dishonesty about Nietzsche has been the moral shock of the year" (*Works and Days*. MSS Add. 46784, December 31, 1895. (EC). fol. 56v. The British Library.

"... his sense of the fact of her life"

In the preface to their rendition of a feminist, homoerotically inclined Mary Queen of Scots in their 1890 verse drama, *The Tragic Mary*, Michael Field confess that they have been "Seized by a passionate desire of access ... Of absolute knowledge we have nothing; her tragedy, clear cut in detail is vague in its determination ... It is therefore possible for a dramatist to transcribe his sense of the fact of her life, to justify the vision of her as it has come to himself" (v–vii *passim*). As in the earlier prefaces discussed in the previous section, here we see Bradley and Cooper engaged in a multi-step creative process: they notice and meticulously research the object of study, are guided by their feelings and lived experience when selecting which facts to preserve, and wholeheartedly embrace their subjective thoughts, feeling, and imagination when embellishing or changing what they don't know for sure. This dialectic of objective and subjective perception owes an enormous debt to Pater, for whom, in the words of Carolyn Williams,

> both aestheticism and historicism are strategies of epistemological self-consciousness and representation, and as such both offer systematic programs for what to look at and how to look. Both begin in skepticism, questioning the very possibility of knowledge, and both turn that epistemological doubt against itself in a dialectical revision of the grounds of knowledge. (3)

Williams continues: Pater "acknowledges from the beginning that the simplest act of perception is an aesthetic act ... He realizes ... that history itself is in part the result of an aesthetic reconstruction" (Williams 4). In *Feeling Backward: Loss and the Politics of Queer History*, Heather Love categorizes Pater's aesthetic historicism as a queer structure of feeling;[9] here, I assert we should do likewise for Michael Field's.

Heather Love identifies in Pater what she calls "feeling backward," by which she means a "disposition toward the past, embracing loss, risking abjection" (30). Love "insists on the importance of

---

[9] See also Elizabeth Freeman *Beside You in Time*. Using Audre Lorde's "The Uses of the Erotic" as a point of departure, Freeman argues that "the sense of time is instrumental to becoming social in an expansive mode [she calls] queer hypersociability" (17).

clinging to ruined identities and to histories of injury," stating that "the longing for community across time is a crucial feature of queer historical experience, one produced by the historical isolation of individual queers as well as the damaged quality of the queer archive" (37). We see this in the implicit and explicit homoeroticism found in so much of Michael Field's *oeuvre*, as well as texts that demonstrate that the absence of mothers or female role models have negative consequences. For instance, in *Fair Rosamund* II, vii, Elinor only gains access to Rosamund by convincing her foster-sister that she is Rosamund's long-lost mother, and after Rosamund stabs herself, she begs Elinor, "to do for my dead flesh the things / A mother would entreat" (Field, *FR* 203).We might therefore say that both Pater's and Michael Field's creative and intellectual processes use history to find community and make art in a way that blends historical and what we today call perversely presentist methods; and objective and subjective viewpoints.

Where Michael Field appears to diverge from Pater, is that Pater's looking backward, for Love and other critics, is characterized by ascesis, queer failure, and withdrawal. In contrast, Michael Field's looking backward as we have seen, is Dionysian, with characters and scenes that so frequently strike their readers as violently passionate, and/or extravagantly tragic. Inspired by the writers they collected in their own "Bacchic library" which included among others the works of Keats, François Villon, Pierre de Ronsard, Angelo Poliziano, Lorenzo di Medici, Anacreon, and Shakespeare (Vadillo "Aestheticism" 21), Michael Field revels in creating characters like *Callirrhoë*'s maenads, whose ecstatic frenzy leads them to engage in *sparagmos* and *omaphagia*: the ripping and tearing of flesh, which then they eat raw. And, though Field certainly provides their readers with plenty of characters who, especially in context of Victorian values of both progress and moderation, could be said to fail—such as both Callirrhoë's and Rosamund's suicides—these characters fail spectacularly, possessing "the glorification of enthusiasm," (which is how they define the myth of Dionysus in the preface to *Callirrhoë*) (xii).

Thus, while it is commonplace to think about closet drama as "theater of the mind,"[10] for Michael Field it also functions as a Dionysian stage on which to "study and touch life," to be that "mirror of ideal presentation" they had described in the preface

---

[10] See Wang, *The Theatre of the Mind*.

to *The Father's Tragedy*, free of the "drawing room conventionalities" they had warned against in their letter to Browning. The closet drama, which affords the ability to write scenes that can't actually be performed onstage, and to tell rather than show, is an excellent vehicle for Michael Field to manifest their own queer structures of feeling: their homoerotic and proto-feminist orientations, and their dedication to living with Dionysian passion, even if critics don't approve of their content or the particular manner of their anachronisms. Thus, through their revisionary poetics, Michael Field reveals the queer-feminist potentiality latent in the closet drama as form.

And indeed, such queer structures of feeling *were* recognized and admired by some of Michael Field's homoerotically inclined contemporaries. For instance, in the first of two notable letters from March 1884, Marc André Raffalovich writes to "Michael Field," gushing, "let me only assure you of my sympathy with the leading or central emotion of both plays: it quite carried me away." Raffalovich's next letter makes perfectly clear (or queer) what he so admires in *Callirrhoë* and *Fair Rosamund*:

> You seem to me to have a different standpoint, a wider application of poetry to feeling. [. . .] Are you—and this is I should really like to know—prepared [for the implications] one may draw from your volume? The purity of ecstasy "pure only from burning lips" leads to Walt Whitman. There is no escape from Leaves of Grass and Calamus and Brooklyn Ferry. Swinburne has sung the magic of rapture and you have taken up the ethics of it.[11]

Raffalovich then goes on to acknowledge that some readers will be displeased but "You have read enough of the Elizabethans to be aware of that." Venturing to include himself in this queer community of Shakespeare, Whitman, and Field, he closes with a copy of his own unabashedly homoerotic *Cyril and Lionel* and expresses a coy wish that "you would tell me something about yourself—Or do you believe too much in the fascination of mystery?"[12]

---

[11] Marc André Raffalovich to "Michael Field," MSS Add. 45851, March 1884. fols. 68v–70v, *passim*. A third letter, from November of that year, is the better-known one where Raffalovich reveals that he thought he had been writing to "a young man of my own age." (fol. 72r.)

[12] Raffalovich to Field. MSS Add. 45851. fol. 70v–71v, *passim*. The British Library.

Granted, closet drama or what Byron called "mental theatre," historically has been characterized by simple plot and austerity (Burroughs 13). Not so for Michael Field, for as Vadillo asserts, "Michael Field's discourse on excess was key to their vision of poetry rather than destroying the beauty of poetry . . . They aimed to reactivate language, stretch it, and reform it" ("Poets of Style" 241). Even in their earliest plays, we see Michael Field exploring the styles of Aestheticism and Decadence—what Vadillo calls the "cultivated extravagance" of their later "Roman trilogy"—with long, complicated plots, luxurious description, language of color, and overuse of metaphor ("Poets of Style" 241). For instance, when Nephele tells Callirrhoë how the maenad Anaitis seduced her for a Bacchanal, Nephele recalls feeling like prey of "a crouching leopard" but also as if Anaitis "empties my young heart as easily / As from a pomegrantate one plucks the seeds (Field, *Call.* 20). Michael Field is fond of metonyms like "Hymen's torches" (2) and saying things like, "Zeus will grant no pause from plague ere the maiden / Haughty to Evius' priest shall try the feel of his altars—/ Knife through the milkless breast or riving the throats spouting vessel" (*Call.* 72). In *Fair Rosamund* they twice employ the aesthetic conceit of Rosamund's hair as "gold made silver in the moonlight" (Field, *FR* 202), or as King Henry puts it, "every crispèd tress/ Will shimmer into argent" (169). With such extravagance challenging the more staid stylistics of the traditional closet drama, Michael Field position themselves among other practitioners of queer aestheticism and decadence, anticipating the famous words of Oscar Wilde's literary executor, Robert Ross, who believed that "overwrought technique" was a sign of "realized perfection" (qtd in Hall and Murray 1) as they portray history (as they had said in the preface to *The Tragic Mary*) according to "his sense of the fact of her life."

Tragic survivors of evolutionary struggle

Critics provide many explanations for why Bradley and Cooper appropriate and revise history as they do. Some cite the influence of Robert Browning's interest in historical subjects; others, as I have already mentioned here, correctly observe that like their poetry, Michael Field's dramas use the distance of the past to critique patriarchy and heteronormativity in the present. Joseph Bristow offers another interpretation in "Michael Field in Their

Time and Ours," where he remarks that the work of Michael Field contains "the marks of a studied antiquarianism that resists what they perceived as the decidedly unaesthetic perils of modernity" (160). While I do think Bristow is correct, I think there's still more nuance to be found here; some further explanation can be discovered in yet another preface: to *Canute the Great* (1887).

Canute's preface, which is worth quoting at length, reads:

> The story of Canute is full of the tragic element of evolution:—I say *the tragic element* in opposition to the still prevalent doctrine, that declension and calamity, rather than development, are essential to the composition of tragedy. The evils of an age of decline cannot be compared with the pangs of a new era; for neither the race nor the individual possess in the term of decrepitude that vitality that gives poignancy to regret. When, on the contrary, a vigorous, aggressive and undisciplined people comes to recognise its barbarism through contact with the civilisation it has defaced, it wrestles with an intolerable shame. In the evolutionary struggle the survivor is himself a tragic figure. Every sunrise brings him into sharper antagonism with the beliefs and habits that beset while they revolt him. He is alienated from his gods, his forefathers, his very dreams. His hopes are not founded on experience, nor his ideals on memory. (5)

Echoing Field's preface, when Oscar Wilde reviewed *Canute the Great*, he called it

> in many respects a really remarkable work of art. Its tragic element is to be found in life, not in death; in the hero's psychological development, not in his moral declension or in any physical calamity; and the author has borrowed from modern science the idea that in the evolutionary struggle for existence the true tragedy may be that of the survivor. (*Woman's World*, 1888)

As this section will illustrate, Field's preface suggests that, rather than mere nostalgia and/or loss, the survivor's tragedy is that he or she may feel keenly that the evolutionary struggle has highlighted problems to be overcome, along with the fact that the old ways no longer serve them well; but they have not yet developed the tools (other than passion) to succeed in the modern world in which they find themselves.

Field's declaration that "in the evolutionary struggle the survivor is himself a tragic figure," provides a concrete explanation for some of the observations that other critics have made about the tragic and often violent outcomes of the Dionysian passions of their closet dramas. All are consistent with Marion Thain's important insights about Michael Field's use of aesthetic paradox. Olverson's views are representative:

> At once life-affirming and utterly tragic, *Callirrhoë* represents the paradoxes of passion ... The coming of the cult of Dionysus signifies a moment of cultural rupture which severely disturbs the social order of Calydon, exposing the fragile, and deeply gendered relationship between the citizens and the polity. ("Libidinous" 760–2, *passim*)

Callirrhoë's dilemma is that the maenadic existence she desires—and the profound changes to her society set in motion by her actions—will be painfully alienating and destructive for the father and brother she dearly loves. Similarly, both Rosamund and Canute act upon their desires and ambitions with good intentions; but their pursuit of love (and in Canute's case, political power) means abandoning values and traditions that are important to them as well as setting in motion consequences that will hurt people they love and admire. Even *Callirrhoë*'s faun, who, as I discussed in the introduction, so charmingly tries to outdance his shadow, can be read as divided against himself and queerly, tragically out-of-time. Each recognizes the complicated problem they face in the moment in which they find themselves; and each recognizes their lack of ability to solve that problem with complete satisfaction.

In this context it's important to note how Michael Field's verse dramas advocate that passionate acts be *publicly* recognized so that their legacy will live on. For instance, after Callirrhoë's death, Machaon reflects upon both Coresus and the eponymous heroine:

> If a man needs god as his ideal self,
> He needs the picture of his life sublimed;
> And we will put
> Before Men's eye the picture of high deeds,
> Their hearts will emulate. (130–1)

Callirrhoë's is a political intervention that will be remembered in the future. *Fair Rosamund* describes a more personal kind of tragic survivorship—after a relationship has evolved to a bad place—but likewise, recording and memorializing extreme passion are important to the central message of Michael Field's adaptation of the tale. For instance, at the end of *Fair Rosamund*, King Henry immediately invokes the language of memorials and emphasizes that their love will not be forgotten: "already is the tender mouth / A rosy marble to the memory / Of all past kisses." (206). He refers to her body as "Lovely portraiture" that has power to slow (his) age; and when her lute catches his eye, he proclaims that the inanimate instrument has "life about the strings / Her spirit's touched it" (206). In metaphorical marble and portrait, in the real instrument she leaves behind, and of course in the "holy spot / At Goddeshill" where Henry will "rear a stately shrine" (208), Rosamund's legacy as one who has moved and transformed a king with her love will be remembered. And of course, while Michael Field's verse drama reimagines a new psychological depth for the context of King Cnut's acquisition of power in England, the fact of his having left a considerable mark upon history is not something anyone can contest, given their title's straightforward reproduction of how historians have represented him: Canute the Great.

Yet legacies are complicated: multifaceted, paradoxical, and open to interpretation. Just as the co-authors' interpretation of Callirrhoë emphasizes different aspects of her tale than legend does, Michael Field also puts a spin on their version of how the Danish King Cnut came to rule England. Their Canute shares few values with the widowed English queen, Emma,[13] or the English alderman, Edric, even though both successfully scheme to enhance Canute's political power. Instead, Field's *Canute the Great* emphasizes Canute's mutual affinities with his purported enemy, Edmund Ironsides. Canute's victory at the Battle of Assandun ends with an intriguing homoerotic scene where Canute and Edmund divide England and pledge friendship: Canute declares, "the heavens seal a vow / That I will live your brother" and remarks upon his deep feelings of "amity" as they clasp hands (59). The scene's parallels to a marriage ceremony intensify as Edmund swears, "I am wholly yours" and they exchange clothes and weapons (59). While the queer potentials of both their affectionate affirmations and their

---

[13] An anonymous review of the *Canute* in *The Spectator* that is overwhelmingly positive (although not about its companion play *A Cup of Water*) makes much of the play's representation of Emma as an unlikable woman.

power-sharing plan as dual kings of England are short-lived, this scene's emotion reads much more authentically than Canute and Emma's declarations of romantic interest in one another elsewhere in the text. Indeed, when Canute discovers that Emma and Edric have had Edmund assassinated in order to make him king over all England, Canute is disgusted with both of them and grieves Edmund:

> I loved his kingdom, loved his people, all
> The other side, the hills beyond the stream;
> I loved him, yea, I hugged him to my heart,
> I felt him royal. (82)

In all of these instances, Michael Field's project of exploring how a survivor can also be a tragic figure involves their own queer-feminist orientation toward the narratives they adapt. And in so doing, their highly subjective re-visions invite the reader to recognize the importance of perspective.

To this end, for example, Michael Field's *Fair Rosamund* provides ample opportunity for the reader to consider how Queen Elinor's perspective differs from Rosamund's, and both from Henry's. Importantly, the consequences, not only of feeling, but of *not* acknowledging the lived (including affective) experience of others is much emphasized, especially in the final actions of the play. For instance, when Queen Elinor confronts Rosamund in the labyrinth, she asks, "Have you thought of me these many days?" (203). Elinor then invokes her age and status, and declares that these things—along with the inevitability of death—"should awe the heart of youth—that churl of nature" (203). Rosamund then kills herself to repay the debt of not acknowledging how her actions would impact her lover's wife. She has loved but she also has harmed; and because she is (in Michael Field's version) a pure and simple child of Nature, Rosamund seeks to act honorably and right the wrong, choosing to stab herself with the dagger rather than die more passively by the cup of poison traditionally associated with this legend. Michael Field's *Fair Rosamund* thereby demonstrates that Elinor, Rosamund, and Henry are all tragic survivors with no options other than to act with authentic feeling; but whether one considers Rosamund's love as stealing something from a relationship that was already in its death throes or as giving new life and hope to a lonely and disappointed king so he can go on and do good things, is a matter of perspective in Michael Field's reclamation of the tale.

In this way, Michael Field's verse dramas become a metatextual field upon which to reflect upon both the narrative at hand and the process of creating narrative. Like so much of Michael Field's work, these early closet dramas, especially *Fair Rosamund*, become a performance of how one participates, phenomenologically speaking, in the projects of history: how perceiving history is a product of the orientations that come from lived experience; how writing history happens in community with others past and present even as it can establish a sense of connection with figures from the past; how understanding history is as an ongoing, Hegelian process; and how engaging with history necessitates *l'engrenage*.

Dustin Friedman argues that through such creative work queer aesthetes gain some "measure of self-determination" (13). Although the situations that drive the characters in their historical verse dramas are obviously different than Bradley and Cooper's lived experience, I think we would do well to consider how Bradley and Cooper, and their authorial persona "Michael Field," were themselves similarly caught in a moment of change, and similarly torn; we can use these closet dramas to reflect upon how Bradley and Cooper similarly were survivors of evolutionary struggle (in this case aesthetic) in a time that they felt was "base with the Vulgarity of Materialism." They too felt the pull of tradition, despite the ways that it disadvantaged women. They too felt the anguish of modernity, of change and of loss, of relinquishing old allegiances and forms, but also evolving toward the unknown. Becoming contemporaneous.

What makes it possible for Callirrhoë, Canute the Great, the characters in *Fair Rosamund*, and Michael Field themselves to negotiate their tragic survivorship is their dedication to the thyrsus—to Dionysian passion. This is the constant, the universal that they see in both past and present—or at least they see its potential to transform both the present moment and the future. Negative, tragic feeling—that too is Dionysian, which Michael Field define as the "glorification of enthusiasm, which [they believed] to be the sap of the Tree of Life" (*Call.* xii). This is what situates them not against the modern, but rather, as Parker and Vadillo's recent collection of Michael Field essays positions them, as "Decadent Moderns." And let's not forget that Bradley and Cooper's entanglement with Dionysian affect in their personal lives paralleled their creative efforts so obviously that it inspired their acquaintance, Logan Pearsall Smith, to publicly refer to then as "Bacchic Maenads" (91). As we see in even their most tragic characters, Dionysian passion constitutes escape, autonomy, and release from repression and oppression, even (or perhaps especially) when it ends in death. Importantly, A. Mary F. Robinson's 1884 review of *Callirrhoë* and *Fair Rosamund* in *The Academy* indicates that, like Michael Field, she believes that "For good or for evil, these periodic outbreaks of contagious ecstasy are parts of the history of the world" (395). For creating space for these tragic figures to re-emerge with a new voice at the close of the nineteenth century, Robinson praises the "young writer with plenty of convictions and plenty of courage" (396).

If we see in Michael Field's work the importance of legacy—of looking/feeling backward in order to find community and to illuminate overlooked and often queer-feminist aspects of the tales and figures from the past—what of *their* legacy? Vadillo has argued, "It may be argued that Bradley and Cooper were the most important, certainly the most prolific, verse dramatists of their time" ("Hot-House" 196). Given their intellectual and aesthetic resonances with major figures such as Pater and Nietzsche, and given the ways that their verse dramas perform a feeling backward that mirrors their own and the late Victorian era's painful difficulties with modernity and change even as they imagine a queer archive, Michael Field perhaps should have attained, in their time, more firm a place among the major thinkers in the transition from the nineteenth century to modernism. But they did not. Only in the past two or three decades, (quite a bit more than the fifty years Robert Browning had told them to wait in 1888) has Michael Field been featured in Victorian anthologies, on websites, in the classroom, and regularly discussed in academic journals—as female aesthetes, and as important female and queer authors. And even so, their slow move toward a more central place in the literary canon continues to owe more to their output as poets and diarists than as dramatists. Like Hegel's owl of Minerva, they have arrived only belatedly; the taste of their own era was against them.

Between 1907 and 1908, when Cooper (at forty-five) and Bradley (at sixty-one) were becoming Catholic, experimenting with devotional verse, yet still ambitiously dedicated to establishing themselves for posterity as both dramatists and poets, *The*

North American Review[14] became the site of a conversation about the unfortunate decline of dramatic literature at the present time. In the course of providing a fairly comprehensive "Retrospects of the Drama," Yale professor of literature Henry Beers opined that closet drama was a perfectly laudable form. But about six months later, Columbia professor of dramatic literature Brander Matthews responded with "The Legitimacy of the Closet-Drama," disparaging closet dramas as deliberate imitations of the Greek and "mere poetic exercises" (217). Matthews criticizes closet drama for "contribut[ing] very little to the reputation of their authors" (218) and sneers, "behind every appearance of the closet drama we can discover a latent contempt for the actual theatre" (222). Matthews concludes, "the closet drama never appears in any period of affluent dramatic productivity" and "the drama is not for the library but for the theatre" (223). Despite their contrasting opinions on the closet drama, both Beers and Matthews mourn the lack of new drama in their current day. Beers laments that "England has lost the dramatic habit" (634). Meanwhile as Matthews reminds his readers that Shakespeare's plays are still very popular and that Ibsen "has shown us that the austerest of themes may be treated in the modern theatre" (223), he seems to be waiting for the right playwright to come along and fill the gap, as long as it's not with a closet drama. In this context of the history of dramatic literature, Michael Field themselves, it seems, are tragic survivors of evolution.

Interestingly, a little over a decade later when T. S. Eliot explores similar issues in "The Possibility of the Poetic Drama" (1920), he, like Michael Field forty years earlier, praises Elizabethan verse drama as a form particularly suited to ideas and emotion and emphasizes that it had been a particularly good fit for "the temper of the age" (57) For Eliot, "to create a form is not merely to invent a shape, a rhyme or rhythm. It is also the realization of the whole appropriate content of this rhyme or rhythm. . . . not merely such and such a pattern, but a precise way of thinking and feeling" (57). These sentiments have much in common with Bradley's 1885 pep talk to Cooper about continuing to write about topics and in forms that would permit them to "study and touch life" just as Shakespeare did. The problem for verse drama in recent times,

---

[14] *The North American Review* served a transatlantic audience of readers and contributors.

according to Eliot, was that "the nineteenth century had a good many fresh impressions; but it had no form in which to confine them" (56)—a situation akin to how Michael Field describes the tragic survivor in their preface to *Canute the Great*. Eliot worries that "by losing tradition, we lose our hold on the present" (55) —a sentiment not opposed to Michael Field's Hegelian-Paterian ideas of history. So, it seems that Eliot and Michael Field would have found much upon which to agree about the implications of history and form for art. Very much like Michael Field, Eliot maintains that "every work of imagination must have a philosophy; and every philosophy must be a work of art"; and he finds hope in the fact that "the undigested 'idea' or philosophy, the idea-emotion, is to be found also in poetic dramas which are conscientious attempts to adapt a true structure, Athenian or Elizabethan, to contemporary feeling" (60) But even by 1920 when Eliot was writing these things, Michael Field had not yet achieved the fame they had hoped for. Eliot's diagnosis that his was a "formless age" suggests that, in addition to the sex-gender politics that quickly relegated all but the most prominent of female authors to oblivion, any attempt to revitalize Greek or Elizabethan drama would immediately be dismissed as imitation. The temper of the age would need to shift once more such that their revisionary poetics could be perceived as *poiesis*, as transformation rather than derivative. Michael Field would be queerly out of time for another fifty or so years to come.

Thinking with fragments: *Long Ago*

Thus far in this chapter I have argued that in their historical verse dramas, Michael Field display a particular investment in portraying the passionate feeling that was so central to their own dedication to living with Dionysian enthusiasm. I have demonstrated how, as they revise stories from the past, anachronistic—especially Elizabethan—language is as central to their project as their fearless revision of historical content. Further, I have advocated that we view Michael Field's aesthetic historicism as a queer structure of feeling that blends both objective and subjective approaches to the objects of their study; that their queer-feminist orientation toward their subjects results in adaptations with striking homoerotic and feminist content; and that in their stylistic extravagance they demonstrate their alignment with other Decadent authors of the *fin de siècle*. In transforming history in such a manner, their revisionary poetics, phenomenologically speaking, requires a willingness to engage the unknown of history; and the doing results in a sense of reclamation and queer community-making that also results in their own sense of queer-feminist self-determination. This is important because, like the characters they imagine (or transform), their lived experience includes a sense of not being aligned with the conventions of their time.

This final section of this chapter will bring these ideas to bear on Michael Field's earliest book of verse, *Long Ago* (1889), which is a collection of poetry based upon Sappho's fragments with each poem preceded by the Greek line that inspired it. This project exercised the co-authors' own ability to read Greek, and benefitted from H. T. Wharton's *Sappho, Memoir, Text, Select Renderings and a Literal Translation* (1884), which included commentary by J. A. Symonds (among others) and made perfectly clear that many of the poems were addressed to women and were homoerotic in nature. Since much has been written about *Long Ago*,[15] here I will focus primarily on the affordances of the fragment as form, highlighting the fragment's potential as queer synecdoche that, in *Long Ago*, renders the collection a series of diverse meditations on transformation, and in so doing lends authority to Michael Field's aesthetic historicism.

Katharine Bradley's interest in Greek dated from her Newnham days; she then taught it to Cooper so they could study it together. By late 1886 Bradley confided to Robert Browning:

> We are working also at a collection of songs and poems, each of which is suggested by one of Sappho's incomparable fragments; and we trust humbly they are not wholly influenced by that richest of inspired women. Do not think we are presumptuous. We only catch the light from her timeless gems in our little, recent mirrors.[16]

In this letter, Bradley's attempt to strike the right tone about their ambitious project is palpable; her implied concerns are in keeping with how other women writers of the period sought to manage gendered expectations by negotiating the boundaries between amateur dabbling and being a professional. For instance, in *Ladies'*

---

[15] See Evangelista, Gorman, and Prins, among many others.
[16] Letter KB to Robert Browning, late 1886. MSS Add. 46866. The British Library.

Greek, Yopie Prins illustrates how Victorian women turned to the passionate lives depicted in Greek texts and thereby demonstrated how a Victorian woman of letters could be both a thinking and a feeling woman (26). And Vadillo observes that many women worked with translations, which permitted them to "fashion a cosmopolitan style which showed the breadth of their artifice and marked their poetries as learned" ("Poets of Style" 234). At any rate, according to reviews, the co-authors' "little, recent mirrors" were received overwhelmingly positively and did much to establish Michael Field as a new poet of growing importance.

While Michael Field's experiments with Elizabethan language and the form of the closet drama were, despite their innovative queer-feminist content, subject to accusations of imitation, their work with the Sapphic fragment was, in terms of form, quite well aligned with valued nineteenth-century discourses. Whereas the closet drama was, as we have seen, considered merely outdated, the fragment signaled importance and intellectual worth. As Robert Preyer, Jonah Siegel, and others have shown, the fragment gestured toward antiquity; and it called to mind a considerable range of wisdom books from the Bible to Thomas Carlyle's 1829 translations of Novalis. Edward Lear's nonsense verse, according to Henchman, demonstrates interest in rearrangement of parts to make new wholes in the context of evolutionary discourse. And Matthew Arnold praises the fragment in "The Study of Poetry" (1880): one should always "have in one's mind lines and expressions of the great masters, and to apply them as a touchstone to other poetry ... Short passages, even single lines, will serve our turn quite sufficiently" (qtd in Siegel, "Among the English Poets" 221). The fragment also resonated with other nineteenth-century cultural forms ranging from the commonplace book to archaeology; and in the context of creative activity, the fragment, like the artist sketch or study, was considered to reside closest to an originary state of inspiration.

The nineteenth-century fragment additionally summoned the weighty history of philosophical thought about the part and the whole, such as that of Bradley and Cooper's most beloved philosopher, Spinoza, who wrote:

> As to the whole and the parts, I mean that a given number of things are parts of a whole, in so far as the nature of each of them is adapted to the nature of the rest, so that they all, as far as possible, agree together.

On the other hand, in so far as they do not agree, each of them forms, in our mind, a separate idea, and is to that extent considered as a whole, not as a part. (Letter 32 to Oldenberg)

As Michael Field scholars well know, Bradley and Cooper's reading of Spinoza influenced their conception of themselves as co-authors: "Spinoza with his fine grasp of unity says: 'If two individuals of exactly the same nature are joined together, they make up a single individual, doubly stronger than each alone,' i.e., Edith and I make a *veritable Michael*."[17] The philosophical currency of the fragment among nineteenth-century thinkers also led some of Michael Field's contemporaries to think about the part and the whole in the context of contemporary aesthetics. For example, Paul Bourget defines the decadence style as, "one in which the unity of the book falls apart, replaced by the independence of the page, where the page decomposes to make way for the independence of the sentence, and the sentence makes way for the word."[18] Influenced by Bourget, in the introduction to *Au Rebours* Havelock Ellis writes, "a decadent style is only such in relation to a classic style . . . The first is beautiful because the parts are subordinated to the whole; the second is beautiful because the whole is subordinated to the parts" (n.p.). Thus, the nineteenth-century cultural work of the fragment accomplishes much for Michael Field: in creating new lyric verse out of the Sapphic fragment, Michael Field signals their ability to read Greek, provides the public with a popular form, and aligns their verse with other philosophical and aesthetic thinkers in the past and at the *fin de siècle*.

With this background in mind, let us now contemplate the actual affordances, for Michael Field, of working with "Sappho's incomparable fragments." Commonsensical thinking might lead one to conclude that one affordance of the fragment as form is that it always already invokes the whole.[19] Where this is the case, the fragment becomes more about the whole than about the fragment, which recedes from view in the shadow of the always already

---

[17] KC to Robert Browning, November 23, 1884. MSS Add. 46866. The British Library.
[18] For a study of Michael Field vis-à-vis parts and wholes, see Huseby. For a different, but equally interesting discussion of Michael Field's thoughts on the fragment in the context of sculpture, see Vadillo's "Sculpture, Poetics".
[19] Cf. Lennard Davis, *Enforcing Normalcy* on the consequences of such thinking, especially, but not only, in the context of ableism.

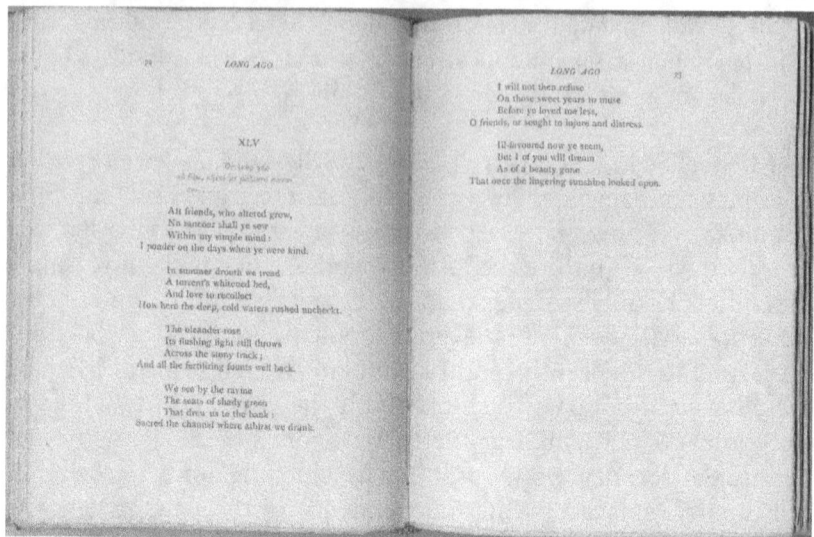

Fig. 1.2 Poem XLV from *Long Ago* (1889). Courtesy of the Mark Samuels Lasner Collection, University of Delaware Library, Museums and Press.

presumed whole. The notion of the whole and unity dominates the now subordinated fragment, which becomes "included" in a real or imagined whole to such an extent that its fragmentary status has been forgotten. It has fulfilled its purpose; it is now unnecessary. But as is so often the case, absences are also powerful, if ghostly, presences. Thus I am more interested in the ways *Long Ago* resists imagined wholeness and the notion of unity, even as it "completes" the fragment.

In at least two interesting and important ways, Michael Field's *Long Ago* precludes the erasure or engulfment or completion of the fragment by the whole. We can look at XLV as a representative example. (See Fig. 1.2). Here we can see, as Evangelista emphasizes, that the Greek fragments in the collection stand out, stand apart, unconnected, uncompleted from the verse they have inspired. Each poem is preceded by the fragment, which is further set apart by being printed in red ink. Second, as Marion Thain observes, the structure of many of the poems, with shortened, indented lines, continue to evoke the fragment: "Michael Field's project of 'completion' does not forestall the lyric sublime or contain the excess of Sappho's fragments, but reflects on it and dwells on it . . . including, ultimately, through the form of the print poem on the page" (*Lyric Poem* 45). It is in these contexts, I want to argue, that the fragment possesses affordances that have queer potentialities, resisting assimilation and erasure by a normative state or goal (such as, but not limited to, wholeness and unity).

My point is that *Long Ago* has much to teach us about affordances of the fragment that lay latent—that might resist unity—even as the fragment appears to invoke unity; and that this resistance is most apparent from the queer-feminist orientation from which Michael Field create their revisionary poetics. The fragment is what we see—indeed it is *all* Michael Field saw—but like Terry Castle's "apparitional lesbian," its faint and confusing existence indicates that there is something else—though we/they may not be exactly sure what that is and likely will never find out. So, an important affordance of the fragment, at least in Michael Field's hands, is a kind of queer synecdoche, where instead of the part that stands in for a unified whole that possesses characteristics that are clear and recognizable because it exists within a norm, the fragment is a part that vaguely gestures at the possibility of something that we don't really know about (and neither does anyone else). Insofar as synecdoche is a subcategory of metonymy, here we would do well to remember how Lee Edelman has written of metonymy as a figure of queer desire: "Metaphor, that is, binds the arbitrary slippages characteristics of metonymy into unit of 'meaning' that register as identities or representational presences" (*Homographesis* 8–9).[20] As queer synecdoche, the Sapphic fragment hints that *there is something queer, here*;[21] or if one already suspected it was there, it confirms that suspicion and further piques one's curiosity. Of course, we can also read Michael Field's intense engagement with the fragment as a form of archive fever[22] that, for these nineteenth-century co-authors, confirms the existence of a fervently desired foremother who possesses ineffable characteristics: that is, a talented and successful female poet and a concrete example of same-sex love. The Sapphic fragment is synecdoche both for such a queer desire and for queer origins—queer mother and originary queer lover.

---

[20] Edelman's reading of queer metonymy also frames Sarah Kersh's excellent essay on Whym Chow.
[21] See Alexander Doty, *Making Things Perfectly Queer*.
[22] Cf. Derrida and Huffer. I will talk more about the archive in the book's conclusion.

Yet, because this particular fragment affords the opportunity but not the obligation or ability to make whole, there is potentiality for completion but not blueprint for what that whole might look like. Thus the affordances of wholeness and unity, with firm boundaries delineating inclusion and exclusion, are uniquely destabilized.

A second, related affordance of the fragment in this context is that, phenomenologically, it necessitates *l'engrenage*. Now, perhaps as with translation, *l'engrenage* is always an aspect of understanding history—at least to a certain extent. But for those seeking to explore the vicissitudes of what we now call queer history at the *fin de siècle*, gearing into the unknown is a necessary precondition of a different order of magnitude. The fragment raises questions that have no answers, but invites contemplation—indeed, provides the liberty to explore and create one's own answers. And as Lynne Huffer provocatively asserts, the inviting quality of the fragmentary unknown entices with strange eros. As she quotes Anne Carson on her experience of reading Sappho: "the drama of trying to read a papyrus torn in half or riddled with holes or smaller than a postage stamp" and Foucault on "the obstinate murmur" of the archive, Huffer describes a queer passion for "geneaology's lacunary events" that Bradley and Cooper surely would have empathized with as they attempted to catch the light from Sappho's timeless gems (Huffer 35–8, *passim*).

This brings us to a third affordance of the fragment vis-à-vis *Long Ago*. In creating mystery, inviting curiosity, and necessitating *l'engrenage*, the fragment in turn invites creativity and experimentation. The fragment affords the opportunity to seek and/or invent a new history, new truths for the past, the present, and the self—in Michael Field's words, "to plead guilty to anachronism" and to be "what o'clock I say it is." This is particularly useful when the fragment one is working with both confirms and raises questions about one's own gender and sexuality.[23] This creative, re-visionary impulse, as with their closet drama, brings Michael Field's queer aesthetic historicism back to the roots of poetics: *poiein*, to make, transform, in both form and content. And indeed, here I want to assert that an important but hitherto overlooked theme of *Long Ago* is transformation, or change.

---

[23] See Friedman.

Many, if not most, of the poems in *Long Ago* exhibit at least one of four different types of change. First, there are the poems that mourn how marriage and the loss of virginity transform the maiden companions of Sappho, as in XVII's "'O whither art though gone from me? / Come back again virginity! // Restore to me my only good / My Maidenhood, my maidenhood!'" (lines 23–4, 31–2). As many scholars of classical Greece have noted, Sappho provides unique insight into the period not only through her celebration of female community, but importantly in her acknowledgment that Greek women resisted the narrative that their sole value was chattel—wives and bearers of children. Similarly, many studies of *Long Ago* rightly observe that Michael Field's verse collection depicts homoerotic desire and activity within the female sphere and, importantly also, as in XVII and also LVII, extreme loss at leaving it behind. In these and other examples from *Long Ago*, the sadness, grief, and life consequences of the transformation that occurs upon leaving the community of maidens is emphasized with repetition: "No living creature may we more delight; / Our maidenhood, our maidenhood is gone" (lines 55–6). Yet, important as this realization is about ancient Greek women, transformation from the virgin state is not the only kind of transformation featured in *Long Ago*.

Second, many of the verses in *Long Ago* explore a change of heart. Sometimes Michael Field depicts love's mutability in a heterosexual context, as in the many poems where Sappho wishes that Phaeon would change his mind about her. Other lyrics notably differentiate between the superior constancy of homoerotic love compared to the inconstancy of heterosexual love, as in XXXIII: "Maid not to you my mind doth change / Men I defy, allure estrange" (lines 1–2).[24] Whereas the speaker says that her "lover's patience tire[s]" of men; between women there "is no thought of pain / peril, satiety" (lines 6–7). Still other lyrics document how emotions between women are also subject to transformation over time, as in XLVI, where Atthis leaves Sappho for Andromeda:

Though Atthis, hateful, flit
From my fond arms, and by

---

[24] *Sight and Song* also asserts the constancy of same-sex (as opposed to heterosexual) love. See Ehnenn, "Looking Strategically."

> Andromeda dare sit,
> I will not let my strong
> Heart fail, will bear the wrong (lines 24–8)

Similarly, LVI narrates the tragic tale of Leto and Niobe, with much emphasis on how close the women were as maidens, and how devastating the change in their relationship was:

> Then were they foes
> As only those
> Can be who once were near
> Each to each other's heart
> Who could not breathe apart,
> Nor shed a lonely tear. (lines 2–7)

Sometimes in these poems about a change of heart, the speaker is musing and mostly detached as in XLV, "Ah friends, who altered grow / No rancour shall ye sow / Within my simple mind" (lines 1–3). But in contrast, sometimes it's clear that the lost love still bears a sting, as in LXVII: "But Atthis loved of yore / Returns, and all my hungry sore, / Death-stricken senses close round her once more" (lines 5–7). Taken together, *Long Ago*'s songs of love—whether love for men or women, friends or lovers—seem to indicate that the only constant about human emotion is its potential to change.

The third category of transformation poems are those that are literally about physical transformation, such as the much discussed LII, which tells of Tiresias who was changed from male to female and back again;[25] LXI in which Dryope is raped by Apollo, who first appears as a tortoise and then as a serpent, and then turns Dryope into a tree/dryad;[26] and several poems that refer to Procne and Philomel's transformation from human sisters into the swallow and nightingale. Also in this group is LX, an interesting version of Leda and the Swan, where Zeus's seduction of Leda and his transformation from god to Swan (and back again) is only implicit. Instead, when Michael Field imagine

---

[25] On Michael Field's treatment of Tiresias, see White, "The Tiresian Poet"; Prins, *Victorian Sappho*; Madden, "Penetrating Matthew Arnold"; and Ehnenn, "From 'We Other Victorians.'"
[26] See Stetz, "As She Feels a God Within."

Sappho imagining the Leda myth, the only transformation that is narrated in an explicit manner refers to an egg that, under Leda's care, hatches a child, and transforms her into a mother. There are several instances in the collection that refer to the physical changes that come with growing up (XXVII), aging (XXII, LI), and the change of seasons (XXV, LX).

Importantly, the fourth and last major type of transformation featured throughout *Long Ago* are the poems that assert that poetry can change both the speaker and listener. From the first lyric about Sappho's maidens, where "the lyre unloosed their souls" (I, l. 10) to the last, where Sappho proclaims, "Men will remember me, I think" as she takes her infamous leap (l. 16), *Long Ago* attests to the power of poetry to make a lasting impression upon history: "The loveliness of word / And healing sound / ... / My dark-leaved laurels will endure (LXII, lines 9–10, 41). In *Long Ago*'s preservation of Sappho's fragments, and Michael Field's meticulous documentation of the provenance of the Sapphic images on the cover and frontispiece (see Figs. 1.3 and 1.4), the co-authors ensure that their beloved foremother "cannot be forgotten whom I sing" (XXXIX, line 26).

In this section my aim has been to suggest that *Long Ago* transforms the Sapphic fragment into a series of poems whose overarching theme, in varied ways, is largely about transformation. Although *Long Ago*'s preface refers to their work as "extensions" of Sappho's fragments, the ambition of their revisionary poetics clearly exceeds that modest claim, and instead performs the intention they expressed in their letter to Browning: that they did not want to be "wholly influenced by that most inspiring of women." Instead, in their hands the Sappho fragment becomes a queer synecdoche that simultaneously preserves a vague and shadowy queer-feminist archive while also engaging the unknowns of that archive and transforming it anyway into something of their own imagining. In so doing they reach back in time to create community, articulate their passionate aesthetic values, and hope to be remembered in the future—in essence, they make/re-make a queer feminist space for themselves. In this sense, what Michael Field do with Sappho's fragments differs little from what they do with their closet dramas: they retell a story from carefully selected bits and pieces of something from "long ago." In the chapters that follow, I will examine how Michael Field's revisionary poetics—especially their aesthetic historicism, their queer-feminist

Fig. 1.3 Long Ago cover (1889). Courtesy of the Mark Samuels Lasner Collection, University of Delaware Library, Museums and Press.

Fig. 1.4 Long Ago frontispiece (1889). Courtesy of the Mark Samuels Lasner Collection, University of Delaware Library, Museums and Press.

orientation, and their fearless willingness to take up and gear into the unknown—results in creative transformative experiments with other literary forms and genres: ekphrasis, lyric, elegy, devotional poetry, and diary.

2

Ekphrastic Poetics in and after *Sight and Song*

> The poet's eye, in a fine frenzy rolling,
> Doth glance from heaven to earth, from earth to heaven;
> And as imagination bodies forth
> The forms of things unknown, the poet's pen
> Turns them to shapes, and gives to airy nothing
> A local habitation and a name.
> —Shakespeare, *A Midsummer Night's Dream* (1600)

This chapter tells the story of the poet's eye—the eye of Michael Field as The Poet—as it is involved in the specific practice of ekphrastic poetics. Here, I try to get into the time and space between looking at an art object and a finished poem about that art object. This is a difficult task, as much happens in that space and time where, as Michael Field's role model, Shakespeare, put it, "imagination bodies forth." For Katharine Bradley and Edith Cooper, the creation of "picture poems" involves a thinking and an imagining not only about the art object, but about the referent for that work of art—across space and across time. Their thinking and imagining, as I have previously argued, takes place from a queer-feminist perspective.[1] Framing this observation with Sara Ahmed's important work on how social norms combine with lived experience to produce one's orientation in the world,[2] we might say that Michael Field's ekphrases illustrate a queer-feminist orientation toward the art object, its referent, their audience, and the world.

[1] See Ehnenn, "Looking strategically."
[2] Cf. *Queer Phenomenology*.

But as Shakespeare writes in the quote that heads this chapter, such a poetic act—an act of *poiein*, of making—is also an act in which the poet's eye becomes engaged in a "fine frenzy rolling." Presumably, the frenzied rolling of the eye makes the poet's mind—and the poet's body—feel frenzied as well. In the previous chapter, I demonstrated how Bradley and Cooper were dedicated to passionate feeling in their life and work, a dedication inspired by their fascination with Dionysus and grounded in a personal philosophy that anticipates, and later, directly engages Nietzsche. For Michael Field, it was of the utmost importance to represent both one's own and one's subject's feelings in art, and in Chapter 1 I described how they accomplished that goal, especially in their closet drama, through their treatment of anachronism; how their queer-feminist orientation toward both their own lived experience and history resulted in their unique re-visions of history, and how their experimentation with the form of the fragment in *Long Ago*'s Sapphic revisions reflected themes of transformation as they reimagined the unknowns of their archive.

This chapter examines how Michael Field's "imagination bodies forth" in the "fine frenzied rolling" of their ekphrastic work in and after *Sight and Song* (1892). Given that *Sight and Song*'s picture-poems expose the heteropatriarchal biases of the art objects that are their referents, along with the centuries of art criticism that subsequently have defined them, and through them, women, what specific characteristics and affordances of ekphrasis help Michael Field communicate that revelation? What characteristics and affordances of ekphrasis facilitate Michael Field's dedication to Dionysian feeling as they seek to render visual art into words? How might the process of re-making what one sees help these two *fin de siècle* female aesthetes invent themselves as queer subjects and as authors? What do they bring to the practice and form of ekphrastic writing at the *fin de siècle*?

In what follows, I will argue that through the *l'engrenage* and orientation of their queer feminist revisionary poetics in *Sight and Song*, Michael Field's ekphrases perform metaleptic leaps that, in their shift from image to word, test the boundaries of objective/formalist vs subjective/anti-formalist modes of interacting with art and complicate the presumption of *paragone*, or rivalry between the sister arts of painting and poetry. They negotiate their outsider status as authoritative viewers of art; challenge the notion of the autonomous art object and the notion of the universal spectator;

bring anti-patriarchal and anti-heteronormative interpretations to the venerable art objects they contemplate; and demonstrate how ekphrasis can be much more synaesthetic—and in particular, haptic—than solely visual. Further, as we will see, much of Michael Field's ekphrastic work in and after *Sight and Song* was in dialogue with other late nineteenth-century theories of vision and the senses, theories that anticipate phenomenology in the tradition of Merleau-Ponty. The second portion of this chapter moves beyond *Sight and Song* to address Michael Field's continued (albeit less frequent) employment of ekphrasis in their later writing and gestures toward the rise of modernist ekphrastic writing that, to varying degrees, resonated with Michael Field's verse.

Ekphrasis and its affordances

The term ekphrasis comes from the Greek ἐκ *ek* (out) and φράσις *phrásis* (speak); in its earliest rhetorical usages it merely meant to provide a vivid description. Whereas Jean Hagstrum reserves the term ekphrasis for poems where the art object is portrayed as actually speaking, and uses "iconic" or "pictoral" for other descriptions of objects, James Heffernan provides (at least to my thinking) a more constructive and now commonly used definition: "the art of describing works of art, a verbal representation of a visual representation" (3). Ekphrasis manifests usually, but not always, in verse,[3] which indeed is the case for Michael Field. As this chapter will show, in some of Bradley and Cooper's later ekphrases, they, like many of their female contemporaries, create ekphrastic verse about items that were not considered high art: photographs, jewelry, crucifixes, and other domestic and decorative objects. In so doing, they expand the notion of what should be considered art, and complicate notions about of the "proper" subject and process of ekphrasis.

Theorizing about ekphrasis historically has taken as its starting point the notion of *paragone*, or rivalry between the sister arts. Such discussions often focus on matters of verisimilitude and the relative abilities of painting and poetry to evoke emotion and to represent space and time. W. J. T. Mitchell famously asserts that ekphrasis demonstrates a desire to overcome otherness and traces,

---

[3] John Hollander uses the term *only* for poems that speak for, to, or about real or imagined works of art.

in the nineteenth century, examples of ekphrastic indifference, hope, and fear;[4] relatedly, Murray Krieger argues that ekphrasis is fundamentally about semiotic contradictions. In contrast, as we shall see, Michael Field's ekphrases are closer to anticipating those modernist female authors whose ekphrases Elizabeth Loizeaux and other feminist critics categorize as relational, networked, and/or mediated rather than paragonal. Meanwhile, most critics recognize that traditionally, ekphrasis manifests gendered dynamics, with a male author speaking for, to, or about a female or feminized art object, often in an objectifying manner.

Indeed, a common ekphrastic device, *prosopopoeia*, or making the art object speak, either directly or through free indirect discourse, is of particular interest when considering gendered aspects of ekphrasis, where frequently the male ekphrastic author or speaker uses *prosopopoeia* to put words in the female art object's mouth. In contrast, some female authors attempt to employ *prosopopoeia* to give voice to a figure or model traditionally thought to be silenced, while some, like Michael Field, find other ways to criticize the silencing of women in art and life and tend to avoid the device all together. Other traditional rhetorical techniques associated with ekphrasis include *enargeia*, or vivid lively description; *descriptio*, or vivid description that sketches potential consequences; and a tendency for the speaker to flatter the object's verisimilitude, perfection, and/or timelessness. Together, these techniques attempt to wield writing to make the art object (and often, its referent) seem real; these matters of mimesis and language's ability or inability to portray experience raise epistemological questions pertinent to both the Victorian and modernist eras.

With this background in mind, but before moving to in-depth examination of Michael Field's ekphrasis, I find it productive to ask, following the recent work of Caroline Levine: what are the affordances of ekphrasis? This question is related to the issues I've outlined above but asking the question in this way invites us to

---

[4] While Mitchell traces a trend in the increasing numbers of picture poems produced in the period—from L.E.L. to the Brownings to D. G. Rossetti and more, it's important to note, as Marion Thain does, that Michael Field themselves did not use the term, which only came back into discourse (and slowly at that) toward the end of the century: "the idea of ekphrasis, then, was important to the cultural development of the fin de siècle, even if the term had yet to gain prominence" (Thain, *Poetry* 68–9).

consider what ekphrasis permits the author, in this case Michael Field, to do in the moment of creation, as what they see (or imagine seeing) is transformed, adapted, revised.

The first affordance of ekphrasis I'll discuss is the following: despite nineteenth-century notions of the autonomous art object, assumptions about universal ways of seeing, and claims about shared aesthetic value, ekphrasis as a form always already invites a dialectical interplay of objective and subjective engagement with the real or imagined art object (and often, that art object's referent). Indeed, consider the Preface to *Sight and Song*, where Michael Field describes their creative process:

> The effort to see things from their own centre, by suppressing the habitual centralisation of the visible in ourselves, is a process by which we eliminate our idiosyncrasies and obtain an impression clearer, less passive, more intimate.
>
> When such effort has been made, honestly and with persistence, even then the inevitable force of individuality must still have play and a temperament mould the purified impression: —
> "When your eyes have done their part,
> Thought must length it in the heart." (vi)

As I've previously argued, *Sight and Song*'s preface begins with a claim to objectivity and formalist analysis only to concede that ultimately, the spectator's associations and subjective interpretation will "mould" one's impression. With the final quote from Samuel Daniels's masque, *Tethys' Festival* (1610), Michael Field suggests that when the evanescent pleasure of beholding the art object passes, continued reflection and feeling can prolong the sensation. This is when, again invoking Shakespeare's words from this chapter's epigraph, "the poet's pen / Turns them to shapes."

We see this dialectic between objective and subjective spectatorship at work in many of the gallery notes that serve as the foundation for Bradley and Cooper's ekphrases. For instance, their objective description of Botticelli's *Venus and Mars* quickly moves to simile and a series of loose associations:

> It is a masterpiece—the tone is perfect, the design has fearless simplicity—it is ideal, it is ironic, it is true. Venus lies alert, her body lifted like a shoot after thunder-rain, triumphant—for she has but received the storm: in him it is spent—a fury and power that he has

lost. He sleeps as if dead—the conch that is blown into his ear through the rust-red locks is silent to his senses—his lids are closely-moulded over his eyes, his lower lip falls with a sharp ridge, his nostrils have the arrested delicacy seen in those of the dying who are unconscious, this fulfilment of love is so like the fulfilment of life![5]

They then conclude, "she is modern, cold, she is sad, she is awake ... where else is there such harmony of line and tint—where is there more firm, more exquisite pessimism?" Here, one might speculate that Bradley and Cooper are doing exactly what their male precursors and contemporaries do—assuming universal values and a neutral, formalist stance while exerting their subjective opinion upon the art object. After all, despite their claims to objectivity, ultimately they make good on their preface's Keatsian promise, "I see and sing, by my own eyes, inspired;"[6] in this instance, they see Venus as a modern woman. But as with the appropriations in Michael Field's closet dramas and *Long Ago* discussed in Chapter 1, by the time the gallery notes become the final ekphrastic product, Michael Field's queer-feminist mode of looking strategically is notable for coming to very different subjective conclusions, often via a different path, compared to their male precursors and contemporaries. Instead of a male speaker fixing and/or speaking for a female or feminized art object, we see in these homoerotically inclined female aesthetes a perspective that, for example, criticizes art history's view of *La Gioconda*, that sympathizes with maenads torturing a faun who teases them, that focuses on winemakers at work instead of the drunken Noah, and that admires the queer beauty of suffering St. Sebastians.[7] Elizabeth Loizeaux defines such feminist ekphrasis as "recogniz[ing] that a woman's place as viewer is established within, beside, or in the face of a male-dominated culture, but that the patterns of power and value implicit in a tradition of male artists and viewers can be exposed, used, resisted, and rewritten" (81).

In his study of empire and nineteenth-century form, Nathan K. Hensley reminds us of the work of Stanley Fish and invites us to think about the shaping power of readerly decisions: "the

---

[5] *Works and Days*. MSS Add. 46779, July 27, 1891. (EC). fols. 56v–57r. The British Library.
[6] From Keats, "Ode to Psyche."
[7] These are some of the examples I discuss at length in "Looking Strategically."

objectivity of any text is an illusion ... of self-sufficiency and completeness" (Fish in Hensley, 25). As I've previously argued, and as this chapter will continue to demonstrate, instead of a single "correct" interpretation, Michael Field suggests alternatives to how centuries of spectators and art critics have viewed the world and Western art. In providing their unique point of view, Michael Field capitalizes on how ekphrasis invites readers to decide what they see. The subjective potential that lies latent in ekphrastic composition is brought to the fore.

For Bradley and Cooper this is a relational way of seeing rooted in embodied lived experience. And it necessitates what Merleau-Ponty terms *l'engrenage*—a taking up and gearing into the unknown—insofar as Michael Field's ekphrases go where no (wo)man has gone before. *Sight and Song*'s proclamation that "the inevitable force of individuality must still have play" is a powerful one; by express virtue of their innovative and daring leap into the unknown, they invite the reader into a dynamic swirl of possible interpretations and model (especially for the female reader) what it might be like to respond to art, oneself. The dialectic of objective and subjective engagement with the art object proves hospitable to situated epistemologies—to women's and queer ways of knowing. The specific outcome of this affordance is an emphasis on the individual that legitimates, in their case, a queer-feminist point of view and bolsters their own subject formation as spectators, thinkers, and subjects with queer-feminist orientation and agency.[8]

We can observe this mode of spectatorship and poetics even prior to *Sight and Song*, in Michael Field's ekphrastic essay "Effigies" (1890), published in *Art Review*, which details two visits Bradley and Cooper (at the ages of forty-three and twenty-seven, respectively) made to Westminster Abbey during 1889. While *Works and Days*' notes on paintings are helpful for shedding light on Michael Field's picture-poems during the period they were writing *Sight and Song*, I don't consider them ekphrastic in and of themselves: they are notes, not yet literary representations. Portions

---

[8] Although he reads *Sight and Song* as undertaking a largely objective perceptual process, in *Before Queer Theory* Dustin Friedman similarly argues that engaging with art permits proto-queer aesthetes like Michael Field to "transform a disabling sense of social alienation into a liberating sense of freedom from social structures" (23).

of "Effigies," on the other hand, are usefully considered prose ekphrasis; they are not art criticism, not gallery notes, but intentional and creative literary efforts in their own right that create verbal representations of the visual representations that are the marble and wax statues in Westminster. Catherine Maxwell has written convincingly about Michael Field's philosophical debate about the efficacy of these effigies *as* representations, along with Michael Field's reasons for strongly preferring the marble to the wax images, so I won't reproduce that here. What I do want to acknowledge is how, in the ekphrastic moments of "Effigies", we see precisely the feminist orientation that can be observed a few years later in *Sight and Song*: how "Effigies" is quite frank about privileging subjective over objective epistemologies.

"Effigies" catalogues both male and female statues, but as in *Sight and Song*, mostly it is the female figures that pique Michael Field's extended interest and critique, especially the waxen effigies of Queen Anne and Elizabeth I. In contrast to traditional ekphrastic conceits that praise the perfection and immutability of the art object, the ekphrases in "Effigies" mince no words in their critique of the waxen images' inferiority to both marble and live bodies; and Michael Field makes little attempt to be objective when describing these "parodies of the flesh":

> Queen Anne sits in stricken comfort, no longer drinking tea, indifferent to the obedience of her "three worlds," as she faces the bit of grey wall that encompasses her. . . . Old Elizabeth, with wretched wizen form and "lack-lustre eye" fills a corner, and turns her head away with a dense glare: she is uninterested in her pearls, once strung by insatiable vanity; she is miserable as a lost spirit in polar hell; her pain and disappointment are ice. (89)

Michael Field also engages in a marked experiment with ekphrastic *prosopopoeia* in a scene where the ghost of Queen Elizabeth confronts her wax statue. An excerpt from this long passage will provide a taste of Michael Field's imagination and seething critical satire:

> Glorianna herself dismounts her pile and goes assured, imperial, through the Tudor Chapel: . . . She sees a distracted, bony face, and eyes stiff with age—a virgin, barren age. The likeness speaks to her: . . . "How handsome you are, dear Self!" it says to her: "you did not

mind when I told you that in the year sixteen hundred. Why, you really have none of these wrinkles which the mirror branded across my heart when I saw them; nor have you a thinness about the jaw; and you do not turn your head like a worried animal. . . . Won't you acknowledge me, Glorianna? I am old Queen Bess, the most beautiful woman of her time—alas, alas!" The royal form addressed is silent; then, with a moan such as we hear among the rocks of a cave, she turns away in soliloquy: "I must have come too near my cousin Mary's tomb for such disaster to have fallen me. I will lie down." (90)

Here, "Effigies" makes clear that visual representations are important, both as art objects in their own right, and because they permit one to "touch sacramentally our accumulated past" (91). The problem, for Michael Field, seems to occur when such visual representations are inaccurate, or unbeautiful. In those instances they are fair game for the critique and re-interpretation that "Effigies" offers in its ekphrastic musings; these anticipate the equally critical work Michael Field will provide in and after *Sight and Song*. Notably, after "Effigies," as we shall see, Michael Field eschews the use of *prosopopoeia*, and instead finds other ways to express their subjective insights about the ekphrastic encounter, and to permit silenced and/or unconventional perspectives to be articulated. This is a technique shared by other *fin de siècle* women writing ekphrases, such as Graham R. Tomson (Rosamund Marriot Watson), and that also anticipates the work of twentieth-century feminist ekphrastic poets such as Marianne Moore, Gertrude Stein, and H.D., who, according to Loizeaux, were engaged in "[changing] the perceived gender dynamics of seeing and saying" (83).

A second affordance of ekphrasis is that it blurs boundaries: not just between objective and subjective epistemologies, visual and verbal, space and time, but also between the senses. In particular, ekphrasis invites synaesthesia; deconstructing boundaries between the senses. Sarah Parker has persuasively argued that synaesthesia is a useful literary device for Michael Field and other decadent and queer writers because it blends and blurs the boundaries between categories. Similarly, Stefano Evangelista suggests that in much of their work Michael Field blends textual and material culture—that they engage, as Hegel, Winckelmann, and others in the German tradition do, "in productive traffic between verbal and visual cultures" ("Greek Textual Archaeology", par. 4). All of this is to say, that, especially given the title *Sight and Song*, which invokes multiple senses at once, we should consider Michael Field's ekphrases more synaesthetically than has been the case.

This is not to imply that vision is not important to Bradley and Cooper's encounters with art objects and their creative process. Indubitably, the nineteenth century was what Isobel Armstrong terms a "spectatorial era."[9] Yet nineteenth-century thinkers were also aware that vision does not wholly account for perception—including our engagement with art objects. As William A. Cohen observes in *Embodied: Victorian Literature and the Senses*, nineteenth-century texts "argue for the materiality of the self and the soul" (16) and, like Merleau-Ponty does a century later, Victorian texts demonstrate how processes of perceiving the world are mutually constitutive and do not engage only one sense at a time. For instance, in *Florentine Painters of the Renaissance*, Bradley and Cooper's friend and mentor, the art critic and historian Bernard Berenson, writes: "Psychology has ascertained that sight alone gives us no accurate sense of the third dimension" and urges that "the first business of the painter ... is to rouse the tactile sense" (3–4). Cohen emphasizes how, for both Victorian texts and Merleau-Ponty, the model of perception now called haptic visuality reveals, "[v]ision in particular operates not as depth perception but as a cutaneous rubbing of surfaces; modeled on the sense of touch, seeing entails a reciprocity between subjects and object" (22). In crossing the boundaries of time, media, and the senses, ekphrasis is a mode of embodied perceiving that for Michael Field, becomes especially useful for exploring decadent and queer embodied thinking and lived experience. Further, we'll see that such synaesthetic and especially haptic engagement with art objects results in ekphrases that exceed visual mimesis, resulting, particularly in Michael Field's later ekphrases, work in conversation with modernist examples of the form.

Related to the affordance of the blurring of boundaries, synaesthetic and otherwise, is a third affordance of ekphrasis: flexibility of form. Historically, ekphrasis is a rhetorical device; its lack of formal requirements leads Heffernan to call it a mode, rather a genre. Yet it has given rise to a category of literary texts, mostly

---

[9] See Armstrong ("D. G. Rossetti"), Crary, Flint and Teukolsky, among others.

(but not exclusively) verse;[10] so it's not unreasonable to think of ekphrasis as a poetic form—a shaping or thematic form—like an ode or an elegy that is determined by a topic rather than fixed pattern of stanzas, rhyme, or meter. Like many shaping forms, then, the ekphrastic encounter is an invitation to write in any form one wishes—verse forms or otherwise. Granted, writing in verse—a distinctly different formal vehicle than the prose of eminent male art historians—provided a way for Bradley and Cooper to negotiate their outsider, amateur status as art critics in the company (and shadow) of the likes of Ruskin, Pater, and Berenson.[11] But it is important to acknowledge that in *Sight and Song* the reader finds sonnets, sestains, ballades, triplets, and more; some of Michael Field's journal entries and published essays (such as "Effigies") are ekphrastic as well. Acknowledging Michael Field's varied use of genre in their ekphrases will, therefore, further reinforce this book's holistic claims that the characteristics of Michael Field revisionary poetics can be observed across their *oeuvre* and across the various genres and forms in which they created. Such observations help us recognize how Michael Field's work resonates with modernist authors who, just a few years later, will similarly destabilize formal conventions of genre and form.

A fourth affordance of ekphrasis and the one that has garnered the most critical attention is how ekphrasis requires a shift in medium, what Michael Field describes as "to translate into verse what the lines and colours of certain chosen pictures sing in themselves" (v). This of course is not a new observation. Here, however, I emphasize the fact of the shift in medium in order to propose that it has particular consequences. I want to propose that we consider the ekphrastic shift in medium as a metaleptic leap—one that affords great opportunity. Here, I am not referring to the rhetorical metalepsis usually applied to poetry, but narrative metalepsis as Genette defines it: a rupture between "the world in which one tells and the world of which one tells" (236). In raising the issue of metalepsis in this way I am influenced by Elaine Freedgood's recent work on metalepsis and the realist novel. In

---

[10] Loizeaux considers ekphrasis a subgenre of lyric (12). Perhaps that's apt for her twentieth-century archive, but seems less useful for thinking about nineteenth-century ekphrases, which often are dramatic monologues or, as with some of *Sight and Song*'s picture-poems, perhaps more narrative than lyric.

[11] See Fraser, *Women Writing Art History*; also Prins, *Ladies' Greek*.

Worlds Enough (2019), Freedgood demonstrates how twentieth-century proclamations about realism in the Victorian novel have obscured how metalepsis provides tools for the reader to lay bare how the world of the so-called realist novel sustains political and social ideologies such as liberalism and colonial enterprise.

What I want to suggest is that ekphrasis in general, but especially in the particular instance of Michael Field, creates another world—what Freedgood calls "another ontological layer" (xvi). While any adaptation, even when in the same medium, invites slippages that can denaturalize ideological assumptions embedded within a cultural artifact (literary or otherwise), each medium has its own rules and conventions; to at least some extent, each medium is a world of its own. Ekphrastic adaptations often contain (hide behind? benefit from?) assumptions about objectivity and formalist accuracy but in their shift in medium inevitably (to repurpose Freedgood) "take us toward other sources of information" (35). Ekphrastic metalepsis, therefore, creates ruptures where the transgression of ontological borders that so often occurs with adaptation becomes even more perceptible. I claim that this observation holds for both the primarily narrative ekphrases in *Sight and Song* and Michael Field's more lyric ekphrastic poems subsequent to that volume.

Finally, a fifth affordance of ekphrasis (and a corollary of the first) is that in this new world, new things are possible. Ekphrasis provides an opportunity for re-vision—to see the art object again, from a different perspective, and to engage what people have previously thought and said about the art object and its referent. In "Looking Strategically" I identified how, following Pater, Michael Field's collection of picture poems employs a revisionary gaze characterized by both objectivity and subjectivity and accomplishes five overarching goals: (1) to criticize the silencing of the female model; (2) to move female figures from margin to center; (3) to celebrate women's auto-eroticism and homoerotic bonds; (4) to critique Victorian sex/gender ideology through the figure of the boy; (5) and to code both male and female homoerotic love through the figure of Saint Sebastian (74). In that study I focused upon identifying *that* these perspectives and possibilities emerge. In this chapter I return to *Sight and Song* in order to further explore *how* such revisionary poetics occur, in terms of phenomenology and form, and how we can best track them and their effects.

To employ a revisionary gaze that creates a new narrative is what Adrienne Rich calls an "act of survival" (18); to do so in a new medium is to take a metaleptic leap into a world with deconstructed boundaries. It is also, as in the examples I discussed in Chapter 1, a critical encounter with an art object (person, character, story, and all it represents and all the criticism that has sedimented upon it), a queer-feminist mode of embodied thinking and feeling across time that necessitates not only a queer-feminist orientation but *l'engrenage*. And Bradley and Cooper were quite aware that they were heading into the unknown and taking risks—in interpretation, form, and content. On May 11, 1892 when they received their first printed copies of *Sight and Song*, Cooper confesses in the diary, "we are terrified" and Bradley writes "We have written the queerest little book in the world. Our teeth chatter with fear."[12] Two weeks later, they describe an evening's conversation with John Miller Gray: "we discussed the theory that a work of art can be criticised by translating it into another, artistic form—The Theory of Sight and Song."[13]

In the discussion of Michael Field's ekphrases that follow, we will observe the co-authors reaching out synaesthetically to try and access and express the unseen, the unheard, the not-discussed, and the unknowable. As we observe them translating—seeing and singing—we'll also observe them pondering, and in many cases inventing, that which is absent, untouchable, ineffable—absent sometimes for heteropatriarchal reasons, sometimes for reasons associated with the formal traditions of aesthetics. As what follows will show, representational friction, a specific form of aesthetic intertextuality pertaining to slippages between the word, the visual medium, and/or the original referent, provides evidence of this metaleptic leap where there are slippages between the ekphrastic text and art object (and/or the object's referent). Thus representational friction operates as a powerful vehicle for critique, especially feminist critique. With all this in mind, let us observe these matters at work in three poems from *Sight and Song* that have not received much scholarly attention; and then I shall turn

---

[12] *Works and Days*. MSS Add. 46780. May 11, 1892. (EC and KB). fols. 89r, 89v. The British Library.
[13] *Works and Days*. MSS Add. May 29, 1892. (EC). fol. 100r. The British Library.

to examples of Michael Field's ekphrases in later, published and unpublished work.

The queerest little book in the world . . .

St. Katharine of Alexandria

Any study of Michael Field's "St. Katharine of Alexandria" that seeks to analyze the picture-poem vis-à-vis its ekphrastic referent is difficult for readers today because *Sight and Song*'s paratextual "museum label" confusingly informs the reader that the painting is by "Bartolommeo Veneto" [*sic*] and was viewed at "Stadel'sche Institut at Frankfurt" [*sic*] (*SS* 31). Granted, Bartolomeo Veneto did paint a Saint Catharine of Alexandria, which is currently housed in Glasgow, but this is not the painting that is responsible for Michael Field's poem in *Sight and Song*.

The painting Bradley and Cooper viewed in Frankfurt in 1891 had been purchased by the museum in 1840 as a "Saint Catherine of Alexandria" by Cesare da Sesto (Fig. 2.1). The attribution changed to "Lombard Master" a few decades later. Then, around 1890, a small group of art critics, with Bradley and Cooper's friend Bernard Berenson prominently at the fore, advocated that the work was actually painted by Bartolomeo Veneto, which explains Michael Field's attribution as such in *Sight and Song*. But the painting no longer exists as it was when Bradley and Cooper viewed it. Notably, what the co-authors originally saw as Saint Catherine's wheel in 1891 was determined by the museum during a 1990 cleaning to be a wall with spikes added in the early nineteenth century—long after the painting's original composition. The spikes were therefore removed by the restoration staff; and today the painting remains in Frankfurt's Städelsches Kunstinstitut as Altobello Meloni's "Narcissus at the Fountain"[14] (Fig. 2.2).

With the poem's referent no longer a mystery, we can now consider how representational friction functions, and indeed, is the primary ekphrastic technique driving the subtle feminist critique in this sonnet. Michael Field's "Saint Katharine of Alexandria," written back at their home on October 10, 1891, reads:

---

[14] The provenance of this painting is given in Sander, pp. 172–86. Many thanks to Stefania Girometti at the Städelschen Kunstinstitut Frankfurt for helping me identify this portrait and pointing me toward the Sander catalogue.

Fig. 2.1 St. Catherine of Alexandria (1510/11). Attributed in 1891 to Bartolomeo Veneto. Oil on poplar. Courtesy of the Städel Museum, Frankfurt am Main.

Fig. 2.2 Narcissus at the Fountain (1510/11). Altobello Meloni. Oil on poplar. Courtesy of the Städel Museum, Frankfurt am Main.

A little wreath of bay about her head,
The Virgin-Martyr stands, touching her wheel
With finger-tips that from the spikes of steel
Shrink, though a thousand years she has been dead.
She bleeds each day as on the day she bled;
Her pure, gold cheeks are blanched, a cloudy seal
Is on her eyes; the mouth will never feel
Pity again; the yellow hairs are spread
Downward as damp with sweat; they touch the rim
Of the green bodice that to blackness throws
The thicket of bay-branches sharp and trim
Above her shoulder: open landscape glows
Soft and apart behind her to the right,
Where a swift shallop crosses the moonlight. (SS 31)

One immediately noticeable feature of this picture-poem is its restraint with the classic ekphrastic feature of *enargeia*, or vivid, lively description. Although, like many of the picture-poems in *Sight and Song*, "Saint Katharine of Alexandria" provides much detail about the painting it references, the tone is markedly detached, thereby emphasizing the divide between spectator and image, and the spectator and the virgin-martyr herself.[15] And although Italian sonnets often move from an objectively descriptive octave to a more subjectively interpretative or explanatory sestet, at first glance this one seems to do the reverse, subtly conjecturing about Saint Katharine's fingers shrinking from the spikes and her feelings of suffering and pity early in the poem, before moving to what appears to be mere surface description of her dress and the surrounding landscape. This detachment (along

---

[15] According to tradition, Saint Katharine was the learned daughter of the king of fourth-century Alexandria. Intent upon remaining virgin, she refused suitors and became Christian after a vision where Mary gave her to Christ in mystical marriage. After she asked the Roman Emperor Maxentius to stop persecuting Christians, he arranged for fifty philosophers and orators to convince her she was wrong but Katharine won the debate. The fifty men, who converted to Christianity because of her intellect and persuasion, were beheaded and she was imprisoned and tortured. When the Emperor's queen and her soldiers attempted to change Katharine's mind, they too were swayed by her convictions. Maxentius ordered the soldiers beheaded and Katharine tortured on the breaking wheel. Miraculously, upon her touch the wheel was destroyed; so instead she was beheaded. For more on the virgin-martyr of Alexandria, see John Capgrave, *The Life of Saint Katherine of Alexandria*.

with other features I'll discuss shortly) produces an effect Julia Saville has provocatively identified as an "austerity of poetics in *Sight and Song*, Michael Field's experiment in ascetic withholding, learned from Pater" (178). According to Saville, Bradley and Cooper attempted to place themselves at a remove from the "feminine affect or Victorian slush" traditionally associated with Victorian poetesses (179) and instead, into conversation with their male Aesthete contemporaries. Granted, Saville asserts that "the Paterian ascesis discreetly signals the male viewer's desire for male beauty within a context of heterodox Oxonian Hellenism" and that Bradley and Cooper's experiment with "self-effacement yields a dividend of multiply dissident erotic perspectives" (Saville 180–1). I agree with those points; but I also posit that the most useful way to read *Sight and Song*'s claims to objectivity are as a legitimizing pose—one that softens unabashedly subjective notions by strategically asserting the volume's seeming similarities with the poetics of their male contemporaries. Thus, as the ensuing discussion will demonstrate, the lack of *enargeia* and sense of detachment of "Saint Katharine of Alexandria" is deceptive. In actuality, the poem provides subtle iconographic and verbal conduits for the spectator to engage intensely with Saint Katharine and to consider the authors' equally intense and subjective reactions to painting.

In addition to its minimal *enargeia*, but producing a similarly double-edged result, Michael Field's "Saint Katharine of Alexandria" refrains from *prosopopoeia*, or dramatic envoicing. As a result, in contrast to much ekphrastic writing, here Michael Field only reservedly imagines what the painting's subject might feel or say.[16] Rather than dramatic envoicing through direct speech or free indirect discourse, the poem's interlocutor refuses to speak for Saint Katharine and thus minimizes further violence against the virgin-martyr. Instead, Michael Field's provocative impressions unfold though symbols, sounds, and inferences that call attention to the representational friction "between signifying medium and subject signified" (Heffernan 136).

Despite the poem's restricted *enargeia* and *prosopopoeia*, closer

---

[16] Other examples of Victorian woman poets who exercise similar restraint with *prosopopoeia* can be found in Julia Margaret Cameron's "On a Portrait," and Graham R. Tomson (Rosamund Marriott Watson's) "A Silhouette" and "A Portrait."

analysis reveals how Michael Field directs the reader to specific details and symbolic linkages within the poem, suggesting a passionate feminist rereading of history and implying that traditional hagiography and iconography provides an incomplete representation of the woman known as Saint Katharine. For instance, as this short poem opens and again near its end, the speaker emphasizes Saint Katharine's intellectual accomplishments by pointing out the painting's bay leaves, symbolic of learning and appropriate for Alexandria's virgin-martyr, patroness of philosophers. Michael Field's diary entry about their gallery visit also highlights the bay thicket and wreath:

> Frankfurt. St Katharine—Bartolommeo Veneto. A dense corner covered with bay. Gold hair that has grown straight in the sweat of suffering—a head full, imaginatively, of the martyr's doom, into the mystery of wh[ich]: she is looking, as the angels look into the mystery of the Cross. One little wreath of bay about her head. Faint, as in softened moonlight the world she has forsaken long ago. The sensitive finger-tips avoid the spikes of the wheel.[17]

Here, in addition to twice mentioning the bay, the journal entry makes contradictory observations about the connection between the saint and the world that ultimately appear in the finished poem as aesthetic paradox. The diary reports Saint Katharine's imaginings of being a martyr and explains the faintness of the painting's upper right-hand corner by stating she has long forsaken the world; yet, it curiously asserts that her fingers avoid the spikes, which seems to imply that her acceptance of martyrdom and renunciation of the world are not quite complete. Here, my reading of the poem alongside the diary leads me to an interpretation that differs from Cheryl Wilson's treatment of it. Wilson writes of *Sight and Song*'s many "Saint Sebastian"s, "Saint Jerome," and "Saint Katharine": "Across all of these poems, Field creates a fairly straightforward equation in which the body is subject to pain but the spirit enables transcendence of that pain. Through the degradation of the body, the spirit is triumphant" (183). It is beyond the scope of this project to discuss the male matryrs here, but with regard to Saint Katharine, I am

---

[17] *Works and Days*. MSS Add. 46779. [Early October?] 1891. (EC). fol. 118r. The British Library.

arguing that in their diary, Michael Field opines that the female martyr's engagement with pain is actually quite ambivalent and contradictory.

The finished poem preserves these contradictions, illustrating what Thain and others describe as Michael Field's penchant for aesthetic paradox as a dominant poetic mode. Here, these paradoxes create representational friction between the poem and the painting and also between Michael Field's ekphrastic rendition and legends, prayers, and hymns that emphasize Saint Katharine's erasure to her martyrdom. These features of the poem raise questions for the reader: for instance, why does the poem connect Saint Katharine with the world and specifically mention that she avoids the spikes when most hagiographies celebrate a saint's willing martyrdom and rejection of the world? Why does the poem create a temporal paradox (another Michaelian characteristic)[18] stating, "She bleeds, each day as on the day she bled" (l. 5), even alliteratively suggesting that she has bled so much her face has become "blanched" (l. 6), yet not extending the temporal paradox to her pity—that emotion so readily associated with both saints and Victorian femininity? Lines 7 and 8 read, "the mouth will never feel / Pity again." If she is perpetually bleeding, why is she not perpetually pitying?

Possible answers to these questions are suggested by close attention to how this sonnet's form helps to deconstruct the deceptively objective tone of its final sestet. "Saint Katharine of Alexandria," like many Michael Field verses, is a modified Italian sonnet; and here, the rhyme scheme creates dual possibilities for reading. On the one hand we encounter a two-part Italian sonnet that ostensibly moves from subjective conjecture in the octave to objective observation in the sestet with a seemingly unremarkable volta at the semi-colon in line 9. On the other hand, the poem also bears resemblance to a four-part English sonnet divided topically/pictorially as follows: lines 1–4, bay wreath and spiked wheel as symbols of her famed intelligence and marytrdom; lines 5–8, eternally bleeding vs never again pitying; lines 9–12, hair, bodice, and bay thicket; lines 13–14, the landscape and boat in the painting's upper right corner. Enjambment across what would be the octave/sestet divide and across the line 12/final couplet divide mimics the visual sweep from point to point across the painting. And here

---

[18] See Thomas, "What Time We Kiss."

is where Field makes things interesting and invites a more empathetic and engaged reading.

In devotional painting, the spectator is supposed to engage in a contemplative journey as a result of the eye's movement across the painting's landscape. Here, seemingly objective descriptions become more profoundly freighted with emotion and meaning after enjambment, sound devices, and imagery suggestively link objects in the visual field. For instance, alliterative and visual patterns create associations across the poem: she **b**leeds causing her gold cheeks to **b**lanch; the similarly golden hair leads across the sonnet's volta to her green bodice and to the darker green bay. This latter movement is driven by alliteration as well: b's and th's, "**th**at to **b**lackness **th**rows / **th**e **th**icket of **b**ay-**b**ranches sharp and trim" (lines 10–11). At this point, the sharp bay branches may motivate the spectator to move circularly back to the start of the poem and create associations between learning and martyrdom—between pointy bay and spiked wheel—and/or the sharp bay thicket may even transform the bay wreath into a crown of thorns. In this movement, what had appeared to be mere objective description becomes ekphrastic *descriptio*, or vivid description that exposes or suggests consequences: in this case, that women of learning will encounter painful difficulties. Michael Field's curious emphasis on Saint Katharine's fingers shrinking from the steel spikes, in this reading, can be explained as her effort to resist such consequences. Michael Field's reading of an object—the wheel's spikes—creates representational friction with feminist implications. Despite the surface appearance of ascetic tempering of subjective impression, the co-authors' message is clear. Meanwhile, to return to our journey through the visual field, the eye is led by contrast from the bay thicket to the glowing open landscape and "swift shallop [that] crosses the moonlight" (l. 14), or what the diary entry describes as "Faint, as in softened moonlight the world she has forsaken long ago." The fact that the bay thicket is what leads us to the boat brings to mind how, even though learning resulted in the saint's embattled engagement with the world, study has also provided her with an escape: heavenly moments on earth that have preceded the final destination "soft and apart" for which she is about to embark.

Finally, to return to the question of why Saint Katharine cannot be perpetually pitying if she is perpetually bleeding, lines 6–8 ("a cloudy seal / Is on her eyes; the mouth will never feel / Pity again") bring to mind not only the cloudy seal of her eyes but the fact that the saint's mouth is sealed as well, through death, because she dared to challenge the Emperor Maxentius. This might lead the spectator to consider the links between emotion, speech, and action and the difficulty of being a woman of intellect and opinion in a male-dominated world that prefers a more self-sacrificing femininity. As Michael Field themselves put it, "we have much to say that the world will not tolerate from a woman's lips" (*WD* 6). But with its shift of medium, this poem creates a metaleptic leap that imagines a different world / world view. The poem's representational friction supports an alternative ekphrastic hagiography and seems to suggest that if the female subject is not permitted to speak or act, then her pity will have limited reach.

The Marriage of Bacchus and Ariadne

As I have discussed elsewhere, many of *Sight and Song*'s picture-poems, like many of the verses in *Long Ago*, resist movement from an all-female realm to a heterosexual one, juxtaposing enduring same-sex bonds with fleeting heterosexual unions. Michael Field's "The Marriage of Bacchus and Ariadne" offers an interesting variation on this theme. They were so fond of Tintoretto's painting (Fig. 2.3) that Bradley gave Cooper a copy for her birthday in 1892, after their work on the poem was complete.[19] At first glance, the poem does seem to provide an objective representation of the painting, and its descriptive elements vary neither from the art object nor from its mythological referent—the tale of how Bacchus falls in love at first sight with Ariadne, who has been abandoned by Theseus, and how Venus enables her to marry the god. In fact, the narrative that Michael Field's provides, rather uncharacteristically for *Sight and Song*, seems to dwell upon Bacchus rather than on the female figures. The vivid description as the poem opens takes pains to accurately represent Tintoretto's version of Bacchus approaching Ariadne:

---

[19] On January 12, 1892 Cooper writes in the diary of the "yet undelivered ... a large photograph of that poetic painting *The Marriage of Bacchus and Ariadne* by Tintoretto, in the Ducal Palace, Venice. I have never had such beautiful presents as these that crown my thirty years." *Works and Days*. MSS Add. 46780. (EC). fol. 12v. The British Library.

Fig. 2.3 The Wedding of Ariadne and Bacchus (1578). Jacopo Tintoretto. Oil on canvas. Courtesy of the Sala dell'Anticollegio, Palazzo Ducale, Venice.

> Dark sea-water round a shape
> Hung about the loins with grape,
> Hair the vine itself, in braids
> On the brow—thus Bacchus wades
> Through the water to the shore. (*SS* 82, lines 1–5)

As it unfolds, however, we see how the poem's *enargeia* is driven more by haptics than vision. Michael Field's description focuses on Bacchus' motion through space as he is compelled to approach Ariadne, and when they observe how curious it is that grapevine, not sea foam, clings to him, they emphasize how heavy the grape hangs about the loins. With no visual detail, the second stanza narrates all he has left behind in order to be with Ariadne as Venus as dictates, or, as the poem says, "to follow Love's command" (l. 20).

Thus, focusing on haptics, and in the last lines, taste, Michael Field brings synaesthesia to their verbal adaptation of the painting. They take advantage of the shift of medium to make sure they tell the reader what they feel Bacchus feeling in the painting: how Venus has compelled him to love Ariadne, and his "Limbs, that push against the tide," (l. 7), his "trembling consent" and pain in his eyes (lines 29, 31), and his yearning for her, which weighs as heavy as the fruit girding his loins. Because of his love for Ariadne, this god has been stripped of his powers. Ironically, when Michael Field asserts, "Therefore he is come in weed / Of a mortal bowed by need" (lines 45–6) they seem to be implying that Bacchus (Dionysus) is now experiencing the overwhelming drive of eros that *he* generally thrusts upon humans, that he is clothed anew, and that in fact it is only when helpless as a human in his love for a human girl that any god can truly "taste of pleasure" (l. 50). This is another notable synaesthetic moment in the poem. The poem's pounding couplets in catalectic trochaic tetrameter further reinforce Bacchus's yearning, despairing, desire, in this instance of sight turned into song.

If this metaleptic leap from sight to song and from the visual object to the haptic narrative turns the tables or at least blurs the boundaries between god and human, Michael Field's ekphrastic adaptation also blurs the boundaries here between male and female power, providing an example of Jason Rudy's observation that nineteenth-century women writers' provocations and pushing of boundaries "was enabled by the metaphors and formal mechanisms associated with embodiment and touch" (91). The published version of the poem is more subtle about this than their notes in the joint diary, which demonstrate equal interest in Ariadne and Bacchus. The diary entry begins:

> Tintoret's Marriage of Bacchus and Ariadne. He comes to her through the sea water; vines hang on his loins; his hair is the vine itself-the terribly shy passion and yearning of nature is in his eyes raised toward his vision of womanhood under the milky crown of stars.[20]

A draft of the poem follows with two stanzas that didn't make it into *Sight and Song*; yet these stanzas are of interest if we wish to

---

[20] *Works and Days*. MSS Add. 46778, [n.d],1890. (EC). fol. 55v. The British Library.

consider what Bradley and Cooper were thinking and feeling as they gazed upon the painting in the Ducal Palace:

Ariadne had been left
Voiceless, of her prince bereft
Looking out across the plain
With one vision on her brain
Of a sail than few: when black
On the distant vessel's track
Rose a form which claimed her breath
Was it loss-effacing death
'Mid the salt-stream of the sea?
She forgot how ships can flee.

Theseus went: now someone came
From the waste and bowed like flame
Toward herself in his desire
Life was in blood like fire
Desolation, barren waves
Had they brought the joy that saves?
Earth with its appeal, its green
Mystic energies was seen
Wooing her, as its young god
Through the ocean-water trod.[21]

This emphasis on Ariadne's story—the sight of Theseus' vessel sailing away—a "form which claimed her breath"—is a "loss-effacing death," a pain that leaves her "voiceless," "bereft," has a more subtle presence in the final poem: in *Sight and Song* the reader only learns that there is "pain / in that stately woman's breast," and that she had been "dishonoured." More important from a feminist perspective are the *new* things in the final poem. Whereas in the first draft, Venus merely "seals his bliss," in the final version Bacchus has no power at all: he is a "medicant / Who has almost died from want." Venus (Love), on the other hand, controls the scene. Michael Field's ekphrasis addresses the episode thusly:

---

[21] *Works and Days*. MSS Add. 46778, August 1, 1890. (EC). fols. 55v–56v. The British Library.

> Love is poised above the twain,
> Zealous to assuage the pain
> In that stately woman's breast;
> Love has set a starry crest
> On the once dishonoured head;
> Love entreats the hand to wed,
> Gently loosening out the cold
> Fingers toward that hoop of gold
> Bacchus, tremblingly content
> To be patient, doth present. (SS lines 21–30)

Nineteenth-century critical commentary on this painting waxes eloquent,[22] often focusing on Ariadne and Bacchus' eagerness to clasp hands. Some critics (then and now) also read the marriage as political allegory celebrating the Doge-as-Venice and the union of Venice and the sea.[23] Michael Field's version, however, employs representational friction and modifies the heteronormative biases of this well-known myth. In so doing, as Bradley and Cooper translate the tale from sight to song they take advantage of ekphrasis's ability, through narrative, to comment upon movement and stasis. In Field's version, Ariadne is not over-enthused to marry Bacchus for his own sake: anaphora in the second stanza emphasizes Bacchus' eagerness to pursue Ariadne, but in contrast she sits "Queenly on the samphire rock" (l. 8) and Venus has to gently pry open Ariadne's fingers to accept the wedding ring. At best, Michael Field seems to be saying, Venus has found a way to rescue Ariadne from the island where she had been abandoned and to distract Ariadne from Theseus' betrayal.

Perhaps it is not surprising that, according to the diary, art critic Bernard Berenson did not care for this particular poem. He accused Bradley and Cooper of confusing

---

[22] Ruskin writes, "Once one of the noblest pictures in the world, but now miserably faded" (qtd in Sdegno, 73). In *New Italian Sketches*, J. A. Symonds writes of the painting, "It is well to leave the very highest achievements of art untouched by criticism undescribed" (183).

[23] In "Celebrating the Most Serene Republic," Giorgio Taglioferro observes that the iconography of *The Wedding of Ariadne and Bacchus*, along with three other allegory Tintorettos from the same period, "offer a dense web of allusion that celebrates the good government of the Venetians" (211).

Ekphrastic Poetics   113

the material of poetry, which is <u>feeling</u> with colour and outline the materials of painting. If we look on a picture til we were on fire with it, the language we used would be poetic. In <u>St. Jerome</u>, we have <u>felt</u> the picture so intensely that unconsciously we have evoked the feeling of a St. Jerome-like the St. Jerome painted or rather moulded by Tura. When ever this burning sensation is maintained there is life in the words we use. Then he gives us a verbal criticism of <u>The Magdalen, The Pieta, St. Jerome, Bacchus and Aridane</u>.[24]

It seems Berenson did not recognize that an emphasis on feeling was precisely what Michael Field were bringing to the conventions of ekphrasis in their revisionary poetics. Perhaps he merely didn't like the fact that, in this version of the tale, Ariadne is not particularly eager to return Bacchus' affection.

A Pen-drawing of Leda

I turn now to the poem that precedes "Marriage of Bacchus and Ariadne" in *Sight and Song*: "A Pen-drawing of Leda." Michael Field's "museum label" attributes the drawing to Sodoma; by 1900, prominent art historian Giovanni Morelli corrected that attribution to Leonardo da Vinci (154–7). Michael Field viewed the drawing at the Grand Duke's Palace at Weimar. It was subsequently acquired by the Dutch collector D. G. van Beuningen and now is held in the Museum Boijmans Van Beuningen, Rotterdam (Fig. 2.4).[25]

Like "The Marriage of Bacchus and Ariadne," "A Pen Drawing of Leda" revises its referent while creating representational friction—a revision similarly made possible by synaesthetic narrative. In the original myth, Leda is passive: Zeus, disguised as a swan, seduces (or rapes) her. As I discussed in Chapter 1, in

---

[24] *Works and Days*. MSS Add. 46780, circa June 25,1892. (EC). fol. 124v. The British Library. For a discussion of Michael Field's treatment of St. Jerome, see Ehnenn, "Haptic Ekphrasis."

[25] Previously, other scholars have suggested that a similar drawing, currently at Chatsworth, is the referent for this poem, but the provenance of the Chatsworth drawing does not support this claim. Instead, *Leonardo Da Vinci Master Draftsman, Catalogue to an Exhibition at The Metropolitan Museum of Art, New York 2003* confirms the provenance of this Boijmans drawing and its presence in Weimar in the 1890s (p. 530).

Fig. 2.4 Kneeling Leda and the Swan (1505/10). Leonardo da Vinci. Pen and brown ink over black chalk. Courtesy of the Museum Boijmans Van Beuningen, Rotterdam.

Long Ago[26] Michael Field retells Leda's tale with a poem that focuses only on the appearance of the eggs and Leda's metamorphosis into motherhood. In *Sight and Song*'s "A Pen-Drawing of Leda" Michael Field modifies the myth anew, in a sonnet with an

---

[26] Michael Field also includes a Leda poem in *Underneath the Bough*: "Leda was weary of her state."

unconventional rhyme scheme, varied line lengths, and a narrative that makes Leda the active partner:[27]

> 'TIS Leda lovely, wild and free,
> > Drawing her gracious Swan down through the grass to see
> > Certain round eggs without a speck :
> One hand plunged in the reeds and one dinting the downy neck,
> > Although his hectoring bill
> > Gapes toward her tresses,
> She draws the fondled creature to her will.
>
> > She joys to bend in the live light
> Her glistening body toward her love, how much more bright!
> > Though on her breast the sunshine lies
> And spreads its affluence on the wide curves of her waist and thighs,
> > To her meek, smitten gaze
> > Where her hand presses
> The Swan's white neck sink Heaven's concentred rays. (SS 81)

This sonnet offers plenty of visual description, but the long lines are the ones that possess notably haptic elements, especially in the first section. Leda "draws" the swan down through the grass (l. 2), her hands "plunge" into the grass and "dint" the swan's neck (l. 4), and though lines 5 and 6 portray the swan's movements toward her, line 7 make clear that, at least in Michael Field's interpretation, it is Leda's will, rather than the swan's (who, here, is never identified as Zeus) that dominates the scene. In addition to preserving Leda's agency, this scene is cleansed of lust and violence, the eggs are pure "without a speck" (l. 3) and after the volta, Nature blesses this coupling via the brightness of the sun's light. Again, the visual and the haptic function in tandem here; light and movement make meaning together as the sunlight directs the spectator's gaze in an erotic caress from Leda's breast to the "wide curves of her waist and thighs" to where her hand presses the swan's neck. To be sure, the poem represents a smitten Leda, but, significantly, one whose desire makes "Heaven's concentred rays" mirror her embrace of the swan and celebrate her own Dionysian passion. Importantly,

---

[27] Lysack, Saville, and Williams similarly note that Michael Field's rendering of Leda in *Sight and Song* minimizes the violence of the original myth and emphasizes her pleasure.

by removing all mention of Zeus from the narrative in their metaleptic leap from image to word, Michael Field's revisionary poetics shift this narrative into a different world that raises the possibility of different rules, revealing, among other things, the potential for ekphrasis to negotiate homoerotic desire. Previous studies have recognized the homoeroticism within some of *Sight and Song*'s other picture-poems, perhaps most obviously "Sleeping Venus." If we are interested in a queer reading of "Pen Drawing of Leda and the Swan," we might conclude that here, Michael Field represents something akin to the animal relations in Oscar Wilde's fairy tales or the love between Stephen Gordon and her horse Raferty in *The Well of Loneliness*.[28] Thus, Michael Field's description of human-animal lovemaking invites queer as well as feminist interpretation.

The initial lines of *Sight and Song*'s preface, with its evocation of the autonomous art object and a universal way of seeing, combined with the paratextual museum labels that precede each poem, at first may seem to suggest that their self-described picture-poems are mere replication akin to the practice of those female copyists who, whether as spectators or art students, were a dedicated and ubiquitous presence in Victorian art galleries.[29] But just as the preface quickly deconstructs itself, each of *Sight and Song*'s picture poems similarly demonstrate that, for Michael Field, ekphrasis is a process that does not merely replicate the image invoked on the museum label. Michael Field's ekphrases are not terribly concerned with making the image come to life, showing what words can do better than images, or assuaging anxiety over semiotic difference. Instead, their ekphrases perform metaleptic leaps into a world that affirms multiple ways of seeing. They imagine a different world that recognizes aspects of the art object that others have not; in so doing they affirm their own self-fashioning as queer-feminist spectators, art critics, and authors. In *Sight and Song* Michael Field acknowledges, where male authors do not, the role of dialectical viewing and creative process, and makes clear that ekphrastic writing takes place in context of (and in conversation, rather than in rivalry with) many influences: museum labels,

---

[28] Later of course, Bradley and Cooper famously figure their beloved Whym Chow as erotic proxy. For an extended discussion, see Chapter 4.
[29] On nineteenth-century copyists, see Codell, "Aura" and Siegel, *Desire and Excess*. For a wonderful study of Victorian replication more generally, see Codell and Hughes.

Ekphrastic Poetics   117

images, referents, other images and narratives about references, and the history of art criticism, as well as their own embodied and lived experience as spectators.

After *Sight and Song*

Fine art ekphrases: three later examples

After *Sight and Song*, Bradley and Cooper did not lose interest in ekphrasis. In fact, on February 15, 1892, after Cooper records a draft of *Sight and Song*'s preface in the joint diary, she catalogues "Pictures for a second series of *Sight and Song* (by Heaven's Grace)":

> Triumph of Chastity – Lorenzo Lotto
> Ecce Homo – Montegna (Louvre)
> Parnasse – Montegna (Louvre)
> The Caniert (sp?) – Giorgione (Louvre)
> Daniel (??) Corregio (Barghese)
> Circe – Dosso Dossi
> The Painting of Christ and his Mother – Corregio (mt Bl. . .)
> The Virgin and St. Anna – Dai libri (Nat Gallery)
> Bacchus and Ariadne – Titian (Nat Gallery)
> The Pieta – Bellini (Brera)
> The Agony in the Garden – Bellini (Nat Gallery)
> St. Sebastian – Dosso Dossi (Brera)
> Caritas – Sodoma (Berlin)
> The Three Astrologers – Giorgione (Vienna)[30]

The second series never materialized, and according to Ivor Treby, only drafts of "Ecce Homo" and "Circe" have survived. The unpublished "On Dosso Dossi's Circe" after *Circe and Her Lovers in a Landscape* (Fig. 2.5) was originally written by Cooper, then copied (and possibly edited) by Bradley into their journal on June 19, 1892:

> How terrible this country, how
>   Alone these creatures round a girl

[30] *Works and Days*. MSS Add. 46780, February 15, 1892. (EC). fol. 48v. The British Library.

Fig. 2.5 *Circe and Her Lovers in a Landscape* (c. 1525). Dosso Dossi. Oil on paper. Courtesy of the National Gallery, Washington, DC.

        Herself now solitary:
For the more quietness doth allow
        The Heron in the swamp to curl
His neck & fish; nor be
    Vexed by that girl with changeless brow.

Her hand is on a runic stone
Pressed flat, & what is written there
    Is in her eyes, her breath,
Though to her very self unknown:
The homestead peeping unaware
        Admonishes of death—
So undisturbed, so overgrown.

Wild beasts that once were men have met
In circle by her—stag and doe,
    Daft howlet & grey dog—
In the deep roadway lions forget
Their wrath: —a frolic puppy so
    Is cowed that as a log
He stretches where he first was set.

Her cloak has July's depth of green:
    Her hair that strays is scarce, & bound
        With flowerets pale & red
In double blinking wreath half seen
        Against the piny shade profound;
And her averted head
    Faces the gray-lit, open ground.

What fresh but ancient awe exhales
From her sweet silence, & is caught
    By fir tree, deer & bird
If men would catch it naught avails
    Save to forget the strife of thought
Turn into brutes & dream unstirred
    For hours within the humming dales.[31]

---

[31] This poem appeared publicly for the first time in Treby's edition of Michael Field poems, *A Shorter Shīrazād* (p. 48).

The formal elements of "On Dosso Dossi's *Circe*" have much in common with many of *Sight and Song*'s ekphrases: the visual field is rendered with careful, seemingly objective detail, and much attention is given to the figures on the periphery, especially nature and animals. Here, especially in the last stanza, synaesthesia translates visual elements into all the senses: looking at Dosso Dossi's *Circe* evokes for Cooper (and Bradley) the feeling that "her sweet silence" "exhales" (lines 30, 29); and as they see the landscape they hear "humming" (l. 35). As in *Sight and Song*'s "St. Katharine of Alexandria" (and "La Gioconda" and "Bust of a Courtesan"), this poem resists *prosopopoeia*; yet even without dramatic envoicing the co-authors' subjective stance toward Circe is clear, sympathetic, and anti-patriarchal in its orientation. This Circe is merely a girl, not the Circe-as-femme fatale portrayed in so many Pre-Raphaelite and Decadent images. The poem sympathetically emphasizes her solitary condition as it catalogues the painting's visual tension between Circe and the circle of wild men now turned tamed animals, between Circe and the "piny shade profound," and between Circe and the "gray-lit, open ground." Circe and her transformative powers remain an enigma as this poem resists—unlike art historians and classics scholars—the urge to explain her, her motives, or her feelings. The reader is only told that Circe herself doesn't understand her power, and that she is sweet nonetheless. In its ekphrastic leap from myth and art object to verse, the world portrayed in this poem is mysteriously freed from the desires and power of men. From Michael Field's perspective, it seems, this is reason for "fresh but ancient awe."

Michael Field continued to create verse about art objects as time went on,[32] with their revisionary ekphrastic practices mounting escalating challenges to the notion of the autonomous art object and the universal spectator. Their two-stage process of observation resulted in even more emphasis on subjective rather than objective modes of knowing: *enargeia* and *descriptio* in these

---

[32] In addition to the examples discussed here, is possible that some of the devotional poems in *Poems of Adoration, Mystic Trees,* and/or the posthumous *The Wattlefold* were inspired by images from the Grimani Breviary, which they acquired at the urging of Fr. John Gray and frequently referred to in their personal writing in their final years. Whether this writing should be considered ekphrastic or merely influenced by the breviary is beyond the scope of this chapter.

Fig. 2.6 Portrait of Composer Adrian Willaert at the Spinet (c. 1550–90). Jacopo Tintoretto. Courtesy of the Colonna Gallery, Rome.

later ekphrases becomes less clinical, less labored, and often more synaesthetic. While still eschewing *prosopopoeia*, the speaker's subjective interpretations nevertheless become more obvious, less visually mimetic, more abstract, and are reminiscent (at least in spirit) of the imaginary portraits of Walter Pater, Vernon Lee, and Oscar Wilde; these, according to Jeffrey Kessler, are a hybrid literary form that imagines fictional figures as simultaneously embodying their historical moment and being effaced by it (377). "On a portrait by Tintoret in the Colonna Gallery" written in 1893, published in *The Dial* in 1896, then reprinted in *Wild Honey* (1908) is representative (see Fig. 2.6).

The poem opens:

An old man sitting in the evening light
Touching a spinet: there is a stormy blow
In the red heavens; but he does not know
How fast the clouds are faring to the night: (*WH* 133, lines 1–4)

A meditation on the subjective nature of perception and of truth, this Italian sonnet could be considered queer in that it insists that unconventional ways of knowing are valid. The first quatrain provides a brief objective description of the painting followed by a declaration about what the subject of the painting does not know. In contrast, the rest of the poem collapses past and present, memory and reality, brown and grey, and sight and sound ("he *hears* the sunset")[33] as it confidently offers Michael Field's interpretation of what the old man is experiencing in terms of emotion and memory.

> He *hears* the sunset as he thrums some slight
> Soft tune that clears the track of long ago,
> And as his musings wander to and fro
> Where the years passed along, a sage delight
> Is creeping in his eyes. His soul is old,
> The sky is old, the sunset browns to grey;
> But he to some dear country of his youth
> By those few notes of music borne away,
> Is listening to a story that is told,
> And listens, smiling at the story's truth. (lines 5–14, emphasis in original)

The lines with the more subjective content also make more sense metrically than the objective, visually mimetic lines. The poem becomes more iambic as the speaker sketches the old man's inner life, and here the metric variations effectively reinforce content: alliteration and spondees represent the heard sunset as a "slíght / sóft tune," line 11 shifts from iambs to anapests as his mind wanders "Whĕre thĕ yéar păssed ălóng," and spondees emphasize that "thóse féw nótes" (of the sunset) are able to transport him into some vague but pleasurable past. Thus, through the metaleptic leaps of this ekphrastic poem, a world is written into being that, despite its boundary-blurring tendencies and embrace of conjecture, makes more sense to the speaker (and the man in the painting) than the "real" world.

Michael Field's later ekphrases also include an unpublished sonnet which appears in the diary on November 24, 1904.

---

[33] The diary entry makes this synaesethetic observation as well.

Titled, "Fellowship, or, Of meeting, or, A Japanese Print"[34] it reads:

> Love, I have found a symbol of our state,
> What to ourselves we are: of this no hint
> As we twain walk together, nor give glint
> Of happy knowledge, or of the eye's debate.
> Behold the pearl embedded in our fate,
> And treasure of our secret in this print
> Of women meeting: face & action stint
> The vibrant joy; nor has one come too late
> And earned reproach; nor is there any word
> Or flutter of the breast, or garment stirred.
> Only one stoops with humbler strain to reach
> The greeting arms bent down to her, & each
> Small hand becomes a ceinture, as the hasp
> Of a fair bracelet fastens on its clasp.[35]

This ekphrastic encounter is even more explicitly personal than "On a portrait by Tintoret." Instead of the third person narration used in *Sight and Song* and all the other ekphrases discussed thus far, this sonnet employs direct address from the spectator to her beloved as it asserts queer kinship with the women in the Japanese print. Here, ekphrastic *enargeia* and *descriptio* offer only vague visual detail, while the poem's emphasis on pearls, jewelry, clothing, and secrets conveys as much about the co-authors' own homoerotic and aesthetic proclivities as about the artwork. Touch and emotion are quite prominent in this poem, yet these haptic features largely function via understatement and reference to secret,

---

[34] I have been unable to identify the referent for this poem. It is likely that Bradley and Cooper viewed the print at the home of Ricketts and Shannon. Upon Shannon's death in 1938, the entirety of the artists' extensive Japanese print collection was bequeathed to the British Museum, but a print that matches the poem is not among their current holdings. According to jewelry historian Helen Ritchie at the Fitzwilliam, which holds many of Ricketts and Shannon's other art objects including the jewelry designed by Ricketts for Bradley, Ricketts and Shannon frequently added to and sold items from their art collection over the years. So it is likely that the print that inspired this poem was sold prior to Shannon's death.

[35] This poem appeared publicly for the first time in Treby's edition of Michael Field poems, *A Shorter Shīrazād* (p. 98).

ineffable truths as Michael Field accentuate the "vibrant joy" and deep connection between the two women that can only be hinted at in the referenced Japanese print. The exquisite, haptic imagery in the final four lines creates a tiny world of tenderness and desire: like a nearly inaudible sigh during an embrace between "friends" who are secretly queer lovers, one can almost hear the click as the "fair bracelet"'s circle is completed.

Ekphrasis and the personal object

Some of Michael Field's later ekphrastic verses, both published and unpublished, depict domestic art objects of a more personal and intimate nature than the fine art discussed in the previous section. As Talia Schaffer has demonstrated, female aesthetes at the *fin de siècle* frequently expressed interest in items that would not have been properly considered "high art"; in so doing, women expanded the notion of what could and should be recognized as an object worthy of aesthetic consideration. The innovative ekphrastic characteristics I've discussed above also appear in Michael Field's picture-poems about photographs and sketches of loved ones, as well as their verse about jewelry and other domestic objects. These further examples indicate that Bradley and Cooper, like many of their female contemporaries, considered beautiful domestic and intimate objects worthy of the same attention as the fine art that otherwise attracted their poetic eye.

Take, for example, the unpublished 1902 poem, "A Miniature," about a portrait of Cooper by Charles Ricketts, completed in May 1901. A few months later Ricketts designed the Pegasus pendant to house the miniature and gave it to Bradley (see Fig. 2.7). The first quatrain of this English sonnet opens with an objective description of the front of the pendant:

> A casket flaming with a thousand flaws
> Of ruby, emerald, & of amethyst,
> With Pegasus the subtle fountain draws
> Down from the clouds to get its bubbles kisst; (lines 1–4)[36]

---

[36] This poem appeared publicly for the first time in Treby's edition of Michael Field poems, *Music and Silence* (p. 138).

Fig. 2.7 Pendant (three views): *Pegasus Drinking from the Fountain of Hippocrene* (1901). Carlo and Arthur Giuliano and Charles de Sousy Ricketts. Gold, enameled in royal blue, green, red, and white, and set with four cut garnets, a cabochon garnet, two large pearls, one small pearl, and a baroque pearl. Courtesy of the Fitzwilliam Museum, Cambridge.

The reader is given the experience of first seeing the flaming jewels on the surface of this decadent object, and then provided the opportunity to examine it more closely. Almost immediately a sense of aesthetic contrast is established: the movement of Pegasus' head from up in the clouds down to the fountain is paralleled with the contrast between flame and water. As the second quatrain unfolds, the speaker extols the beauty of the pendant using words that evoke spiritual sublimity such as "wonder," "enshrine," and "behold":

> A wonder of enamel & pure gold;
> Yet tarry not, push the closed doors ajar,
> Enshrined a miniature thou shalt behold:
> Forget all crusted things of curve and star; (lines 5–8)

But as the poem zooms in for closer and closer examination of the pendant, it is clear that the most beautiful aspect of this art object is the miniature enclosed within, and it is beautiful because of the sitter's personal qualities and her relationship to the speaker:

> For thou are with a face where thought is young,
> And Love primaeval as when Heaven was starred,
> A face that gives itself & must belong
> To those that stone, so solitary, marred;
> And yet a face that needs not anything,
> But rises as from God's own fountain-spring. (lines 9–14)

Like "A Japanese print," this interlocutor derives aesthetic and other pleasures from the beautiful art object by recognizing something of personal relevance that not all spectators will fully understand or be familiar with.

The unpublished "To Pearls: on a net" (1905) operates similarly.[37] The poem is not about a fine art object, yet nonetheless begins with a traditional second-person address to the pearls, trying to intervene in the art object's silence: "Bright pearls, you need to speak / And yet too shy—" (lines 1–2). It quickly becomes clear that, since the pearls cannot, the speaker will voice admiration for the beloved wearer:

---

[37] *Works and Days.* MSS Add. 46794. January 13, 1905. (KB). fol. 9r. The British Library.

> Lo, hanging by,
> In dimpled line, her cheek,
> Your voices open as doves' bills, to laud
>   The lovelier sky
> Than any feathers of their wing or breast:
>   Tress you the hair untressed,
> And, from your filletings of golden cord,
>   Appear & reappear
>   By brow & eye!
> She must not put you off by night
> all the long night must keep—
>   Yet soft! If so she lie
>   With all her beauty dear
>   Lit by your light,
> There must I kneel in dark idolatry,
>   Nor ever sleep. (lines 3–18)

As the poem develops, the pearls, like the Pegasus pendant, become a vehicle for expressing homoerotic attraction and devoted love for Cooper. Echoing Shakespeare with the phrase "Yet soft" at line 14, the pearls inspire a fantasy of Bradley as a courtly lover who gazes upon his lady all night.[38] It's important to note, though, that although the pearls are a means for talking about the beloved, the poem is not just about Cooper; it's about both the pearls *and* Cooper. Here we see a key characteristic of Michael Field's ekphrasis, especially their later work, in full swing: The art object(s) *and* the spectator/author, the visual *and* non-visual aspects of the art object, together make the ekphrastic encounter "real" and meaningful. It's not just what one sees—it's what one feels, and desires, and thinks; yet, not everyone will have the same perception of the object—visually and otherwise. As Loizeaux says of the twentieth-century women writing ekphrasis that Michael Field seems to anticipate, "Ekphrasis is more dynamic, polyvocal and multiply responsive than the poet–work-of-art–audience triangle might suggest" (26). Put another way, it moves "away from a logic of 'either/or' and toward an embrace of 'both/and'" (Keefe 136). "A Japanese Print," "A Miniature," "To Pearls," and even

---

[38] Reading this poem, I can't help thinking of Carol Ann Duffy's "Warming her pearls."

"On a Portrait by Tintoret" all employ this revisionary approach to ekphrasis.

Lest one think that Bradley and Cooper permit themselves such subjective ekphrastic reflection only in work not intended for publication, consider "Suggested by A Picture," which was published in *Mystic Trees* and references a photo of Bradley and Cooper's friend and confessor, Father Vincent McNabb. Although most of *Mystic Trees* was written by Bradley (see Chapter 5), Ivor Treby notes that a letter to Cooper's sister Amy "makes clear that this piece was a collaboration—as Henry writes, "Cut out by me and stitched by Michael" (Field, *UR* 208):

> It is the brows, the infinite, soft confusing
> Of wave on wave and lovely current there;
> It is the brows, the marge of the soft hair
> In reedy level; or it is the eyes
> Where plumes of sea-birds wrangle with the skies;
> It is the mouth where bitter shadow lies,
> Where in the twilight there are nymphs that mourn
> As at the birth of Christ and grow forlorn—
> O face, take heed what freedom you are losing!
> This cowl is as a cage
> For such soft passion's rage;
> And when the temperance of youth is gone
> You will be terrible to look upon. (Field, *MT* 90)

The fact that the poem is inspired by a photo is important to our consideration of ekphrases about objects that are not fine arts. For the most part, nineteenth-century photography was considered an objective representative of reality, and thus especially useful for journalistic reporting and scientific documentation.[39] Although the work of selected photographers, such as Julia Margaret Cameron, was beginning to be accepted in some Victorian circles as fine art, most photos were not thought to possess the same aesthetic prowess and depth as painting or sculpture, and therefore not considered worthy of the kind of interpretive or philosophical examination that fine art would inspire. Nevertheless, in "Suggested by a

---

[39] For excellent studies of Victorian photography, see Martin Meisel's *Realizations*; and Jennifer Green-Lewis's *Framing the Victorians* and *Victorian Photography*.

Picture" the blazons in the octave quickly transform the facial elements in the photo into metaphors for deep reflection: they stage a series of escalating contests between conflicting ways of being. Locks of hair mixing with eyebrows become waves crossing in a current; the eyes recall the paradox of a creature of the sea taking flight in air; and importantly, the shadow about the mouth juxtaposes the pagan and the Christian. As this modified sonnet moves from *enargeia* to *descriptio* at the volta in line 9, the speaker's opinions and fears for the dear friend in the picture are further, and more clearly, articulated.

Another unpublished poem, "The salt cellar sonnet" (1905) references a crystal bowl Bradley gave to Ricketts intending for him to display it filled with shells.[40] The poem largely refuses visual *enargeia*. Instead, it wryly focuses on *descriptio* (the fact that Ricketts filled it with salt and put it in the pantry) and more generally the theme, so apt for Michael Field's ekphrases in general, that things sometimes are not what they seem:

> How have you curbed my proud imaginings,
> And all my perfumed hopes put out of sight!
> So then this crystal bowl no chalice is
> No cruet from the altar; & with salt
> You fill it, putting it to offices
> Of service; & no honor in default: (lines 3–8)

Yet ultimately the poem celebrates friendship, gesturing in particular to the quirkiness of their relationship and the secret affinities the two queer couples share in their fellowship:

> For I will take it as a lovely sand
> That thou mayst stir from the spoon's silver tip,
> Inscribing there, from imprint of thy hand
> Terms of renewed and secret fellowship.
> Yea, take it as thy plaything, to acquire
> Its preciousness confirmed to thy desire. (lines 9–14)

Several other similar ekphrases, published and unpublished, exist in Michael Field's later *oeuvre*, perhaps most notably including

---

[40] This poem appeared publicly for the first time in Treby's edition of Michael Field poems, *Music and Silence* (p. 164).

at least one unpublished poem (1904) about the synaesthetic star sapphire ring Ricketts designed for Bradley[41] and "A Crucifix," from *Mystic Trees* (1909) which I discuss in Chapter 5 as an example of devotional poetry.

I close this chapter with the unpublished "Image and Superscription" (1903) after a sketch of Ricketts (Fig. 2.8).

> Shadow & whispers & half audible
> Secrets that dart as minnows from the sight,
> The eyes rich in communion with the light,
> Or gathering if as simples for a spell:
> As a whole sea had travailed on a shell
> The curves of the worn cheek are infinite
> And are at rest: only the ear is bright
> As with suspicion of incredible
> Dealings with thought. What may the impact be?
> What of thy sinuous & gliding power?—
> Moving as though many regions of the spirit
> As with a flame, wilt thou not in thy hour
> Create a finer sense we may inherit,
> Or re-create some lost felicity?[42]

This unpublished sonnet is rough but provocative, in that it uses the ekphrastic encounter as an attempt to capture the kind of thought that engenders artistic creation. In the introduction I discussed how *Sight and Song*'s "L'Indifferent" takes on the difficult task of depicting two embodied moments of "flow:" the spectators' absorption in gazing at the painting and the dancer's absorption in the dance. Similarly, this ekphrastic representation of the sketch of Ricketts dedicates itself to the task of representing not merely a person absorbed in thought, but the nature and consequences of creative thought itself. The sitter's imagination is fed by light, in a process that is holy, magical, and mythical by turns (lines 3–5). The bubbling of imagination evokes both sight and sound—"Shadow and whisper"—and is compared to darting

---

[41] The "Sabbatai" ring is mentioned more than a few times in the diary during this time.

[42] This poem appeared publicly for the first time in Treby's edition of Michael Field poems, *Music and Silence* (p. 154). Treby's notes identify the Bodleian Ricketts sketch (Fig 2.8) as the referent.

Ekphrastic Poetics 131

Fig. 2.8 Sketch of Charles Ricketts. Pencil on paper. Courtesy of the Bodleian Library, Oxford. MS. Eng. misc. c. 654/3 fol. 27r.

minnows. The poem keenly conveys the elusiveness both of the act of imaginative thought and trying to describe it. In so doing, as in so many of the other ekphrases I've discussed in this chapter, Michael Field gears into (*engrener*) the ineffable and the not easily grasped, to some extent prefiguring the experimentation and epistemological crisis that will become characteristic of modernism. At the poem's conclusion, as in the poems in and after *Sight and Song*, the speaker's investment and standpoint is clear; and here, direct address helps to strip away presumptions of pure objectivity during the lived experience of the ekphrastic process. In so doing, these later ekphrases reinforce (if there was ever any doubt) that Michael Field's earlier picture-poems from *Sight and Song*, despite their omniscient third-person narration, also represent a spectator-author with a critical eye and legitimate, albeit unique, insights.

3

"Come and sing": Elizabethan Temper, Eco-entanglement, and Lyric in *Underneath the Bough*

All art constantly aspires to the condition of music
—Walter Pater, "The School of Giorgione," (1877)

Mick and I were just two waves at our dance on the shore.
—[Edith Cooper], *Works and Days* (1896)

In the other, Heraclitean universe, being in your body is more like having a volume out from the library, a volume subject to more or less instant recall by other borrowers—who rewrite the whole story when they get it.
—Val Plumwood, *The Eye of the Crocodile* (2012)

When in 1889 Katharine Bradley and Edith Cooper first conceived of the project that eventually became *Underneath the Bough*, they wrote to John Miller Gray of "our new and beautiful Elizabethan songbook—which aspires to treat of Victorian themes in Elizabethan temper" (in Bristow, "Lyrical" 50). Their project was inspired by three texts. The first was William Byrd's 1589 *Songs of Sundrie Natures*, a title Michael Field also used while they were working on their collection.[1] The second was Thomas Campion's *Works*, a collection of verse and essays from the early 1600s which, thanks to A. H. Bullen's 1889 edition, garnered new interest among the Victorians in the Renaissance poet, musician, and physician. The third influence, more properly medieval than

---

[1] MS Eng poet d.60 is a fair copy of *Underneath the Bough* with explanatory notes in Cooper's hand, with the working title "Songs of Sundry Nature." Archive of "Michael Field." Oxford, Bodleian Libraries.

Renaissance, was Edward FitzGerald's popular Victorian translation of *The Rubáiyát of Omar Khayyám*, which ultimately gave *Underneath the Bough* its final title and epigraph:

> A Book of Verses underneath the Bough,
>   A Jug of Wine, a Loaf of Bread – and Thou
>   Beside me singing in the Wilderness –
> Oh, Wilderness were Paradise enow! (FitzGerald (1872) 130)

From 1859 to 1879, Edward FitzGerald published *The Rubáiyát* in four significantly different revisions and reorderings; although they did not initially win much attention, these eventually became quite popular among the Victorians, and particularly beloved by the Pre-Raphaelites, Swinburne, and Tennyson, from whom FitzGerald also sought editorial advice.

Like *The Rubáiyát*, *Underneath the Bough*'s three editions proved to be particularly recombinant; this chapter focuses on the first edition, which was divided into four books of songs.[2] In terms of the collection's "Elizabethan temper," as I argued in Chapter 1, Michael Field's dedication to the accurate portrayal of feeling—both positive and negative—convincingly explains their decision to write in the style of the Elizabethans: Bradley and Cooper asserted that that particular style is suited to the expression of emotion. Recall that in an 1885 letter to Cooper, Bradley writes:

> Do not desert Shakespeare and the Elizabethans ...we must seek to study and touch life as ... Shakespeare studied and touched it, and our speech must always be utterly different from ordinary speech; because ordinary speech is not transfigured by emotion, and the ordinary speech of an Age like ours is base with the exceeding Vulgarity of Materialism. (Bickle, *Fowl* 149)

For Michael Field, to be "transfigured by emotion" is both a necessary precondition for art and a key element of their fierce

---

[2] Because I am more interested in the context and process of Michael Field's adaptations and appropriations of other works and genres, rather than their revision of their own work, this chapter will only address the first edition of *Underneath the Bough*. For treatment of *Underneath the Bough*'s revisions and subsequent editions, see Bristow, Fletcher, Murray, and Richardson, among others.

personal dedication to the Dionysian thyrsus and all it represents. Chapter 1 explored this at work in Field's historical verse drama; one of this chapter's goals is to note how similar impulses in *Underneath the Bough* are facilitated by appropriations of thinkers such as Byrd, Campion, and Khayyám.[3]

But what of the "Victorian themes" that Michael Field said would be treated with this Elizabethan temper—such transfiguration of emotion? This is the question that most piques my interest, because at first glance, *Underneath the Bough*'s themes appear solidly universal rather than uniquely Victorian. Joseph Bristow identifies them: the first book, erotic love; the second, death; the third, poems that Michael Field's journals show commemorates their intimacy; and the fourth, verse that either mourns or seeks to repossess lost love (Bristow, "Lyrical" 54). Certainly this is one way to describe the topical divisions within the *Underneath the Bough*'s first edition.

In this chapter I suggest that the *Underneath the Bough*'s "Victorian themes" should more properly be understood as ecological and Decadent themes, specifically what Dennis Denisoff describes as "the eco-political potential pulsing through the pagan vein of Decadence" ("Dissipating Nature" 433). Granted, for many Victorians, "nature was something to be held in opposition to the human—something separate from society ... that one might view from an Aesthetic distance" (Denisoff, "Natural Environments" 7). And, of course, much Decadent literature posits the self "against nature." Yet Denisoff also identifies a different strand of Decadent ecopaganism at the *fin de siècle*, a "species intersubjectivity held by Pater and other contributors to pagan Decadence" ("Dissipating Nature" 432). Thus, while Chapter 2 focused on ekphrasis as a mode for Michael Field to explore subjective, queer-feminist epistemologies in the context of the long history of heteropatriarchal art criticism, in this chapter I will posit *Underneath the Bough* as an exploration of that individual subject's inextricable relation with the natural world, in all its multiplicities. What Denisoff describes as ecopaganism

---

[3] In his essay on Wordsworth's influence on Michael Field, Alex Murray argues that Bradley and Cooper felt their representation of nature in *Underneath the Bough* was too dispassionate, and it was only in subsequent revisions that added poems included the Dionysian impulses they were striving for. As this chapter will show, I identify significant moments of passionate entanglement with nature in their earliest edition as well.

possess two important characteristics that, as we shall see, can also be found in *Underneath the Bough*: a "symbiotic relationship between life forms that are reflected in eco-paganism's efforts to diffuse self-identity within a larger natural collective"; and negotiations of both the natural and the unnatural that can be understood as both decadent and queer ("Dissipating Nature" 437–8, *passim*).

This chapter also considers how (what we might term) Michael Field's nature poetry or environmentalist impulses can be understood vis-à-vis other nineteenth-century ecologies. Recently, scholars of nineteenth-century environmental writing have made much of the Victorian invention of ecology, of Darwinian and other scientific discourses that gesture toward human and non-human interdependence on both large and small scales (despite Victorian ideas that the human should be, somehow, above nature),[4] and of texts and theories that acknowledge the Victorians' growing awareness of deep time. For example, the essays in Nathan K. Hensley and Philip Steer's collection *Ecological Form* address the many and various conceptual dilemmas that arose as thinkers in the early years of the Anthropocene sought to understand and model human entanglement with the natural world at the precise moment that many of them were also aware of how nineteenth-century "advancements" were contributing to that world's pollution and other forms of what we today would call unsustainable practices. Hensley and Steer catalogue how in Shelley, D. G. Rossetti, and Robert Browning "the natural world gladly shrugs off its human traces (Hensley and Steer 13). And Elizabeth Carolyn Miller convincingly demonstrates how some Victorians' concerns about extraction ecologies complicate the era's otherwise dominant rhetorics of progress and reproductive futurism. As we'll see, in Michael Field's *Underneath the Bough*, such conceptual dilemmas are less pronounced: entanglement seems a way of life—between Bradley and Cooper as lovers and life partners, certainly, but also with nature, the past, and even with death. Granted, such entanglement is messy: random, unpredictable, multifaceted, and at times contradictory, as this chapter will show. But this is where we can identify, in *Underneath the Bough* as in their

---

[4] For instance, Denisoff observes that those considered "too close" to nature, such as pagans, indigenous people, the Irish, were considered less human. ("Natural Environments" 7)

other works I have discussed thus far, Michael Fields's characteristic *l'engrenage*—a phenomenological willingness to gear into and take up the unknown—in the case of Underneath the Bough, through their eco-entanglement.

If Michael Field's ecodecadence diverges from more frequently discussed strands of Victorian discourse, environmentalist and otherwise, Underneath the Bough's lyrics also differ significantly from many of the trends that have been identified in nineteenth-century women's nature writing. Underneath the Bough does not resemble texts in which women use nature writing to assert their right "to conceptualize and broadcast scientific knowledge" or to insert the domestic into scientific discourse (Harris-McCormick par. 1). Nor does Underneath the Bough have much in common with the garden-centric focus of many Victorian female poets such as Edith Nesbit, Violet Fane, A. Mary F. Robinson, and Mary Howitt who, as Fabienne Moine observes, deploy the garden as refuge or prison, as women's private space either within or against gender convention, as symbols of respectability, as commentary upon modernity and threats to Englishness, as a way to celebrate the new hybrid existence of life in suburbia, or as "denunciation of the threats of unbridled capitalism" (Moine 142).

Instead, in Underneath the Bough Michael Field takes a capacious and entangled approach to writing nature, voiced through a lyric speaker characterized by decadent, queer stylistics. Synaesthetic, archaic language, historic and mythic figures, and references to the animate and inanimate natural world and its energies facilitate the lyric speaker's expression of great emotion associated with varied passionate entanglements, and in so doing manifests affinities with both their Renaissance role models and *fin de siècle* ecopaganism. For Michael Field, as we shall see, nature is universal and thus somewhat objective in its transhistoricism; but their appropriation of and experimentation with the earlier lyric modes of Byrd, Campion, and Khayyám/FitzGerald render all experience—including ineffable experience and experience in nature—accessible for a uniquely subjective and queerly boundaried aesthetic of heightened emotion and entanglement.

To be sure, Bradley and Cooper's diary and letters do not provide copious detail about their intent to appropriate Byrd, Campion, or Khayyám/FitzGerald. Nevertheless, their references to Byrd and Campion at formative stages of their project, their invocation of Campion in Book Three, and their quotation of Khayyám in *Underneath the Bough*'s title and epigraph are provocations that should not be dismissed. This chapter takes up Bradley and Cooper's appropriations of these earlier lyric voices, then, as invitations that will proceed, as Michael Field does, throughout their *oeuvre*, in the spirit of *l'engrenage*.

Hearing Byrd's counterpoint: the lyric "I" in relationship

Of lyric's many affordances, here I will focus upon one that is sometimes overlooked: *the speaker—the lyric "I"—is in some sort of relationship with the addressee.* J. S. Mill, of course, famously supposes a lyric speaker who is so self-absorbed in his [sic] emotions and ideas, that instead of being heard, "poetry is overheard" (95). Mill asserts, "the peculiarity of poetry appears to us to lie in the poet's utter unconsciousness of a listener. Poetry is feeling confessing itself to itself, in moments of solitude" (95). Northrop Frye similarly asserts that "the speaker turns his back on his listeners ... lyric is internal mimesis of sound and imagery and stands opposite the external representation of sound and imagery which is drama. Both avoid the mimesis of direct address" (231). As for Mill, even when the poet seems intent upon direct address, the addressee is often more in the poet's mind than truly present—an idea to whom the lyric "I" is speaking. That said, however unconscious of a listener the lyric poet may be, there still is an audience.

When *Underneath the Bough*'s speaker calls out, "Come and sing, my room is south" (Field, *UTB* 80), that invitation is issued to someone. And this is the issue, the affordance, around which this chapter revolves: the fact that the speaker is in relation with the addressee, regardless of whether that audience is present or eavesdropping, and whether that audience is a beloved, Nature, or some other specific or unidentified listener including God, a figure from the past, Time, or Death. In calling attention this affordance in this chapter, I build upon Yopie Prins's work on *Long Ago*, in which she argues that Michael Field's lyrics challenge not only gender, but also a genre characterized by singleness. Emily Harrington's *Second Person Singular* makes a similar foundational claim about relation, the I-Thou, and experimentation with boundaries in Victorian women's verse

(3), as does Devin Garofalo,[5] who following Isobel Armstrong, explores how certain strands of Victorian lyric "[are] emphatically plural and distributed, vulnerable and permeated by external—and distinctly nonhuman—energies" (756). In other words, in this chapter I am interested in the characteristics of lyric's affordance (however subtle) of documenting the felt presence of those with whom the speaker is in relationship. As I consider Michael Field's innovations with lyric in this chapter, including moments where, contra Mill and Frye, their song *does* employ direct address, I will be exploring how their revisionary appropriations of Byrd, Campion, and Khayyám aid Bradley and Cooper in crafting a unique voice for their lyric speaker. But before we turn to the characteristics of the speaker, let us first consider: How might we characterize the relationship between the speaker and Michael Field's various addressees—both human and non-human?

As many critics have noted, *Underneath the Bough* features a fluidity of pronouns, and varying attitudes toward the addressee, who is sometimes a female beloved, sometimes a male, sometimes nature, sometimes a more abstract entity. Sometimes, as in the first poem of Book Three, the speaker and addressee are perfectly aligned: "We are bound by such close ties / None can tell of either breast / The native sigh / Who try / To learn with whom the Muse is guest" (66); sometimes, as in the second stanza of "As two fair vessels, side by side" the relation between speaker and addressee is combative: "*And this is hate* / We cried" (90, emphasis in original). In an unsigned *Athenaeum* review later attributed to Augusta Webster, the reviewer observes that these correspondences and fractures between poems and across sections makes it extremely difficult to discern a coherence narrative throughout the *Underneath the Bough*: "try any two poems to pair together as written from exactly the same point of view and you fail" (Webster in Thain and Vadillo 369). Like Elizabeth Helsinger, who writes of the importance of silence in the nineteenth-century lyric, especially women's lyric, Robert Fletcher observes in Field's songbook, "A desire to tell and not to tell, a wish to control their

---

[5] Garofalo's excellent essay examines *In Memoriam*. Although it is beyond the scope of this chapter's focus on Renaissance songbooks to do so, tracing Tennyson's influence upon *Underneath the Bough*'s ecological impulses would be a promising project.

own story and the realization that they can do so only through the cooperation/co-optation of others" (167).

For Fletcher, the narrative discoherence of Field's songbook is fundamentally transgressive and has much to do with the collection's homoeroticism:

> The four books of *Underneath the Bough* invite the reader to segment the volume into discrete narrative fragments ... None tell the truth about Bradley and Cooper. Rather, they overlap, conflict, qualify, and confuse one another *in toto* both fitting the culturally safe (and significant narratives) and leaving room for the representation of transgressive desire. (165)

I largely agree with Fletcher's conclusion, but also want to assert that we gain important insights about the dynamic between Field's speaker and addressee if we consider this relationship in the contexts of, first, Michael Field's debt to the notion of Renaissance counterpoint found in William Byrd's works such as *Songs of Sundrie Natures*; and second, the queer and decadent characteristics that thinking contrapuntally brings to Michael Field's ideas about human interactions in and with nature.

By the late 1880s, when Bradley and Cooper were making note of Renaissance songbooks in *Works and Days* and in their letters, the Victorians had succeeded in reviving Byrd and many of his contemporaries in both print and performance. J. A. Westrup notes how several decades prior, "The Musical Antiquarian Society, which flourished from 1840 to 1847 and by its second year had nearly 1000 members, issued the five-part Mass, the first book of 'Cantiones Sacrae' and 'Parthenia'" (127). Victorian music afficionados such as Richard Terry, H. B. Collins, Whittaker and Kennedy-Scott dedicated themselves to the revival and Dr. Fellows, author of English cathedral music, was particularly influential. By the end of the nineteenth century the Brompton Oratory had revived the Masses and Arkwright had published Byrd's *Songs of Sundrie Natures*, which Bradley and Cooper also used as an interim title for *Underneath the Bough*.

It is highly likely that Bradley and Cooper first became motivated to familiarize themselves with Renaissance music in the late 1880s as part of the research they were doing as they were writing *The Tragic Mary* (1890), which features a scene with the lyric "She was a royal lady born"—a lyric they reprinted in *Underneath* the Bough.⁶ Bradley and Cooper's writing process for their historical dramas involved intense library research and travel; indeed, their diaries and letters provide excellent documentation of their effort to better understand Queen Mary as they visited Edinburgh. Granted, as Chapter 1 argues, Michael Field seemed nonplussed, even celebratory of the fact that such research could never yield completely accurate results; of their work on Mary Queen of Scots, the preface of *The Tragic Mary* proclaims, with characteristic *l'engrenage*, "Of absolute knowledge we have nothing ... It is therefore possible for a dramatist to transcribe his sense of the fact of her life, to justify the vision of her as it has come to himself" (v–vii *passim*).

Nevertheless, over the next few years Bradley and Cooper continued to immerse themselves in Renaissance music; obtaining copies of Campion, of Bullen's *Elizabethan Song Book*, and attending concerts. In May, Bradley wrote to J. M. Gray:

> Of course you know Bullen's *Elizabethan Song Book*. To our shame we only the other day won it for our own. We are nursing with it—I mean letting it sing to us in every moment of rest or respite. Oh that my name could be put at the end of that song by the divine Campion— "The fair Queen Proserpine!" What a fall! And that cradle-song [I did not think there was a cradle-song in the English language] "Upon my lap my sovereign lies."⁷

On February 27, 1892 they attended a "consort of Viols, with the Lute and Harpsichord, hosted by Mr Arnold Dolmetch and Mr. Herbert P. Horne."⁸ Notably, Bradley and Cooper did not care for the timbre of the ancient instruments, complaining "How strange the tones of these old instruments—what far-off, tinkling youthfulness! ... Men must have been half-crickets when this music satisfied them."⁹ Nonetheless, during these years Bradley and Cooper seem to be taking seriously Walter Pater's dictate: "all art constantly aspires to the condition of music" ("Giorgione" 528), even sharing their philosophy of poetry in an

---

⁶ For an extended discussion of this poem, see Witcher, "A Royal Lady."
⁷ KB to J. M. Gray (May 7, 1889). MSS Add. 45853. The British Library, London.
⁸ Small invitation card inserted into *Works and Days*. MSS Add. 46780. fol. 50r. The British Library, London.
⁹ *Works and Days*. MSS Add. 46780. fol. 53r. The British Library, London.

1890 letter to J.M. Gray via their own translation of Verlaine's *Ars Poetica*:

> Music! Before all else be that your mark;
> And out of love for it choose the rare,
> Uneven metre, that melts in air,
> That is not like the couplet print and stark.
> ....
> Music, still music, music set above,
> Ought else beside! Let your verse take wing,
> And feel itself free as a soul to spring
> Toward unattempted skies and undreamt love. (lines 1–4, 29–32)[10]

Thus, I would argue that their concertgoing and other studies of Renaissance music had lasting effect on their own stated goals of creating a "songbook." I would further assert that we can perceive this influence specifically in how the lyrics in *Underneath the Bough* adapt the musical technique of William Byrd's counterpoint.[11]

According to classical pianist and William Byrd expert, Kit Armstrong, Byrd's experimentation with motifs and variations brought multidimensionality to Renaissance polyphonic music and made him "the most contrapuntally eloquent of composers."[12] Armstrong emphasizes that in contrapuntal music, when the bass or rhythmic voices imitate the treble, this does not make the voices individualized, but does the opposite: "That a voice should follow and imitate another is an *interdependence*." Analysis of musical counterpoint in Byrd (and other composers) therefore considers the contrapuntal voices on a continuum of stronger and weaker imitation, evaluating whether each variation possesses the same context in terms of pitch, harmonization, rhythm, and/or opposite vs parallel movement.

If we think about *Underneath the Bough* as manifesting contrapuntal thinking, the "inconsistencies" in Field's collection of lyrics begin to represent a passionately interdependent world, rather than an incoherent one. Understood as imitative counterpoint, we

---

[10] KB to JM Gray (1890). MSS Add. 45854. fol. 50. The British Library, London.

[11] Here I will be very clear that I am not referring to counterpoint in the sense that G. M. Hopkins does, but rather in the way that, in polyphonic music, imitative voices introduce new or related ideas as musical variations on a theme.

[12] All quotes from Kit Armstrong are taken from a January 6, 2018 lecture on Byrd's counterpoint, <https://www.youtube.com/watch?v=7axwDzY21Qw>.

can view lyrics like "No beauty born of pride my lady hath," "My love is like a lovely shepherdess," and others as offering variations on a theme, or, as Armstrong describes Byrd's counterpoint, "successive points of meaning ... musical material presented in an imitative texture each one of a different character." Field's "Once his feet among the roses" unfolds as call and response; "O wind, thou hast thy kingdom in the trees" compares varied aspects of nature as "all thine instruments in tune" (*UTB* 7, line 5); and most of the lyrics in *Underneath the Bough*'s Book Two present multiple perspectives on grieving and death. Webster's *Athanaeum* review notices these variations on a theme as well, "in poem after poem, death will be found appearing other than before—the treatment modified by the immediate theme. Love is set forth in sundry ways" (in Thain and Vadillo 369). Given their investment in "being contemporaneous" while paradoxically looking to past forms and narratives for inspiration, Michael Field must have been particularly pleased with Webster's assessment: "A peculiarity of these poems is that while they are of antique mould, ancestral not merely in form but in expression, they are in feeling distinctively modern" (in Thain and Vadillo 369).

Perhaps the collection's emphasis on multiple perspectives—a characteristic that will continue to gain popularity in literature, art, and philosophy with the rise of twentieth-century modernism—is one of the things that struck the *Athanaeum* reviewer as "distinctly modern"; this, I would argue, has much to do with *Underneath the Bough*'s revisionary representation of the lyric I-in-relationship and the felt presence of the addressee. Michael Field's appropriations of Byrd's contrapuntal style illustrates how, contra Mill, *their* lyric addressee is *always* present, albeit in varied degrees. For instance, "My love is like a lovely shepherdess" and "No beauty born of pride my lady hath" might be considered similar poems insofar as each unfolds with assorted descriptions of the beloved; and one might even conclude that although the speaker might prefer the beloved to be present and to listen, she need not be. On a second look (or listen) however, and keeping weak vs strong counterpoint in mind, we can conclude that the addressee is more present than we might otherwise think: these are no mere visual descriptions of a static, objectified beloved. Rather, in both songs, with each variation, the beloved makes a significant impact upon her surroundings (as well as upon the speaker), often via similes and metaphors that convey movement, such as comparing her voice to a flowing stream that brings "peace and fertility" (75, lines 2–4).[13] Thus the poem documents the speaker's lived experience that there are two *interdependent* presences here. That said, "My love is a lovely shepherdess," with four fairly parallel sestains and only minimal metric variation in the second and third stanzas, suggests weaker variance compared to "No beauty born of pride," in which each couplet differs from the others in its meter and/or layout on the page:

> No beauty born of pride my lady hath;
>   Her voice is as the path
> Of a sweet stream, and where it flows must be
>   Peace and fertility.
> Who loveth her no tumult hath or pain;
> Her cloudy eyes are full of blessed rain,
>   A sky that cherisheth; her breast
>   Is a soft nook for rest.
>   She hath no varying pleasure
>   For passion's fitful mood;
> Her firm small kisses are my constant food,
> As rowan berries yield their treasure
>   To starving birds; her smile
>   Gives life so sweet a style,
>   To die beneath its beams would be
>   To practice immortality. (*UTB* 75–6)

Note how the description of erotic passion and pleasure spills over from the sole abba rhyme at lines 9–12 and into the final two couplets of the poem, as the iambic trimeter of lines 13 and 14 give way to the extended pleasures of the Elizabethan double entendre "to die" in the final iambic tetrameter couplet. Here then, Michael Field's variations on a theme mix archaic language with modern approaches to rhyme, line length, and meter in order to make "my lady"'s presence insistently felt.

Contrapuntal influences play out somewhat differently in "Irises," since this poem is not addressed to anyone specific. Yet two voices nonetheless seem present, describing flowers in a vase that no doubt were a gift from one half of Michael Field to the

---

[13] The fertility in this case presumably refers to ideas and literary output, as in the frequently anthologized poem, "A Girl."

other. In terms of placement of long and short lines, the two stanzas appear visually similar on the page; yet metrically are somewhat different. As two variations on an aesthetic theme, each stanza catalogues a distinct set of observations. The voice in the first stanza documents color and light; the second focuses more on motion and texture:

>   IN a vase of gold
>   And scarlet, how cold
>   The flicker of wrinkled grays
> In the iris-sheaf! My eyes fill with wonder
> At the tossed, moist light at the withered scales under
>   And among the uncertain sprays!
>
>   The wavings of white
>   On the cloudy light,
>   And the finger-marks of pearl;
> The facets of crystal, the golden feather,
> The way that the petals fold over together,
>   The way that the buds unfurl! (*UTB* 107–8)

Despite the differences between the stanzas, both observations document how the aesthetic impression depends upon all elements working in concert: light and matter, the white and grays of the flowers in the red and gold crystal vase, the combined effect of the blooms and the leaves. Yet these contrapuntal elements are harmonic and interdependent rather than independent, with the last two lines perhaps implicitly invoking the two viewers standing together, commenting on something they are viewing simultaneously. Thus, where Chapter 2 emphasized how Michael Field's ekphrasis features a strong dialectic interplay between objective and subjective vision; Michael Field's experiments with contrapuntal elements of Elizabethan-style song also anticipate modernism's fascination with perspective and with freer rhyme and meter.

While *Underneath the Bough* is Michael Field's "songbook," it is also the collection most invested in nature. Byrd's contrapuntal influence upon *Underneath the Bough* in my view, provides Michael Field with an aesthetic approach to representing not only the multiplicities within their own life and work partnership (and their sometimes contentious relationships with others, especially Berenson), but also the affinities, discontinuities, and entangled interdependencies they experienced—in an embodied way—in and with nature. These entanglements are what I am suggesting we consider to be *Underneath the Bough*'s "Victorian themes." Kate Thomas describes such impulses as the "seasonal polyphonies and polyamories" in Michael Field's depiction of the natural world ("Vegetable Love" 36). For instance, each stanza of "In the moony brake" pairs the joyful action of the doubled lyric voice with an action of varied elements in nature: violets sleeping while "we laugh and leap" in the first stanza, woodbine leaves, compared to doves, "Roost upon the bare / Winter stems" while "we shout and sing," in the second stanza, etc. (Field, *UTB* 12). As each stanza uses contrapuntal imitative texture to articulate subsequent variations upon the greater Dionysian theme, the entangled world that Denisoff terms "pagan ecodecadence" emerges into view. The lyric "we" in this song is in joyful relationship—but not just with one another. Rather, "we" also exists symbiotically with all the varied natural entities that "In the moony brake" describes.

There are many such examples in *Underneath the Bough* where the lyric I/we is diffused in this way "within a larger collective" (Denisoff, "Dissipating Nature" 437) and smaller spots of nature are represented as "a complex ecosystem that sustains life" (Murray 444). One is "If the sun our white headlands with flame," which employs contrapuntal call and response within each stanza as the lyric "we" imagines multiple instances of forgiveness between and among human and non-human nature (*UTB* 15). Importantly, in this book of "songs," many of the poems deliberately invoke sound and music as their variation and counterpoint document nature's intra-actions and interdependencies.[14] In "A shady silence" the barking of hunting hounds disturbs natural elements—rocks, streams, and stars; gnats, bats, and fir trees—in an otherwise peaceful night (Field, *UTB* 104). As the echoes leave their imprint upon the land, past, present, and future merge as Michael Field invokes old and newly made ghosts, which like the echoes, "walk in hosts / Long after the live echoes pass away"

---

[14] In this sense, *Underneath the Bough*'s portrayal of nature resonates with Stacy Alaimo's queer ecological thinking about transcorporeality: the notion that "all creatures, as embodied beings, are intermeshed with the dynamic, material world, which crosses through them, transforms them, and is transformed by them." It also anticipates Jane Bennett's notion of vital materialism, which connects all human and non-human bodies.

(*UTB* 107). Similarly, human, avian, and sylvan existence is overlaid in the context of history's effect on the present in the following short verse:

> To field where now the forests fail
>   The nightingale comes back,
> To the soft footsteps of the wood so clinging
>   As if there were for singing
>   One track.
>
> The poet, as the nightingale,
>   Must haunt the olden track,
> Must sing of Love where Love first heard his singing,
>   Though there's no bringing
>   Love back. (*UTB* 116)

Here, the speaker juxtaposes the hauntingly sad love songs of both poet and nightingale with the trace—both visual and aural—that footsteps leave in a wood. The visual effect of the three elements coexisting in one place, over time, resembles that of notes that align and realign on musical score; even while the "one track" being sung evokes choral unisons and harmonies. Thus, sound combines with vision and/or feeling to create intense aesthetic impressions in these songs which, like the synaesthetic picture poems I discussed in Chapter 2, decadently blur boundaries between (and create unexpected affinities among) categories.

Michael Field's contrapuntal ecodecadence also highlights the queerness of the natural world. Like the erotic interactions and interdependences already discussed in "No beauty born of pride my Lady hath," *Underneath the Bough*'s speaker delights in erotic depictions of orgiastically entangled grasses and flowers and of bees penetrating foxgloves and violets. "Say if a gallant rose my bower doth scale" provides one interesting example of how nature's queer decadence offers inspiration that justifies departing from cultural norms. The first stanza depicts a rose that refuses to grow as intended on its trellis:

> Say, if a gallant rose my bower doth scale,
>   Higher and higher,
> And, tho' she twine the other side the pale,
>   Toward me doth sigh her

> Perfume, her damask mouth—
> *Roses will love the south—*
> Can I deny her? (*UTB* 23, lines 1–7)

From a plant that is both gallant and gendered female, to the speaker's eroticized attraction to both the aroma and the "damask mouth" of the rose, to the willful agency accorded to the flower, this is a very queer stanza, indeed. Additionally, the italicized line and the dashes suggest that here, the lyric "I" is not only in relationship with the rose, but also with the addressee, with whom, perhaps, she is in conversation. The stanza depicts the simultaneity of multiple perspectives, impulses, desires, conventions, and a decision in the process of being made.

This song's other stanza creates a human parallel to the first stanza's tale of human-vegetable desire:

> I have a lady loves me in despite
>   Of bonds that tie her,
> And bid her honest Corin's flame requite;
>   When I espy her,
>   Kisses are near their birth—
>   *Love cannot love in dearth—*
>   Say, shall I fly her? (*UTB* 23, lines 7–14)

Where the previous stanza depicts a rose that refuses to climb a trellis, this stanza depicts a mutual attraction between an ungendered speaker and a lady—an attraction that tempts them to disregard the conventional heteronormative "bonds that tie her" to "honest Corin." Again, the italicized line and dashes suggest a conversation between the lyric "I" and the addressee, who may or may not be the lady in question; again, multiple perspectives are presented. The poem provides closure for neither variation on this theme of whether to fulfill one's desire. Rather, the purpose of this song seems to be to celebrate the intensity of feeling that comes from the entanglements that can be experienced within the human and non-human natural world.

Kate Thomas identifies such impulses as a queer becoming that, for Michael Field, "interrupts association of fecundity with temporal linearity ... literally moving our gaze sideways getting us to notice generational adjacency and simultaneity" ("Vegetable Love" 36). "A calm in the flitting sky" for instance, is one of many poems in *Underneath the Bough* that mirrors Bradley and Cooper's loving intergenerational coexistence. The first stanza reads:

> A calm in the flitting sky,
>   And in the calm a moon,
>   A youngling golden:
> 'Mid windy shades an olden
>   Oak-tree whose branches croon
>   As the orb sails by.
>   Heigh ho!
> Youth and age, the soft and dry,
>   While breezes blow. (Field, *UTB* 17–18)

Here, against the lovely backdrop of a moon that evokes joy as it "sails by," the commingling of young and old elements in nature makes an aesthetic impression upon the speaker and resonates positively with the age difference between the two co-authors themselves. The next two stanzas convey more traditional perspectives about age vs youth; yet each stanza nonetheless returns to images of "the blithe new moon, / That westward slideth, / And on the white wind rideth": as well as the jolly refrain, "Heigh Ho!" (Field, *UTB* 18). Thus the poem suggests that an unconventional, queer orientation to age difference (in this case via the moon) provides a frame that reveals the beauty and joy of these unconventionally joined elements in nature.

'Welling from Elizabethan spring': Campion, passion, history

The problem for the female lyric speaker in the Victorian period, of course, is the problem of the poetess. As Meredith Martin and others have observed, during the nineteenth century women poets were increasingly praised for their ability to write short, powerful lyric poems so that the terms "poetess" and "lyric" became practically synonymous (Martin 31). Poetesses were often praised as songbirds, yet such a descriptor suggests that the speaker, who is not human, is less important than the song or what the audience might think of the song. Thus, "EBB, Eliot, Webster, and other famous poetesses chafed against the suggestion they were mere songbirds" (Martin 36). Bradley and Cooper worked hard, starting with the very name of "Michael Field" itself, to distance themselves from such a Poetess tradition.

In such a context, when we think of the lyric poets that Michael Field might have found to be useful alternatives to the songbird poetess, the strongly introspective and revolutionary voice of the male Romantic poet as solitary genius might suggest itself as a contender. Yet it is the Renaissance rather than the Romantics to which they turn. To this end, Alex Murray notes that Michael Field specifically reject Wordsworth's more rational engagements with nature in favor of Dionysian passion in their revisions of *Underneath the Bough*. I observe these impulses even in the poems of the first edition, as this section will show. Also relevant to this chapter's larger concern with how *Underneath the Bough* represents the lived experience of a lyric I-in-relationship with the addressee is Marion Thain's discussion of J. A. Symond's essay on the lyric genre. There she observes "Symonds's idealization of the Elizabethan age as a time when lyric poetry was still inherently connected to sense of song and a vocal encounter with an audience" (*Lyric Poem* 21).

For Michael Field, Thomas Campion (1567–1620) proves to be an excellent model for a desiring, playful "I" who speaks and sings to an audience. Campion was a Renaissance poet, musician, and doctor who wrote in neo-Latin and English, often composed music to accompany his lyrics, and had access to the royal court. Of the many Elizabethan writers whom we know influenced Bradley and Cooper in the late 1880s and early 1890s when they were writing the poems they would eventually include in *Underneath the Bough*, Campion appears several times in their joint diary, *Works and Days*. For instance, in 1891 Cooper mentions reading Campion aloud to Bradley;[15] and the year before she tantalizingly refers to "the Campion incident"—a source of conflict between the Michaels and Robert Browning.[16] The details of this incident

---

[15] *Works and Days*. MSS Add. 46779, November 8, 1891. (EC). fol. 134r. The British Library.

[16] Cooper is vague about this disagreement with Browning. The entry is part of a long retrospective about Browning after his death and this portion merely recalls that he found Whitman "dangerous," an assessment Cooper would have found shocking if not for "the Campion incident." In fact, Bradley and Cooper don't go into many specifics about any of their Elizabethan influences other than Shakespeare. *Works and Days*. MSS Add. 46778. January 2, 1890. (EC). fol. 5r. The British Library.

seem destined to forever remain a mystery, thus in this section I will have to approach Michael Field's use of Campion in the spirit of conjecture and *l'engrenage*, much as they themselves geared into figures from history while navigating those figures' and histories' varied unknowns. Yet, as a Dionysian, lyric precursor, Campion seems a reasonable enough choice for the Michaels, especially given that he was, like they were, a poet caught "between the two worlds of classical and English literature," and a lyricist whose work manifests a "fusion of classical tradition and vernacular language" (Manuwald 30).

Much of *Underneath the Bough*, like Campion's *Ayres*, conveys the exquisitely intense joys and sorrows of life, especially love. In fact, Campion presents himself as the first love poet in Britain, proclaiming: "And let them celebrate the first poet from the name of Brutus to sing sweet elegies and his own love affairs" (qtd in Manuwald 33).

Of the intense sensations of love's passion, Campion sings:

And as her lute doth live or die
Led by her passion so must I ! (*First Book of Ayres* VI, Bullen 11)

and

Then come, sweetest, come,
My lips with kisses gracing!
Here let vs harbor all alone,
Die, die in sweete embracing! (*First Book of Ayres* XVII, Bullen 20)

Similarly invoking the all-encompassing sensations of both emotional and sexual union, Michael Field sings:

Thee, whose sweet soul I con
Secure to find
Perfect epitome
Of Nature, passion poesy?
From thee untwined, I shall but wander a disbodied sprite,
Until thou wake me
With thy kiss-warmed breath, and take me
Where we are one. (*UTB* 71)

and

> I have all the charact'ry
> Of thy features, yet lack thee;
> And by couplets to confess
> What I wholly would possess
> Doth but whet the appetite
> Of my too long-famished sight (*UTB* 73–4)

As for the pain that love can sometimes inflict, Campion extols his grief's passion: "Break now my heart and dye!" (*Third Book of Ayres* X), and:

> Blame not my cheeks, though pale with loue they be;
> The kindly heate vnto my heart is flowne,
> To cherish it that is dismaid by thee,
> Who art so cruell and vnsteedfast growne:
> For nature, cald for by distressed harts,
> Neglects and quite forsakes the outward partes. (*First Book of Ayres* XIV, Bullen 18)

Michael Field's lyric speaker similarly explores negative passion in *Underneath the Bough*: "Alas! / My heart is frozen up with scorn / Is broken with neglect" (91) and:

> Yet sometimes Love awakes
> On a black hellish bed,
> and rise up as hate:
> He drinks the hurtful lakes,
> He joys to toss and spread
> Sparkles of pitchy, rankling flame,
> He joys to play with death; (*UTB* 24)

Shared affinity for Dionysian outburst notwithstanding, it is important to note that mostly, the causes for the authors' emotional states differ. Campion's speaker is frequently spurned, or at least teased and denied sex by his lover, while Michael Field's speaker often experiences extreme sorrow imagining a separation that either will not actually happen, will happen through death in the distant future, or, will simply be of short duration:

> Already to mine eyelids shore
> The gathering water swell

> For thinking of the grief in store
> When though wilt say Farewell. (*UTB* 67)

Field's verse, in a departure from Campion, concludes with the resolve "that we must live together" (67). Thus, as Fletcher also notes, "Michael Field both appropriates and subverts the cultural narratives of desire that serve as frames for *Underneath the Bough*'s lyrics" (165). For Fletcher, while many of the poems, especially in Book Three are "utopian expressions of same-sex desire and fulfillment," the collection also "explore[s] the homoerotic within and through heterosexuality" (171, 172). By re-appropriating poetic forms and cultural/historical narratives from a queer-feminist perspective, Michael Field's passions emerge in *Underneath the Bough* via many of the same strategies I previously identified in the earlier chapters that analyze *Long Ago* and *Sight and Song*.

For example, unlike Campion and his contemporaries, but like Michael Field's experiments with ekphrasis, *Underneath the Bough*'s blazons are not just visual, they are synaesthetic, and they frequently document the actions, rather than just the appearance, of the female beloved. I discussed a few of these in the previous section; here I want to shift to songs that not only describe but require the participation of the addressee. Most obvious would be the oft-discussed "A Girl," which performs not only love's passion but also the practice of literary collaboration. Of the girl, the speaker sings:

> Such: and our souls so knit,
> I leave a page half-writ—
>   The work begun
> Will be to heaven's conception done,
>   If she come to it. (*UTB* 69)

As many critics have already offered rich analysis of "A Girl," here I'll simply present it as a point of departure from which to consider another interesting song that requires the participation of the addressee: "An Invitation," or, "Come and sing my room is south."

"An Invitation" unfolds contrapuntally, with nine five-line stanzas providing varied enticements for the addressee to join the speaker. It opens:

> Come and sing, my room is south;
> Come, with thy sun-governed mouth,
> Thou wilt never suffer drouth,
>   Long as dwelling
> In my chamber of the south. (*UTB* 80)

Unlike "No beauty born of pride," where each example creates imitative texture by appearing in a variant meter, the stanzas of "An Invitation" are metrically parallel, following a 7-7-7-4-7 syllabic pattern, with an incantatory, trochaic rhythm reinforcing the speaker's summoning of the beloved. Yet the aaaba rhyme scheme creates opportunity for each stanza's topic to take on a different timbre, with the open sounds of "south", "mouth," and "drouth" in stanza one and long /ō/ rhymes in stanzas three, five, and seven contrasting with the long / ī / rhymes in stanzas two and eight, long /ē/s of stanzas four and nine, and short /ĭ/s of stanza six. Each reason to come sing with the speaker thus appears in a different tone, yet all combine to promise a pleasurable experience.

Stanza five of "An Invitation" sets the stage for the second half of its argument. The speaker and beloved alone will not attain their desired goals—at least not all of them. They need the inspiration that comes from

> Books I have of long ago
> And to-day; I shall not know
> Some unless thou read them, so
>   Their excelling
> Music needs thy voice's flow. (81)

This stanza documents layers of collaboration—both between the Poet-Lovers and with the historical narratives found in these books. Notably, Cooper's notes about *Underneath the Bough*'s poems in a notebook then titled *Songs of Sundry Natures* says that "An Invitation," composed on January 22, 1891, was "Written in anticipation of the new study at Durdans."[17] Thus the invited interactions and promised pleasures in this poem are inspired by previous experiences Bradley (now forty-four) and Cooper (now twenty-nine) have had together and hope to repeat in their new

---

[17] Archive of "Michael Field." MS Eng poet d.60. fol. 72. Oxford, Bodleian Libraries.

study, including the coy nod to their own *Long Ago*, published in 1889. These pleasures are physical, emotional, and intellectual; and as in "A Girl" they are inextricably linked to the pleasures of artistic creation as the songmates sing and write together, as the enticements that unfold from stanza five to the end make clear. The poem thus blends past and future, visualizing both the new study and the continued interactions that will continue within it.

Reading is reading aloud, and is music, in this poem. Reading together is also foundational to writing, with Thomas Campion named first in a select panoply of songwriting influences:

Campion, with a noble ring
Of choice spirits; count this wing
Sacred! all the songs I sing
    Welling, welling
From Elizabethan spring. (Field, *UTB* 81)

As "An Invitation" brings together poets from past and present, and experiences from an imagined, historical past, a more recent, personal past, and those anticipated in the new study in the near future, the reference to "books today" might mean books created or soon to be created by the speaker in this lyric (such as *Long Ago*) or books written by their contemporaries, Flaubert and Verlaine, invoked in stanza seven. The final two stanzas reference Bradley and Cooper's studies of the renowned Latin and Greek lyricists they have already emulated, like Sappho, or hope to, like Catullus and Cynthia's lover, Propertius.

Campion's appearance at the head of the list of historical influences deserves more analysis, however, since he, like Michael Field themselves, frequently weaves together the personal and the universal, using classical themes, from varied sources, to address contemporary issues. According to Gesine Manuwald, Campion's 1601 *Book of Ayres* "uses classical terminology and concepts to characterize and thus ennoble his own poetry" (30). There, Campion often begins with a famous Latin line "and thus activates a certain context but then completes the poem in a different direction" such as "My sweetest Lesbia" which derives from Catullus (Manuwald 32). But while Catullus's poem is about living life and enjoying it, Campion's becomes "a general defense of life devoted to love and peace, comparing it to a soldier, also incorporating work of other Roman poets" (Manuwald 32).

"A Spring morning by the Sea" and "King Apollo" provide two examples of how Michael Field appropriates Campion's bold historical methods and topics in *Underneath the Bough*, queering an otherwise heterosexual narrative of a male spectator gazing with intense sexual desire upon a sleeping woman. A letter dated March 31, 1885 from Bradley (then thirty-nine) at Sidmouth to Cooper (then twenty-three) details the genesis of Michael Field's queer pastiche in these two poems:

> Ah my Deare, I awoke at half-past five this morning [and imagined you asleep surrounded by books]. By and bye I looked out on the sea: the sun was spreading a golden net on the water and two tiny fishing-boats lay outside the glittering mesh; again I curled myself up in my bed, and wrote to
>
> My Deare Asleep
> I did not take me to the sea,
> When the winged morning wakened me
> With beamy plumes: I used them right
> To bear me in an Eastern flight
> Of arrowy swiftness to the bed
> Where my beloved still slumbered
> Lying half poet and half child
> The twin divineness reconciled.
> And I, who scarce could breathe to see
> Her spirit in its secrecy
> So innocent, drew back in awe
> That I should give such creature law;
> Then looked and found God standing near,
> And to His Rule resigned my Dear.
>
> But I had not said all about it, nor how its little mouth lies open—its pretty shorelines dimpled by its dreams. Then I grew pagan and invoked
>
> King Apollo
> When my lady sleeping lies,
> Her sweet breath her lips unbar;
> This is when Apollo spies,
> With dreams footfall, not to mar
> The dear sleep,

> Through the rosy doors ajar
> He with golden thoughts doth creep.
>
> Ah Pretty, Pretty! There are thousands of such songs in my heart. There is in me a mine of love—enough to make the fortune of innumerable hearts,—and it is all possessed by the P.
>
> It is now after ten—my Pretty is creasing its brows it is thinking about things in themselves[18] and Tracking the secret paths of reason. Before me lies—the dazzling phenomenon the sea, fitter I think for the gaze of the mild blue eyes than foolscap and blotting paper!! (in Bickle, *Fowl* 113–14)

Bradley's thoughts in this letter are a mélange of Campion's *Ayre* VIII "It fell on a sommer's day," and his sources: Ovid and Propertius. In Campion's *Ayre*, "sweete Bessie," half-asleep, spies Iamy gazing upon her with desire. Iamy takes a "soft kisse" while she pretends to remain sleeping,

> Iamy then began to play,
> Bessie as one buried lay,
> Gladly still through this sleight
> Deceiu'd in her owne deceit,
> And since this traunce begoon,
> She sleepes eu'rie afternoone. (*First Book of Ayres* VIII, Bullen 12–13)

Campion's fantasy of the willing Bessie, desirous of Iamy's attentions not just this once but "eu'rie afternoone" is a variant of Ovid's *Amores* 1.5, in which Corrina comes to the speaker's bedchamber during the afternoon siesta, with her hair down and in an unbelted tunic. She pretends to be unwilling as the speaker pulls off her tunic, and the speaker describes her beauty in great detail and then alludes to the sexual pleasures that followed. Campion's *Ayre* also derives from Propertius 1.3 in which Propertius comes to Cynthia while she sleeps but does not act upon his tremendous desire for her because he fears her anger should he disturb her. She awakens and scolds him anyway, because she had cried herself to sleep, longing for him and worrying he had been delayed by another woman.

---

[18] This is a reference to Kant.

Michael Field's "A Spring morning by the sea" and "King Apollo" preserve each source's assertions that it is normal (contra dominant Victorian ideology) for women to experience erotic desire; but Field locates that desire in the *female* gaze—explicitly in the first instance and via cross-gender identification in the second. Yet in these poems, unlike in Campion and Propertius, the sleeping woman is not disturbed; though it is likely that the deferred desire in Field's poems is a metaphor for Bradley and Cooper's physical separation rather than a reflection of a fear that the speaker's amorous attentions will be unwelcome. Queer desire reframes the heteronormative passions of better-known Renaissance and classical narratives, with Michael Field's speaker drawing back like the waves Bradley sees on the shore. Yet the intensity of erotic (and historical) entanglement remains clear—note Apollo's golden thoughts, perhaps resonating with what Bradley describes as the "glittering mesh." Thus, this incident provides an example of what Marion Thain observes in Michael Field: a tendency for the aesthetic lyric to blend the personal and the universal. The lived experience that Bradley documents in her letter is deeply specific, subjective, and queerly oriented; yet Michael Field frames the resulting lyrics within a transhistorical narrative that will guarantee these unconventional co-authors a more general appeal. Nonetheless, this is *poiein*, a creative transformation, in which Michael Field challenges the notion of a universal spectator-actor as they participate queerly in the projects of history.

But let us return to "An Invitation," which sets the stage for creatively weaving together such passionate historical moments in its mention of Campion, French and Latin poets, and Sappho. It is important to note that in addition to orienting desire in a transhistorical narrative, the poem also orients the speaker (and addressee's) singing in a palpable setting: in the "chamber of the south," and in that room's relation to the natural environment. In the first stanza the sun saturates the room and the mouth of the addressee, which, like the beloved's mouth in "A Girl," the speaker clearly desires for its beauty, its ability to speak of love and ideas, to read and sing, and to kiss. The second stanza of "An Invitation" promises that the yellow-scarlet woodbine, with its honeyed scent, will always suit the addressee's mood; while the third stanza anticipates the bliss of kisses shared three ways between the two songmates and the fragrant myrtle: human and non-human interactions from which "lovely dreams will grow!" Both woodbine and myrtle connote love and devotion within the Victorian language of flowers, while the synaesthetic decadence of these human-vegetable relations promise to beget daring new songs. Thus as the nine stanzas of "An Invitation" develop contrapuntally, queer entanglements connect the speaker, addressee, nature, and history resulting in intense physical, emotional, and creative pleasures.

Throughout *Underneath the Bough*, such queer impulses and species intersubjectivity can especially be found where classical and environmental images come together. To cite just two more examples, In "Invocation" the doubled lyric "I"—"We thy nymphs who in a ring / Dance around thee, carolling" catalogue the flowers, fruits, creatures, even sunbeams that all "express" Apollo's features, and are invoked in their highly individualized praise of him (*UTB* 4). And the ecopoetics of "Cowslip Gathering" enacts a pagan marriage between "twin maiden spirits" who yearn no longer to be divided and so Nature facilitates their consummation: "So led us to a tender, marshy nook ... / In the moist quiet, til the rich content / of the bee humming in the cherry trees / Fills us; in one our very being blent" (*UTB* 67–8). In these songs, we see, hear, smell, and feel what both nature and historical narratives have in common: their disparate elements—no matter how varied—coexist and wield effect—not in unison, but contrapuntally, symbiotically. And, as in D. G. Rossetti's famous notion of a sonnet as a "moment's monument," in these lyrics passions—erotic, aesthetic, and otherwise—are passed on, sometimes chronologically, sometimes sideways intergenerationally, or as palimpsest. Thus *Underneath the Bough*'s songs perform how, in nature, poetry, and the retelling of history, humans experience all manner of entanglement with each other and with non-humans, with the living and the dead, and the space between objective and subjective lived experiences becomes blurred.

Khayyám's queer energies

Finally, let us turn to the text that gave *Underneath the Bough* its title: *The Rubáiyát of Omar Khayyám,* as translated by Edward FitzGerald (1809–83). If Campion provides Michael Field with a model for a desiring, playful lyric speaker who revises history, and if Byrd's counterpoint suggests a formal approach for representing a speaker and addressee entangled both with each other and with the natural world, Fitzgerald's translations of the twelfth-century Persian astronomer Omar Khayyám (1048–1131) are useful because in both form and content, the *Rubáiyát*, like *Underneath the Bough*, celebrates a *carpe diem raison d'être* that reflects Victorian science about matter and energy, and queers life, death, and time.

Throughout, *Underneath the Bough*'s Dionysian impulses mirror the *carpe diem* passions of the *Rubáiyát*: Michael Field proclaims, "Let us wreathe the mighty cup, / Then with song we'll lift it up" (*UTB* 7). The co-authors joy at flowers and bees, imagining wildly dancing fauns and nymphs, contend that "Mortal if thou art beloved" (5) one can scoff at age and death, and accept that some things are unknowable: "Love doth never know / Why it is beloved, / And to ask were treason: / Let the wonder grow!" (13). The temper or tone of lyrics such as these echo *The Rubáiyát*: "Ah, my Beloved, fill the Cup that clears / Today of past regret and future Fears" (FitzGerald 139). Supping from, or as the speaker sometimes put it "kissing the cup"—whether understood as drinking, making love, or simply making merry, is to be passionately in the moment or, in FitzGerald's words: "Ah, make the most of what we yet may spend, / Before we too into the Dust descend" (144). Even before publishing *Underneath the Bough*, Michael Field indicated that they felt affinities with FitzGerald; their 1889 short essay "Mid-Age" in *The Contemporary Review* begins with an epigraph comprised of the last two lines of the sixth rubai: "The Bird of Time has but a little way / To flutter—and the Bird is on the wing" (Field, "Mid-Age" 431).

Michael Field's adaptation of musical influences enables them to establish the natural environment as a site of Bacchic entanglement, as we have seen. The queer energies in *Underneath the Bough* are thus both natural and contra convention—against the grain—and bring to mind Havelock Ellis's gloss of Bourget's definition of decadence as analogous with "the social organism which enters the state of decadence as soon as the individual life of the parts is no longer subordinated to the whole" (xvi).[19] Consider, for instance, how in "Butterfly Bright" (Field, *UTB* 19) both a

---

[19] The ideas in Ellis's introduction to Huysman's *Au Rebours* (1884) are taken from Paul Bourget's essay on Decadence and Baudelaire. Ellis later reprints these in *Affirmations* (1897).

butterfly and a bee gorge themselves in a garden, each in their own fashion. The second and third stanzas read:

> A blessed thing
> To poise and cling
> Mid the sweets without
> A thought of the morrow,
>   To quaff and to bask,
>   While the busy rout
>   Grows dull at its task
> Of heaping up riches and sorrow.
>
> O, let me be
> That creature, free
> From the thought of the hive,
> That doth never stint her
>   Gay soul of its fill;
>   But warm and alive
>   Feeds, feeding until
> The fall of the leaf and the winter! (*UTB* 19)

Cooper notes that "Butterfly Bright" was inspired when "We twain saw a ruddy butterfly and a bumblebee on the great disk of a sunflower at the same moment."[20]

The *carpe diem* impulses of "Butterfly Bright," like the *Rubáiyát*, negotiate the space between the personal and the universal and destabilize the boundaries between the human and non-human world.[21] Like several of the poems discussed in the previous section, the (dual) speaker and the multiple elements described

---

[20] Archive of "Michael Field." MS English poet d.60. fol. 60. Oxford, Bodleian Libraries.

[21] Andrea Gazzaniga reads *Underneath the Bough* as domesticating nature and employing a poetics of enclosure that permits the collaborators to sing together "away from social pressures." Such a reading would align with the discourses that Fabienne Moine observes in the garden poetry of many of Field female contemporaries and does indeed reflect Bradley and Cooper's rather isolated *personal* lifestyle at the time. But in contrast, this chapter focuses on the more capacious energies that *Underneath the Bough* shares with FitzGerald and its other influences. Even where *Underneath the Bough*'s verses describe domestic, enclosed spaces, I argue, bold and capaciously entangled energies are found—energies that cannot be enclosed or contained.

interact contrapuntally to form the aesthetic impression documented by the song. Here, the butterfly, the bee, and the speaker all exist in the same moment, yet none of the individual elements are, to use Bourget's/Ellis's words, "subordinated to the whole." Indeed, in opposition to more anthropocentric descriptions the Victorians often deployed when talking about the environment, "Butterfly Bright"'s speaker concludes that human modes of existing—subordinating to human social expectations—are inferior to that of the butterfly and the bee. Thus Michael Field profess an ideology of entanglement while rethinking the relationship between the speaker and the world—both the natural world and the man-made world. Such ideas bear similarities to *The Rubáiyát*'s themes of random synchronicity and symbiosis, as in rubai XXVII and XXIX:

> They say the Lion and the Lizard keep
> The Courts where Jamshyd gloried and drank deep
>   And Bahrám, the great Hunter—the Wild Ass
> Stamps o'er his Head, and he lies fast asleep
> ....
> And this delightful Herb whose tender Green
> Fledges the River Lip on which we lean—
>   Ah, lean upon it lightly! for who knows
> From what once lovely Lip it springs unseen! (FitzGerald (1872) 137, 70)

As Kristin Mahoney observes, "Bradley and Cooper were not alone in their desire to rethink the distinction between human and non-human animals at the turn of the century" ("Queer Community" 38). In gesturing, with their title, toward FitzGerald and Omar Khayyám in *Underneath the Bough*, Michael Field ally themselves with other queer texts and other homoerotically inclined thinkers and aesthetes, who "wished to radically rethink all forms of kinship and alliance. Queer discourses concerning community at the fin de siècle contributed to a broader rethinking of the ethics of interrelation that in term fostered greater thoughtfulness about the natural world" (Mahoney, "Queer Commnity" 38). "Butterfly Bright" is particularly instructive when read alongside some of the other contrapuntal poems previously discussed in this chapter's Byrd section. All focus insistently on the energies of the elements described in relation to one another. In some, the natural elements, as we have seen, interact and commingle in orgiastic Bacchic revelry; in others like "Butterfly Bright," the energies of poising and clinging, quaffing, and basking—actions of pure desire free from any other influence—coexist with the speaker-spectator in a politics of non-interference.

To better understand the complexities of how *Underneath the Bough* "treats of Victorian [environmental] themes," it is useful to understand how the songbook is in conversation, not only with the contrapuntal dynamics found in its Elizabethan musical precursors but also with how FitzGerald represents the entangled energies of Khayyám's rubai. As Tyson Stolte has convincingly argued, FitzGerald "offers the *Rubáiyát* as proxy battleground over the meaning of atoms, the implications of thermodynamics, and the legacy of Lucretius" (356). Stolte recounts how FitzGerald was greatly influenced by Lucretius' atomism, which the Victorians perceived as congruent with their own theories about the circulation of matter and transformation of energy.[22] "Omar's Genius," for FitzGerald, was the twelfth-century astronomer-poet's anticipation of a thermodynamics that explains conservation of matter and energy as relationship over the *longue durée* (Stolte 362–3). Consider, for instance, rubai XXII:

And we, that now make merry in the Room
They left, and Summer dresses in new Bloom,
    Ourselves must we beneath the Couch of Earth
Descend, ourselves to make a Couch—for whom? (FitzGerald 141)

In the *Rubáiyát*, then, as in *Underneath the Bough*, the entanglements of human and non-human bodies, objects, and indeed the entire universe, can be perceived as an exchange of matter and energies. While my efforts in this chapter, thus far, have been focused on how musical forms and metaphors perform entanglement in *Underneath the Bough*, Stolte observes, in *The Rubáiyát*, the circulation and exchange of images (flowers, wine, dust, bodies) and rhymes, especially the effect of the shifting third lines of the four-line rubai stanza (Stolte 364). As might be expected, in their concerns with representing—indeed, performing—the energies of

---

[22] For foundational work on Victorian sciences that make connections between the environment and energy, especially thermodynamics, see, among others, Allan MacDuffie and Barry Gold.

a dynamic world, Field and FitzGerald's texts share much more than the phrase "Underneath the Bough."

Both texts call to mind Victorian scientific ideas about the world; and both share a *carpe diem* philosophy, with expansive yet non-linear views on time. These commonalities, combined with *Underneath the Bough*'s mixture of Christian and pagan themes and *The Rubáiyát*'s unwillingness to take a clear stance on atheism resulted, unsurprisingly, in both texts being noted for their "modernity." These characteristics also align with how Havelock Ellis writes of decadence in his introduction to Huysman's *Au Rebours*:

> the energy which in more primitive times marked the operations of the community as a whole has now simply been transferred to the individuals themselves, and this aggrandizement of the individual really produces an even greater amount of energy. The individual has gained more than the community has lost. An age of social decadence is not only the age of sinners and degenerates, but of saints and martyrs, and decadent Rome produced an Antinouis as well as a Heliogabalus. (iv–xv)

As *Underneath the Bough* and *The Rubáiyát* create space to rethink queer alliance in and through entangled natural energies, they also explore concepts that we would associate with what we term queer temporality. Victorian concerns about the environment and its energies, like our own, largely have to do with reproductive futurism: stewardship, sustainable industry, and questions of what the world will look like for offspring—for future generations that bear resemblance to ourselves. In contrast, Khayyám/FitzGerald's and Michael Field's impressions in and of the natural environment are situated in queer time. Non-reproductive, non-teleological, and oriented toward feeling in the moment, temporality in these verses contrasts the priorities of the heteronormative life cycle.[23]

Field's and FitzGerald's queer temporalities also suggest ways to interpret their speakers' "inaccurate" use of history and translation. Annmarie Drury argues that a philosophy and aesthetics of accident drives *The Rubáiyát*, making possible its *carpe diem*

---

[23] For foundational thinking on queer temporality see Edelman, Halberstam, and Freeman.

themes and repudiation of divine providence. In other words, like Michael Field, who (like Campion) takes liberties with history, FitzGerald's translations of "my Omar" result more from felt affinities with his precursor than mastery of Persian; *The Rubáiyát* "privileges chance and randomness over predictability and determinacy" (Drury 40).[24] Thus FitzGerald's appropriations, like Michael Field's, exhibit what Linda Hutcheon would term privileging fidelity to tone rather than to content and permits room for queer reading—for the subjective as well as the objective.

While Drury focuses more on FitzGerald's Orientalism and doesn't explore the implications of his queer affinities with Khayyám in depth, Benjamin Hudson does, providing provocative groundwork for additional points of overlap between *Underneath the Bough* and *The Rubáiyát*. Hudson suggests that FitzGerald embraces a stance of dilettantism; he argues that presenting his work as that of an enthusiastic amateur permits FitzGerald to justify the poems' "clash with dominant ideologues of its time" (161), especially its anti-teleological poetics, its religious skepticism, and "its ambiguous, eroticized network of multiple fragmented bodies" (172). While Michael Field surely would have not welcomed charges of amateurism, they do repeatedly proclaim the impossibility of fully knowing history—as Chapter 1 demonstrates, they adopt a phenomenological stance of *l'engrenage* toward their historical subjects. Just as their prefaces to their historical verse dramas assert sentiments like "It is what o'clock I say it is," the verse in *Underneath the Bough* (as elsewhere in their *oeuvre*) takes risks, as we have seen, with historical adaptation, suggesting similarities with Jack Halberstam's queer failures and José Esteban Muñoz's notion of a backward glance that enacts a future vision. Thus, queer approaches to temporal connections—to both recent memory and distant, mythological pasts—are deployed throughout *Underneath the Bough* to depict intense erotic desire on the one hand and to manage missing a beloved on the other, even when it's merely the thought of being away for a weekend that is being managed. As Mahoney theorizes, "Relocating oneself imaginatively, aesthetically, or geographically frequently allowed queer subjects to extricate themselves from British ideologies of gender and sexuality" ("Queer Community" 38).

---

[24] For Drury, this accounts for the unpredictability of rhyme in the third line of each rubai.

As we will see in the next chapter, even Michael Field's elegies—in and after *Underneath the Bough*—emphasize that relations with the departed are not broken, but changed. Meanwhile, verses where the speaker contemplates her own death reflect a Ruskinian organicism where little distinction is made between animate and inanimate entities:[25]

> Endowed by thee
> Death, let me enter privacy
> Unmorose and fellowly
> To mix, with the free pleasure
> Of stars and spring
> And magic, unfamiliar things,
> My beauteous leisure. (Field, *UTB* 48)

In death, as in life, one is not solitary but tied to the universe, at least in the dynamic world of *Underneath the Bough*, as in FitzGerald's queer rendering of *The Rubáiyát of Omar Khayyám*.

Echoes of the future

Like their earlier ekphrastic collection, *Sight and Song* (1892), *Underneath the Bough* portrays perception, affect, and thought as both objective and subjective, simultaneously universal and individual. Much as *Sight and Song* recasts its painted referents for a more modern age, in *Underneath* the *Bough* Michael Field's lyric "I" departs from the Renaissance speakers that are its verse influences: Byrd, Campion, and Omar Khayyám, as well as the self-absorbed Romantic lyric speaker who, for J. S. Mill, can only be "overheard." The co-authors find universal appeal and relevance in the prior lyric utterances they appropriate, but their contrapuntal revisions feature a lyric speaker who is queerly entangled with the beloved, with nature, with history, and with the departed. Their ecopagan impulses, perhaps like those of other *fin de siècle* thinkers such as Edward FitzGerald and, as Denisoff suggests, Walter Pater and Vernon Lee, can thus be understood as a queer bridge between the anthropocentrism of what is more traditionally thought of as Victorian environmentalism and the later ecologies of the twentieth and twenty-first centuries.

---

[25] See Kreisel.

We can glimpse Fieldian notions of entanglement with the natural world in the transcorporalities and vital materialisms of our own (queer) ecologies, and what Val Plumwood identifies as the Heraclitean characteristics of the human-non-human natural world. Plumwood, an Australian philosopher, ecofeminist, nature writer, and explorer, famously survived a crocodile attack, which led her to write in "Prey to a Crocodile":

> Before the encounter, it was as if I saw the whole universe as framed by my own narrative, as though the two were joined perfectly and seamlessly together. As my own narrative and the larger story were ripped apart, I glimpsed a shockingly indifferent world in which I had no more significance than any other edible being ... Thus the story of the crocodile encounter now has, for me, a significance quite the opposite of that conveyed in the master/monster narrative. It is a humbling and cautionary tale about our relationship with the earth, about the need to acknowledge our own animality and ecological vulnerability. (n.p.)

Plumwood's words resonate with Michael Field's poetry about not being afraid of death but instead embracing it as a return to the ever-exchanging energies of the universe:

> Then take the life I have called my own
> And to the liquid universe deliver;
>   Loosening my spirit's zone
> Wrap round me as thy limbs the wind, the light, the river. *(UTB 39)*

Many of our notions about Victorian environmentalism and the relations of the Victorian to nature maintain a strict separation between the human and the non-human. Whether we are thinking about Decadence "against nature," or nineteenth-century texts that fetishize the purity of nature, or those who, however conflicted, were engaged in extractive enterprises, or nineteenth-century women describing their gardens as refuges, prisons, or laboratories, this chapter has demonstrated that Michael Field is oriented toward nature differently. Instead, *Underneath the Bough*'s treatment of "Victorian themes" provides a queer ecological intervention characterized by human-non-human entanglement and interspecies subjectivity. As Plumwood reminds us:

> To the extent that we hyper-separate ourselves from nature and reduce it conceptually in order to justify domination, we not only lose the ability to empathise and to see the non-human sphere in ethical terms, but also get a false sense of our own character and location that includes an illusory sense of autonomy. The failure to see the non-human domain in the richer terms appropriate to ethics licenses supposedly "purely instrumental" relationships that distort our perceptions and enframings, impoverish our relations and make us insensitive to dependencies and interconnections (*Environmental Culture* 9)

As we consider Michael Field's elegiac relationship to death and mourning in the next chapter, we'll see that natural elements in their poetry continue to play an important role as they revise elegiac conventions, their representations of their relationship to one another, and the very notion of Michael Field, Poet, itself.

4

"Our dead": Michael Field and the Elegiac Tradition

> No more shall wayward grief abuse
> The genial hour with mask and mime;
> For change of place, like growth of time,
> Has broke the bond of dying use.
> —Tennyson, *In Memoriam* (1850)

> I owe a longer allegiance to the dead than to the living: in that world I shall abide forever.
> —Sophocles, *Antigone* (c. 441 BCE)

By the early spring of 1908, Katharine Bradley and Edith Cooper's beloved dog, Whym Chow had been dead for twenty-six months. Their first book of verse in fifteen years, *Wild Honey from Various Thyme* (1908), had recently come out; and despite the widespread praise they were enjoying from Britain's literati, they were annoyed at how the volume and "Michael Field" had been represented in the local press. Catholic converts now for about a year, they also worried what their new friends and mentors in the Church would think about the diverse collection of poems in "the Honey-book": pagan nature poetry and Sapphic love lyrics dating as far back as 1893; more recently composed devotional verse; and a considerable quantity of elegy. The elegies mourn a variety of subjects: Cooper's father James, who had tragically disappeared in a mountaineering accident in 1897; their religious shift away from the Bacchic life that had sustained their intertwined identity as Poets and Lovers for so many years; and, of course, Whym Chow, whose loss still had the ability to throw them into episodes of acute mourning. Yet despite their ongoing grief over the death of the chow, "Michael" and "Henry" were hard at work writing religious poetry, collaboratively composing historical verse dramas to be published "by the author of *Borgia*," and taking trips to consult with clergy at various cathedrals and abbeys, in order to delve deeper into the intellectual and spiritual mysteries of Catholic theology.

This complex tapestry of events and emotions provide a backdrop that may help us interpret a curiously paradoxical and elegiac moment recorded in the joint diary during a trip they took that Lenten season, a journal entry that indicates, among other things, the extent to which Bradley and Cooper continued to be devastated by Chow's death, and that has considerable implications for understanding the last decade of their work:

> And on the couch and up and down the stairs and by the inn-door-always beside us is our bright Whym Chow: all the sun on the couch falls on him and when we are happy we are happy among us three. An inn was always the Light place for Whymmie—the stagnancy of the lodging house being as a disease to him and his beloved ones. How good we can take him with us now into the very presence of the God to whom he has been allowed to lead us—our guardian angel of the little Torch, our Flame of Love—Whym Chow.[1]

With its claim, in material detail, that the deceased dog has accompanied them to the inn, where he frolics in the sunbeams, jumps on the couch, and is happy they are not in a lodging house, this is admittedly a highly eccentric passage, although certainly not an isolated one. In fact, it is representative of the rhetoric Michael Field had always used and continued to use when writing about Whym Chow—in both poetry and prose—long after his death and indeed, until their own. But are we to read it and other, similar effusions, literally or symbolically? What is the logic behind this seemingly illogical, paradoxical description of the deceased dog's presence at the inn? How does this passage stand in relation to Michael Field's other representations of themselves and those they have mourned? How do their elegiac texts, as a whole, fit into an elegiac tradition; and how do they compare to other Victorian representations of death, loss, and mourning?

---

[1] This is the Tumbledown Dick Inn in Farnboro, where Bradley and Cooper stayed as they visited St. Michael's Benedictine Abbey. *Works and Days*. MSS Add. 46798, March 1908. (EC). fols 51r–54r. The British Library.

None of these considerations are unrelated to those concerns of gender and sexuality which, to date, have been so central to and so fruitful for Michael Field studies. Although I use the term with some reservation, all of the texts I will examine are "personal elegies," a phrase that begins to highlight how these poems differ from the poetics of public lamentation and succession to power that characterize much traditional elegy. And as Sandra Gilbert and Susan Gubar, Peter Sacks, and Celeste Schenck, among others have noted, elegies that take the personal as subject have been characterized as deploying a feminine strategy that modifies the elegiac mode; in contrast to the public elegy's masculine impulses and conventions, which traditionally, have been problematic and/or inaccessible for women poets. As we shall see, there are indeed aspects of Michael Field's approach to mourning that run contrary to masculine tradition and patriarchal norms; they reject elegiac tradition to some extent in favor of continued modes of eco-entanglement, yet they also continue to employ the Dionysian and Decadent tropes favored by homoerotically inclined male Aesthetes.[2] Thus, as should not be surprising when considering the work of the "dear Greek women"[3] who preferred to be known as "Michael" and "Henry," the representation of gender and desire in the elegies, as in the rest of their *oeuvre*, is sometimes playful, often contradictory, always complex. As we proceed to look for trends in Michael Field's texts about mourning, we will also be focusing on the departures, the elements that we might consider, in context, to be odd, eccentric, indeed, queer.

The relatively small amount of scholarship that, to date focuses on Michael Field's unique writing about Whym Chow and the trinity that the two Poet-Lovers believed that, with him, they formed, has resulted in several important and compelling conclusions. Ruth Vanita argues that the dog functioned as an erotic proxy for Bradley and Cooper's same-sex love. Similarly, Marion Thain observes that Whym's role in their poetry "helped them overcome significant anxieties about their erotic relationship in context of their Catholic conversion" (*Poetry* 188) and that "their

---

[2] See, in particular, Martha Vicinus's provocative work on Michael Field's identification with the figure of the boy; and Frederick Roden's equally groundbreaking study of their appropriation of both male and female homoerotic imagery to convey devotional pleasure and desire for union with God.

[3] One of Robert Browning's pet phrases for Bradley and Cooper.

identification with the Trinity can be read, in part, as a defensive gesture at a time when they were extremely concerned with accommodating all aspects of the life and their relationship within the Church" (*Poetry* 192). Frederick Roden coins the term "lesbian trinitarianism" to demonstrate how Whym Chow enabled Michael Field to "fully embody a female-centered Christianity" (198), a "canine catholicism" in which intense homoeroticism, religiosity, and dog-love could all be subsumed into art; and through which, after the chow's death, ongoing and aestheticized sacrificial offering became central to their narratives of individual and joint theology. Sarah Kersh examines how *Whym Chow* revises the amatory sonnet tradition through the use of metonymy and Carolyn Dever argues, "the poets write the story of the death of a family and the death of romantic love, along with the death of the dog" (187). My aim in posing the aforementioned questions is to continue to develop an explanation for the striking Whym Chow writings that is in line, for the most part, with these previous arguments, while also contextualizing the Whym Chow texts specifically within and against Victorian elegiac convention and the revisionary characteristics of Michael Field's own work.

As their poetry, letters, and journals indicate, over the years Michael Field maintained a complex and devoted relationship with "their dead": from their youthful pagan celebrations of and otherworldly "communications" with Cooper's mother, Robert Browning, and Shakespeare, to the "Longer Allegiance" sonnet cycle of *Wild Honey* for Cooper's father, to their sublimely prolonged and eroticized mourning of Whym Chow. In order to begin to answer the questions I have posed, it will be necessary to comb through some of these varied elegiac texts—to parse their dead, as it were—in order to gain a greater understanding of Michael Field's overarching conception of the work of mourning in their life and writing. Ultimately, I suggest that these texts, individually and in sequence, come together to create a kind of elegiac scaffold that functions, albeit in a fluid and shifting way throughout their lives, as a framework that makes possible not only Michael Field's many representations of grief and mourning, but also their explorations of what it means to live and die in relation to others—a topic I began to explore in the previous chapter on ecodecadent entanglement in the lyrics of *Underneath the Bough*. Additionally, as we shall see, Michael Field provides exceptional and important examples of Victorian elegy, examples that deserve study because, both within and against dominant discourses of death and mourning, they shed light on their era's elegiac forms of literature and other practices of grief. Overall then, I wish to show that the life and work of Michael Field offers a unique opportunity to think about Victorian elegy from both margin and center, as well as to consider the *telos* of mourning (or more accurately, the potentially multiple *teloi* of mourning) both then and today.

"The grave and memory shall not drag on"

Mourning has, or is supposed to have, very specific relationships to ideas of time and place. For Freud, as well as psychological theorists before and after him, normal experiences of grief, as expressed through mourning, follow a specific progress narrative over time: an emotional and behavioral chain of events unfolds whereby the grieving individual gradually can withdraw their attachments to the lost loved object and return to everyday life. In "Mourning and Melancholia" (1917) Freud writes, "the [absorbing] work of mourning is completed [and] the ego becomes free and uninhibited again" (154). Although the stages of grief may vary within different psychological traditions, most theories of bereavement agree: if the process of mourning is interrupted in its happening, it ceases to be mourning and becomes pathology, a problem.

The work of traditional elegy, as numerous scholars have shown, helps the bereaved move through this process of mourning and into readiness to form new attachments. Thus, a feature of the elegiac poem is that it engages in a series of procedures and resolutions, in which previous attachments are substituted for new ones. Peter Sacks observes that in elegy, "at the core of each procedure is the renunciatory experience of loss and acceptance, not just of a substitute, but of the very means and practice of substitution" (8). Thus, among other strategies and affordances, the elegy may provide a series of symbols of consolation; or, the elegy itself can become what is substituted for the deceased.

In terms of place, the one who mourns is confronted with the fact that the loved one is gone: they once were *here* but now are *there*. *There* may be a specific graveyard, another town or country, or more abstractly, missing; *there* might be the afterlife, or perhaps *there* is a combination of these places, with the material body perceived to be below the earth, the spirit, above. Regardless of the details in all their cultural specificities (although not to dismiss them), the lost love object, now *there,* occupies a new place in space as well as in memory and mind; what is gone and mourned has made a passage, through space, from *here* to *not here.* In fact, "few elegies or acts of mourning succeed without seeming to place the dead, and death itself, at some cleared distance from the living" (Sacks 19).

When we consider Victorian practices of mourning, we see both examples of and exceptions to these ideas about time and space. Regarding time, for instance, the Victorian widow commonly was expected to feel numbness first, then "episodes of severe anxiety and psychological pain, known as the pangs of grief," then apathy and depression, and then ultimately, to "reorganize her life and establish a new social identity" (Jalland 231). Similarly, Tennyson's popular elegy for Arthur Hallam, *In Memoriam* (1849), moves through a three-year mourning process, in which emotional growth, marked by three Christmases, is traced in some of the following ways: from numbness and anguish to being able to celebrate holidays and weddings; from repeated crises of faith to having hope for the future of humanity; and, from youthful homoeroticism, considered within dominant ideology to be a developmental stage, to a letting go of same-sex love that will make possible adult heteronormativity. Tennyson's speaker proclaims: "No more shall wayward grief abuse / The genial hour with mask and mime; / For change of place, like growth of time, / Has broke the bond of dying use" (CV. lines 9–12). Notably, there are numerous Victorian testimonies to the therapeutic value of recording memories of the loved one in detail;[4] thus, the act of writing, such as journaling or writing an elegy, was perceived then, as now, as a valuable part of the (teleological) work of mourning. Such literary acts, like the Victorian ritual of wearing, then leaving off, mourning dress, help to ensure, or perhaps even to quicken, the desired outcome—the cessation of mourning—the ability to attach to a new object—after an appropriate passage of time.[5]

---

[4] Jalland 288. Among others, also see Sacks.

[5] Sacks and Clewell both address the theoretical underpinning of prescriptions for the mourner to "move on." Joseph and Tucker, as well as Jalland and Wheeler, provide examples of specifically Victorian injunctions about the end of mourning; and Mangum extends this even to pets, as will become relevant to our discussion later.

In terms of place, in mourning, Victorian juxtapositions of *there* (heaven) and *here* (earth) are frequently firm binaries. However, while in classical elegy the space between dead and living and the necessity of keeping those two places separate is often figured through processional motifs; the Victorians often reinforce the logic of the here/there binary with the concept of reunion. For example, *In Memoriam*'s speaker portends he won't see Arthur "Till all my widow'd race be run" (IX. l.18; XVII. l.20); nonetheless, the lines convey he believes he *will* see him again. Similarly, in Coventry Patmore's "A Farewell," the speaker looks forward to when he and the beloved departed will "Amazèd meet; / The bitter journey to the bourne so sweet" (lines 22–3). Victorian discourses of mourning therefore will sometimes depict the survivors traveling, after death, to join the departed in the hereafter, which may be figured as a place of worship and praise (such as the Tractarian unseen world) or as home, (often quite a material one) (Jalland 271).

Yet, for the Victorians, these themes of mourning's logics of time and space exist in many variations and with complications, including paradoxes, that create tension in time's relationship to space, in the context of mourning. Spiritualist beliefs and practices, for instance, muddy the boundary between the *here* and *there* of life and death, producing a sense that the departed is simultaneously *no longer here* yet *still here*, and in turn, perhaps facilitating the temporal process of mourning in some cases and forever stalling it in others. Additionally, Michael Wheeler observes how verb tenses in Victorian literary and religious representations of death and mourning often complicate linear time (xiii). In addition to the horizontal dimension of the temporal process of everyday existence, Wheeler demonstrates how much of Victorian literature and culture reflects a notion of "the eternal present" which:

> collapses earthly time ... Thus the mourner's or elegist's experience of separation—I/you, life/death, earth/heaven, is subsumed in a larger scheme of Christian faith, the "double consciousness" of which holds the this-worldly and other-worldly in creative tension, and which speaks of a kingdom that is here *and* elsewhere, of a paradise that is now and not yet. (xiv)

Thus, as an ironic counterpart to Spiritualism's belief in a departed one who is *no longer here* yet *still here*, Victorian Christians could and did believe that the mourner, through faith, is both *still here* and *already there*.⁶ And so did those Victorians whose ideas of religion were less orthodox, especially those whose elegiac writing combined elements of the sacred with those of the profane. Recall, for example, D. G. Rossetti's still-bereaved lover, who sees his Blessed Damozel lean across the divide of heaven and earth, and whose sense of time since her death is both collapsed and telescoped. Thus, those Victorians who found themselves engaged in the work of mourning—that is, struggling to let go of the lost love object—experienced this engagement within and against a frame of time and space that was simultaneously linear and fluid, concrete and permeable.

Michael Field's elegiac writing reflects many of the Victorian ideas about mourning vis-à-vis time and space that I have just outlined; in particular, they demonstrate intense investment in and diverse depictions of both temporal and spatial paradox. The reason for Field's embracing of paradox, as Marion Thain has argued, is in part stylistic, related to the co-authors' self-fashioning as Aesthetes:

> Paradox is the hallmark of [the Aesthetic] moment . . . Michael Field's work can best be read through Bradley and Cooper's manipulation and apparent reconciliation of conflicting concepts . . . The impossible desire to combine the diachronic with the synchronic are at the heart of Michael Field's aesthetic; and achieving that combination, or the illusion of that achievement, is Bradley and Cooper's greatest aesthetic triumph. (*Poetry* 16)

Yet there are also philosophical and spiritual underpinnings for the elegiac employment of paradox that strives to relate to the absent beloved, and to the past, such that "the grave / And memory shall not drag on my desire" (Field, *Wild Honey* lines 11–12).

Phenomenologically, their elegies, like the previous forms discussed in this study, provide yet another example of what Merleau-Ponty refers to as *l'engrenage*—in this case, a gearing into and

---

⁶ See also Tracy Miller on Matthew Arnold's poetry of place and elegy. Framing her discussion with Gaston Bachelard's ideas about the associative possibilities of space, Miller writes, "This relation between place, memory and the imaginary inhabitation of the spaces of our past renders space and place portable" (164n 7).

taking up of the unknowns of death and the afterlife as well as the unruly vicissitudes of grief. As the next two sections will demonstrate, as Michael Field's beliefs, interests, and personal problems shift over time, the queerly oriented paradoxes that they employ to gear into the unknowns of death and mourning shift as well—with varying degrees of "success" regarding their consolation for loss.

Longer allegiances, Aesthetic paradoxes

Michael Field's elegiac texts can be described in two distinct stages. This section will address the earlier set, which includes verse and diary references to those they termed "their dead": Cooper's mother and their friend and mentor Robert Browning, who both died in 1889; Cooper's father, (killed in a tragic mountain accident in 1897); and on occasion, Shakespeare.[7] In the following section I will examine the latter set of elegiac texts, written in response to the 1906 death of their beloved canine companion, Whym Chow.

Michael Field's earlier elegies largely represent death and mourning, especially in relation to time and space, in the typically Victorian ways described above, albeit with additional pagan attributes characteristic of much of their other work. They trace a movement whereby, over time, grief and feelings of loss fade and are superseded by renewed joy in life and looking toward the future. In these elegies, the dead have of course moved to another place; but notably, in a variation on paradoxical Victorian thinking about death and "the eternal present," the dead also are still very much with the co-authors, often because the dead now reside in Nature—a heaven on earth—which is also home to the speaker.

Those written after the death of Cooper's mother, Emma, who was Bradley's elder sister, are representative. The 1889 lyric,[8] "Bury her at even," published in their 1893 collection *Underneath the Bough* reads:

---

[7] Michael Field wrote other elegies as well, for noted figures such as Swinburne and Christina Rossetti, but they did not consider them to be "their dead."

[8] According to Cooper's notes on this poem it was actually written of "little Evelyn Barnett" and published in the *Academy* in June of 1889. But after Cooper's mother died in late August of that year, it was "Read to the Little Girl [Amy Cooper] after tea of the burying of our dear white relic [Emma Cooper] and said by me just outside the front door, with Amy by, under the many stars. The poem was then reprinted in *Underneath the Bough*. Archive of "Michael Field." MS Eng poet d.60. fol. 12. Oxford, Bodleian Libraries.

Bury her at even,
That the stars may shine
Soon above her
And the dews of twilight cover:
Bury her at even,
Ye that love her.

Bury her at even,
As the shut of flowers
Softly take her;
They will lie beside nor wake her:
Bury her at even
At the shut of flowers.

Bury her at even
In the wind's decline;
Night receive her
Where no noise may grieve her!
Bury her at even,
And then leave her! (*UTB* 41–2)

Here, the steady falling rhythms of the trochaic lines are gentle; rather than stalking or pounding; they rock the deceased subject(s) of the poem, easing her passage through time and space. They also ease the passage of the speaker through the mourning process, as the poem's repetitions do, which is characteristic of the elegy as a form. The only irregular line, line 3's "soon above her" suggests a certain urgency: the speaker wishes "her" to be buried at twilight, knowing the stars will soon appear, which implicitly conveys the need to complete the interment before darkness completely falls; perhaps the speaker even wishes her to be buried *this* "even," instead of waiting for tomorrow. Yet, "soon's" sibilant connection with "star" and "shine" in the previous line and "above her's" rhyme with "cover" and "love her" in the lines that follow renders this urgency both beautiful (in the first case) and lovingly gentle (in the second), like the falling of dew and the shutting of flowers. In stanzas two and three we see that the flowers, perhaps like the stars, become guardians that "take" or escort the deceased into the literal and euphemistic "Night"; and curiously, here Night (a time) also becomes an abstract place. Yet, it is a hospitable and considerate one: the beloved's place of final rest is not in darkness, but is partially lit by starshine and twilight;[9] and the everlasting silence that "receive[s] her" is not eerie, merely free of the trouble of wind and noise. The speaker may leave the beloved deceased in Nature and proceed with life, as indicated by the classical elegiac reference to flowers growing on the grave.

A similar poem, "I laid her to sleep," written in September 1889 and published in *Underneath the Bough*, narrates how mourning at Emma Cooper's gravesite is cut short by the cheerful sight of a squirrel playing in the sun, which is described with bouncy play between iambs and anapests.

> I laid her to sleep,
>   And I came to weep
> By her forest-grave; but I found
>   That a squirrel gay
>   At its noiseless play
> Was springing across the mound.
>
>   The sun made a mote
>   Of gold on its coat,
> On its pretty hind-legs it stood;
>   Then without a sound
>   Leapt over the mound
> To its home again in the wood. (*UTB* 53)

Here, the lively rhythm makes it impossible to dwell for long in the sadness that motivates the opening of the poem. Using alliteration and assonance, the speaker "finds" in the "forest" that, at this "grave," one cannot, in fact *be* grave, as the speaker's attention shifts from the deceased to the "gay" squirrel at "play." As is fitting for the co-authors, as Aesthetes, the brief narrative is driven by aesthetic observation of movement and light. Yet, from the opening euphemism of "sleep" to the common woodland creature's antics to the poem's close associating the squirrel's "home" with "her" eternal one, the short poem remains firmly in the realm of the familiar, simple aspects of Nature, rather than in the realm

---

[9] Peter Sacks notes, in classical elegy, "a heritage of powerful contradictions associated with the original positing of any imagery of light on the far side of darkness, or of the presence in the space of an absence" (34).

of its mysteries. The "noiseless"-ness of the squirrel links this poem with the previous one, with silence again as comforting fact, rather than oppressive absence. Thus, in these poems, the place of death and sadness quickly becomes a place of life, beauty, and simple joy. As is typical of Michael Field's pagan-inspired writing of the period, in both lyrics the dead can be eternally present because Nature becomes their home. Thus, these two elegies manifest Michael Field's insights about eco-entanglement, present in so much of *Underneath the Bough*.

Bradley and Cooper's collaborative diary also clarifies their attitude toward the practice of mourning, frequently documenting how they keep an altar for their dead, dressing it with pictures, bits of nature, and books and objects loved by the departed. They ritualistically observe birth and death days, recalling memories, reading poetry and the Bible, and creating their own Bacchic rituals—from garlanded dances to libations to shared kisses over outdoor altars. For instance, on Easter day of 1890, Cooper, then twenty-eight, spends the day in remembrance of her mother:

> I read with her in the Blue Room—she was certainly with me . . . for as I sat in the old place and read her chapter out of Corinthians I to her, all my tears were wiped away and a firm joy given to my being. I could no more cry than I did after she kissed me at the moment when she lived and was dead. I felt no glory like that—but a close understanding blessedness, a familiar thrill of union and intercourse. . . . I fell into a small, soft sleep, with my mouth open! It was the gentle close of "an hour's communion with the dead." more vivid and immanent than usual.[10]

These rituals of mourning, although eccentric, are not qualitatively different from other quotidian practices recorded in Michael Field's diary or verse; and they assert that, in almost Spiritualistic fashion, the dead are with them: *no longer here* and *still here*.

Notably, although Cooper generally is considered the more mystical of the two co-authors, Bradley documents a similar experience celebrating Shakespeare on April 23, 1891:

---

[10] *Works and Days*. MSS Add. 46778, April 6, 1890. (EC). fol. 26r. The British Library.

And for his sake P[11] and I went up the hill to the savage country where the juniper grows. We almost touched the beech trees on the verge; we saw the steadying horizon hills of the plain; the wind walked free, not enslaved as among coverts. This morning I planted in the earth, I had communion with her. And tonight P has read the sonnets to me. How accessible he is, how close. And like us. Yet how much greater by suffering! Loving and being loved—it is only with God that this brings peace. I recall the old anniversaries of his birthday in Warwickshire. What has he not been to me! What may he not become? We forsake his methods to achieve his results. We thank heaven for him: we ask for his gentleness of nature.[12]

One of many remarkable elements in this passage is the easy sliding between God, Shakespeare, and savage (elsewhere Dionysian) Nature, all to create the effect of the material presence of the Bard, over various times and places. The rhetoric of connection—to the trees, to the earth, to Cooper, and to the deceased Shakespeare—is prevalent; in Chapter 3's discussion of *Underneath the Bough*'s entanglement and transcorporeality, I noted a similar rhetoric of connection, which as Schenck and Stone among others observe, is also a feature of feminine elegy. Notably, connection and communion in this passage, as in Cooper's passage about her mother, is associated with freedom, happiness, peace, and limitless potential, as opposed to enslavement or being stifled; it also is in keeping with Bradley's fascination, at the time, with Spinoza, who "with his fine grasp of unity says, 'If two individuals of exactly the same nature are joined together, they make up a single individual, doubly stronger than each alone,' i.e., Edith and I make a *veritable Michael*" (Field, WD 16). In addition to the rhetoric of merging, with the declaration, "How accessible he is, how close. And like us," we see what critics have called Michael Field's "tropes of likeness," which Ruth Vanita has shown follows Shakespearean models of love that feature a homoerotic economy of likeness in opposition to heterosexuality (102). Thus, these early rituals honoring the dead share impulses with Bradley's musing on New Year's Eve, 1891,

---

[11] P = Puss = Cooper.
[12] *Works and Days*. MSS Add. 46779, April 23, 1891. (KB). fol. 36r. The British Library.

"[we] are knit up into one living soul";[13] and with the language of much of the poetry that celebrates their love, life, and literary collaboration, like the closing lines of *Underneath the Bough*'s famous poem "A Girl," "Such: and our souls so knit / I leave a page half writ-/The work begun / Will be to heaven's conception done / If she come to it" (88).[14]

The following poem from *Underneath the Bough*, written about two months after the death of Robert Browning, further explains their elegiac rituals, literally outlining, as a philosophy, the practices of grief and mourning that Michael Field adopts during this period:

> Others may drag at memory's fetter,
> May turn for comfort to the vow
> Of mortal breath; I hold it better
> To learn if verily and how
> Love knits me with the loved one now.
>
> Others for solace, sleep forsaken,
> May muse upon the days of old;
> To me it is delight to waken,
> To find my Dead, to feel them fold
> My heart, and for its dross give gold. (*UTB* 32–3)

From a Freudian perspective, one sees how the work of mourning is accomplished in this poem, but with a twist. Rather than substituting a new object-attachment altogether for the lost loved one, the speaker substitutes a new kind of relationship with the departed, which is made possible by focusing on "how / Love knits me with the loved one *now*" (my emphasis). Absence, paradoxically, and unconventionally for the elegiac form, becomes presence. It is clear that the speaker believes this is a superior way of dealing with grief than dwelling on thoughts of the past with the beloved; memory can only be enslavement, a "drag," a "fetter" that, at best, might yield some "comfort" or "solace" during sleepless, grief-obsessed

---

[13] *Works and Days*. MSS Add. 46779, December 31, 1891. (KB). fol. 161v. The British Library.

[14] For extended readings of "A Girl," see, among others: Ehnenn, *Women's Literary Collaboration* 30–1; Laird, *Women Coauthors* 23–4; White, "Flesh and Roses" 50–1.

nights. Instead of such poor treasure, this speaker's loss is compensated with "delight" in an ongoing, transformed relationship in the present with "my Dead," which is clearly figured, as in the two previous diary entries, as a physical interaction that is as real as (or perhaps superior to) communing with the living: the speaker "feel[s] them fold / My heart, and for its dross give gold."

Chris Snodgrass assesses such impulses in Michael Field's writing in the following way:

> This valuing of a basic Otherness carried over readily into the Field's religious sensibilities, not least in their allegiance to a cult of the dead. When Browning offered his sympathy to Katharine at the loss of her sister Lissie, she replied, "Ah, how good to have one's dear ones not outside one any more," suggesting that for the Fields the dead could be in more intimate relation with the living—inside their hearts-than people who were still alive. (174)

And indeed if the diaries are any indication, after an initial period of grief, in many ways Bradley and Cooper *were* happier with their relationships with "their dead," posthumously, than when their loved ones were living, a point to which I will return in a moment. In her extended discussion of *Underneath the Bough*, Marion Thain describes this transformed and ongoing relationship with the absent Other as "elegy without a corpse," which she further explains as Bradley and Cooper's "certainty of presence. This presence is paradoxical in the context of the elegy; but, as usual with Michael Field, this is not an indication of confusion or doubt: it is a paradoxical certainty" (*Poetry* 111).

The co-authors' representations of paradoxical presence, and related tropes of merging and likeness have, of course, been topics of interest since the inception of Michael Field studies; they are foundational to discussions of the diaries, the lyrics describing Bradley and Cooper as writers and lovers, and indeed, their collaborative persona, including the very name of "Michael Field." Early readings of Michael Field's work, along with their proclamations, "the work is a perfect mosaic. We cross and interlace . . ." (Letter to Havelock Ellis, quoted in Sturgeon, 47), and "I am away from my own identity,"[15] initially prompted critics to make

---

[15] Cooper, writing of Bradley's absence. *Works and* Days. MSS Add. 46780, February 14, 1892. (EC). fol. 46r. The British Library.

claims literalizing and romanticizing their oneness, such as Mary Sturgeon's in 1922, "they are a union so complete" (62), and Lillian Faderman's 1981 assessment that they achieved "absolute, perfect equality" (213). However, more recent analyses, including my own, have reinterpreted the co-authors' claims to oneness, not as literal, but as literary conceits that function as interpersonal and textual strategies.[16] Yopie Prins, for instance, envisions Michael Field's lyric voice as a chorus: "the intertextuality of their relationship, the very possibility of crossing and interlacing, depends on difference between the two, and it is this asymmmetical doubleness produced by writing together that allows their work to be 'joined' and them to be 'closer married'" ("Sappho Doubled" 180); while Virginia Blain finds in their texts an oscillation of voices that only creates the appearance of unity, an illusion of singleness. Meanwhile, Marion Thain observes that because elegy underpins the Victorian lyric, even in Michael Field's writings that are not strictly elegies, absence paradoxically becomes presence: "Bradley and Cooper are interested in how the lyric poem necessarily exists within space and time, in the same way drama does ... Michael Field's poetry is 'staged,' just as Bradley and Cooper's [joint] persona is contrived" (*Poetry* 115). Each critic concludes that, in "Michael" and "Henry's" celebrations of their erotic and creative life partnership, representations of tension and difference operate in tandem with those of likeness and merging; furthermore, the importance of difference to the ongoing negotiations of desire that fueled the Michaels' long-term relationship cannot be understated. "Difference was crucial to their articulation of their relationship, even if they shared those roles equally," reports Thain (*Poetry* 106); and Blain asserts:

> They lived together, worked together, wrote together, holidayed together, slept together, were converted together, and almost died together, in what seems a perfect orgy of togetherness; yet they were never simply one person. In fact, they were two quite different people, with quite different poetic talents and impulses. (242)

The consequence for their writing, as many studies of Michael Field to date have shown, is a curiously complicated and often paradoxical articulation of authorship and (inter)subjectivity.

[16] Ehnenn, "Our Brains."

Here, I further develop Thain's argument that elegy underpins the Victorian lyric,[17] and that it takes particular form, in the Michaelian lyric, in a dialectic between presence and absence. I agree that, in Bradley and Cooper's writing about one another, we see crucial traces of difference operating alongside insistence on unity and sameness; and that this results in rich and paradoxical tensions within the texts. This observation is important for analyzing their writing about "their" dead because I think what occurs there, vis-à-vis unity and sameness, presence and absence, differs from what occurs in their lyrics about each other. It seems that in their early elegies, the kind of interpersonal difference and interlacing that is so important in their other work becomes erased; it is as if, in these elegies of transformed relationship and eternal presence, the larger difference between the living and the dead (the fact of death) subsumes all other tensions that may have existed between "the Michaels" and Cooper's parents, or Browning, in life. Thus, Cooper speaks of the "familiar thrill of union and intercourse" with her mother without the accompanying feelings of being stifled that her diaries and letters indicate she often experienced when her mother was alive. Both "Michaels" could have a much more intimate and carefree connection with Browning during their Bacchic communion with his memory than they did before his death, when they certainly treasured his mentorship, but also expended much energy correcting his misunderstandings of them as collaborative authors, and often worried he would reveal their identity. And as we shall see, after his death, they could enjoy a positive emotional connection with Cooper's father, James, free of the caustic arguments they had had in life about topics ranging from socialism to their devotion to one another.

It is important to emphasize that, in these poems and diary entries, the phenomenological sense of connection with the dead is articulated as "real," not metaphorical, as evidenced by Bradley's jealous diary entry after Easter 1897 when she complains how lonely and miserable she felt the previous day, which Cooper spent with her dead. Bradley grumbles: "I am treated no better than an old Pagan cow on this day. It is unjust"; she then painfully adds that Cooper, uncharacteristically, did not apologize for

---

[17] For more on the "funereal" tenor of Victorian life and literature, see Joseph and Tucker.

making her feel slighted and abandoned.[18] Though the lived experience of connection is real and lasting, Bradley's peevishness is the exception rather than the rule, since, importantly, the outcome of Michael Field's mourning process, both in ritual and in writing, is to reinforce their love for one another through and after communion with their dead. As in Romantic elegy, for Michael Field eventually "the mourner" (or in this case the mourners) "displaces the mourned as principle subject" (Wheeler 225).

We see this displacement particularly at work in *The Longer Allegiance* sonnet cycle, which was inspired, at least in part, by the process of mourning Cooper's father James, who died during an 1897 hiking accident. *The Longer Allegiance* appears as a distinct section of *Wild Honey from Various Thyme*, bringing together under one umbrella the varied themes of the previous elegiac writing we have examined thus far. What I would like to focus on here (since I will address *Wild Honey*'s Chow poems in the next section) is how *The Longer Allegiance* employs the affordances of elegy to craft a progress narrative whereby the poets work through their libidinal attachment to the events surrounding James's death. While the diaries document his disappearance during a summer walking holiday in Switzerland,[19] Bradley and Cooper's understandable frantic and obsessive reaction, and their relief and grief when the body was discovered the following October, the sonnet cycle stages a series of visits to and meditations upon the woodland site of James's fall and death.[20] In so doing, it praises the untamed yet enduring powers of Nature, God, love, death, and memory, asserts the paradoxical presence of the deceased, and ultimately substitutes a celebration of their poets' own love and life together for their grief.

The opening poem, "The Torrent," contains classic elegiac questions and protestations of anger, indignation and sorrow: "And here thy footsteps stopped? / . . . / Is it on these round eddies I must

---

[18] *Works and Days*. MSS Add. 46786, [April 19],1897. (KB). fol. 43v. The British Library.

[19] For a study of mourning and the absent body in the Victorian novel, see Jolene Zigarovich.

[20] Cooper and Bradley traveled to Zermatt during the summer of 1897, after James's disappearance; but the body was not found and they left Switzerland, only to return after his body was finally recovered on October 25. They made a third trip back to Zermatt on the anniversary of his death the following year. See Donoghue 94–102.

spend my passionate conjecture?" (137, lines 1, 8–9). Similarly, "Possession" opens with complaint and indignation: "Thou hast no grave. What is it that bereaves / That has bereft us of thee? Thou are gone!" (138, lines 1–2). In both poems the speaker acknowledges that James now belongs to Nature—figured as wild in the first poem: "this writhing swell / Thus surging, mad voluminous, white stream, / Burst starving from the hill" (137, lines 1–3); but gentle in the second:

> The forest with its infinite soft leaves
> May have received thee, or thou wandered'st on
> The tender, wild, exhilarating flowers
> Crowning thy broken pathway; . . . (138, lines 3–6)

In both of these lyrics the natural world reflects the emotion of the speaker, which is also signaled in the title: "The Torrent" connects the speaker's torrential pain to the "writhing," "surging" mountain waters that, later in the poem, create "clanging music" (137, line 11); while "Possession" implies that the grief that now possesses the speaker is analogous to the relationship between James and Nature. This latter is complicated; on the one hand, Nature now possesses James: "The forest with its infinite soft leaves / May have received thee" (138, lines 3–4). On other hand, James, even though he did not desire or ask for it, through his death now has a "hold" on the Alpine hills and valleys, an event that is articulated in abundantly rich imagery with positive economic and aesthetic implications:

> . . . Thou has made no plea
> For rest or possession; and thy hold
> Is on the land forever: thine the gold
> Brimming the crystal crests, the gold that fills
> The vales, the valley's fountain purity
> And thine the inmost meadows of the hills. (138, lines 9–14)

Line 10's use of "and" instead of "yet" is curious; softening the tension between the past and the future. Similarly, Bradley and Cooper did not ask "to be bereft of thee"; but in keeping with their philosophy of grief and death as expressed in poems like "Others may drag at memory's fetter," they imply that eventually the outcome of their anguish will be golden and pure.

As *The Longer Allegiance* sonnet cycle unfolds, the co-authors employ many additional elegiac conventions. For instance, in "The Torrent" and the third poem, "Falling Leaves," the space between the living and the dead is accentuated through references to England as a place that is contrasted to the Alps. In the first poem, the speaker recounts how she received word of James's death, abroad, while she was "in the grey, azure iris-bed" he had left for her to tend; in "Falling Leaves" the speaker crosses "an English street" (139, line 2) to a garden where, among the autumn trees, she meditates on her sorrow and her deceased loved one, now lying far away "among thy hills" (139, lines 2, 14). Repetition, another way elegists conventionally move toward acceptance of death and consolation, is also a key feature of the verses honoring James; for example, note the anaphora as the speaker of "Falling Leaves" gazes upon the linden trees in the English garden:

> The leaves are falling—ah, how free to die!
> The leaves are falling, life is passing by,
> The leaves are falling slowly at my feet,
> And soon with dead summer, soon—how sweet!—
> They will be garnered safe from every eye. (139, lines 4–8)

The choice of the word "garner" in line 8 reminds the reader that autumn brings harvest even as it brings decay; and from this point on, the energies of the sonnet cycle become increasingly focused upon the resolution of mourning and ultimately, how the poets grow closer to each other through the experience. The next poem, "The Forest," employs many of the features of "Bury her at even" and "I laid her to sleep": the sonnet provides consolation by emphasizing Nature's beauty, calling attention to the eternal cycles of the seasons (which mirror the cycle of both human and woodland life and death) and by repeating the idea that when James fell to his death, "He lay asleep" (140, lines 1, 5) in the forest setting. The sixth sonnet, "Turning Homeward," the last of a cluster written in 1897, features classic elegiac images of closure as the poets recall leaving the Alps: "cover[ing] up thy grave" (142, line 6), the road they take "descends," the doors of the huts in the valley are "shut / All closes as we saw thy coffin close / And we are turning homeward" (142, lines 8–9). The sonnet then concludes with images of rebirth: we find that the torrential waters that opened the sonnet cycle in "Torrent" are now "shrunk"; and the speakers see "Two lusty lambs, pressing their mother's teat, / Drink and are glad: we feel another year" (142, lines 13–14).

The *Longer Allegiance* sonnet cycle continues with poems referencing the co-authors' 1898 return to Zermatt, interspersed with a few poems written the previous year. At this point, the cycle's narrative arc begins to incorporate Bradley and Cooper's personal mythology about grief, mourning, and what happens to them as a couple as the result of their newly transformed relationship with the dead. "The Heavenly Love," for instance, asks that "the grave / And memory shall not drag on my desire!" (148, line 10); and "April" again meditates on the cycles of nature as "I invoke / And fall on the profoundness of the dead" (152, lines 13–14). Meanwhile "A Bacchic Theatre" mirrors a ritual that Cooper documents in the joint diary:

> Michael and I climb to our Bacchic temple by the Matterhorn Ridge, where we exchanged rings last year, where we read the funeral service to our undiscovered Dead, flinging clods of thyme into the torrent . . . [in reading *Alastor* aloud we feel] the high wild sacredness, the sense of motion that is beyond our directing, that we can follow into regions of life larger than we can of ourselves conceive. . . . in that mood we grow and increase in happiness. Little moths dance about in religious eddies and the air twinkles itself. . . . one is able by moments to feel how it is with the blessed. We kiss over solemn altar stone in this midst of our peculiar little Bacchic theatre and re-dedicate ourselves to life and love . . . We feel that all we have suffered and enjoyed in our suffering yet enjoying lives can be expressed by our god . . . and we will be as free as the forests and streams in our verse.[21]

The sonnet that results, reads:

> There is a spot given of a god to be
> A tiny, sylvan theatre—a seat;
> Most common flowers are growing at our feet.
> Wild thyme and little tufts of barberry,
> With shoots of willow herb: in tragedy
> We flung them earthy on the stream to meet,

---

[21] *Works and Days*. MSS Add. 46787, July 31, 1898. (EC). fol. 74r, 74v. The British Library. For an extended study of the "marriage" ceremony referred to from the previous year, see Bickle "Living Willfully."

> To hallow our lost dead: but now we greet
> A tomb, as fair as the tomb of Semele
> Drest fragrant with the vine, to life we spring;
> We grow, increase in happiness; the air
> Is twinkling itself: we have in sight
> The solemn fir-trees thickening up the height;
> We have the exultation, the despair,
> And all the lonesomeness of love to sing. (WH 155)

Both recountings of this Bacchic event document a pagan, eco-decadent entanglement with the natural environment, with the dead, and with each other. It is both "tiny" and "theatre"—both deeply, uniquely personal, yet with a dramatic and tragic tenor worthy of classic tales that have universal appeal. Here, in this theatre, thyme's ritual merges the present and the previous visit. In this place, time—past, present and future—become intertwined, as do the joint speakers' complex emotions. Like Semele, mother of Dionysus, theirs is a tale of both sacrifice and resurrection, despite "despair," "we grow, increase in happiness." The journal entry makes clear this is a rebirth of their relationship—both as lovers and as authors.

The many poems of *The Longer Allegiance* are simply too numerous and complex to even begin to treat in full here; but as a brief gloss, about midway through, the focus shifts away from the specifics of James's death and the poets instead explore their more general and universal connection to the dead as a foundation for their love for one another. Continuing to employ a paradoxical dialectic of absence and presence, the remaining poems celebrate the unity of all things, living and dead, in God and/or in Nature; articulate the point of view of the dead toward God and toward the living; sing the praises of beauty and wisdom in present experience as opposed to dwelling in the past; express the poets' deepening love for one another after several bouts of severe illness, and in the last poems, as we will see in the next section, begin to respond to the death of Whym Chow. Some of these in the second half also frankly express homoerotic desire, bringing together the pagan and Christian, and references to physical, spiritual, and post-mortem union in literally productive ways, as in "Unity."

In "Unity," the poets locate themselves at Ostia, an ancient Roman site, and together, "Perceive[d] the rule of the great peace." They entreat one another:

> Love, were it possible that thou and I,
> Being one day together soul to soul,
> At shore of some wide waters, in the flush
> Of roses tinging them, might so draw nigh
> That we might feel of our accord the hush,
> Binding all creatures, of God's pure control! (WH 167, lines 9–14)

This is a Paterian quest for experience—for ecstasy and its aftermath. As in the Dionysian impulses discussed in Chapter 1, here Bradley and Cooper desire the active pursuit ("of our accord") of an utterly complete union with one another—perhaps through physical consummation or perhaps through death—which they believe will beget an experience of the all-consuming awareness of God's unifying presence. Similarly, the final poem of *Wild Honey*, the second in the cycle with the title "Good Friday,"[22] invokes both the pagan, "the flood of Styx" (*WH* 194, line 2) and the Christian, "the deep-blooded crucifix" (l. 7) and then concludes:

> A Power is with me that can love, can die,
> That loves, and is deserted, and abides;
> A loneliness that craves me and enthralls:
> And I am one with that extremity,
> One with that strength. I hear the alien tides
> No more, no more the universe appals. (WH 194, lines 9–14)

Both "Unity" and "Good Friday" are, on the surface, about union with the Divine, here depicted as a lonely Power that both craves and enthralls the speaker. Yet, we must not forget that the speaker, Michael Field, is not one, but *two* who become "one with [and perhaps in] that extremity, / One with that strength," thereby making this poem, like so many of their others, about queer intersubjectivity and co-authorship. To apply terms that Walter Pater used in his conclusion to *The Renaissance*, this elegiac sequence culminates in what could just as easily be viewed as an aesthetic, as opposed to a religious, manifesto: *The Longer Allegiance*, in helping the Michael Fields mourn, also moves them from the

---

[22] According to Ivor Treby's catalogue, the "Good Friday" lyric that roughly marks the end of the first third of *The Longer Allegiance* was written in 1899, while the final poem was written earlier, in 1897.

"impression of the individual in his isolation" to the "fruit of a quickened, multiplied consciousness" (Pater 218, 220).

Thus, in each of these examples, Michael Field's process of writing and the temporal repetition of ritual facilitate the "normal" trajectory of mourning. Pagan, Christian, and sometimes ghostly tropes are appropriated and melded to create temporal and spatial environs in which the poets continue to co-exist with "their dead"; and these experiences are documented within a recognizably domestic and generally outdoor setting. The *Thyme* in *Wild Honey*'s title helps time become a place. Mourning—letting go—is accomplished by detaching from the deceased as they were and substituting a transformed relationship with the dead, here and now. The dead are represented as gone but not really gone—as at once absent and present—since Bradley and Cooper's life and love involves rituals for/with the dead and talking, and importantly, writing about them.

With Sophocles' *Antigone*, whose words title the sonnet cycle, Michael Field proclaims: "I owe a longer allegiance to the dead than to the living: in that world I shall abide for ever." Indeed, through their elegies for James, as for Emma Cooper and Robert Browning, the dead and the living do share the same world. For "Michael" and "Henry," this belief is a phenomenological and spiritual philosophy of life: an elegiac Aesthetic style and a practice of the self that makes possible, and becomes inscribed within, their writing in both drama and verse. Their "longer allegiance to the dead" informs their sense of themselves as co-authors and the rhetoric they use to represent their relationship; it provides them with a spiritual practice; ameliorates their griefs; creates pleasurable community with their dead and with one another; and celebrates their homoerotic bonds and desires. Michael Field's enduring allegiance to their dead thereby provides scaffolding for their ongoing allegiance to one another, through the exercise of paradox that makes possible the productive management of sameness and difference, absence and presence, self and other—as in the important lyric from *Underneath the Bough*, "It was deep April," where, "My Love and I took hands and swore / Against the world to be / Poets and lovers evermore," only to then head into the Underworld, scoffing at those "who spent no hour among the dead."

The "Asian bacchant"

So far, these Michael Field texts comprise a relatively sanguine approach to the process of mourning. When we read the diaries beside the poetry, we see that in a fairly straightforward and Freudian sense, as per *Mourning and Melancholia*, Bradley and Cooper's mourning is "successful" and their elegies have helped to make it so. Their practices of mourning may appear colorful, but grief over Emma Cooper, Robert Browning, and James Cooper subsides; and the co-authors' attachment to one another is augmented as a substitute for the deceased.

However, when Bradley and Cooper's dog, Whym Chow, unexpectedly took ill in 1906 and had to be put down, it catapulted them into a veritable orgy of mourning so prolonged and extreme that it alienated most of their friends.[23] Mourning Whym Chow appears to contribute to their subsequent conversion to Catholicism, which, as the next chapter will demonstrate, resulted in topical, if not stylistic, changes in their writing.[24] The tragic event also resulted in nearly one-hundred tear-stained diary pages reliving the dog's last days and a substantial quantity of poetry (mostly by Cooper). A few of the poems, as I noted earlier, were included in *Wild Honey*; with some revision, Bradley republished those along with most of the others in *Whym Chow: Flame of Love* (1914) after Cooper's death in a gesture to mourn and honor both the dog and her Fellow. I now turn to a sampling of these poems, since their representations of bereavement and the lost love object differ from Michael Field's other elegiac texts. Here I argue that because the queer function of the Michaels' relationship with Whym Chow renders it different than their relationship with the rest of their loved ones, mourning him creates problems that the co-authors attempt to negotiate with literary tropes that differ from those in their earlier elegies. Their mourning of Chow, in Freudian terms, "fails"; yet to paraphrase Jack Halberstam, it

---

[23] Dever observes how, after Chow's death, "the world quickly splits into the good and the bad": the good being Marie Sturge Moore and the household serving boy; the bad including Forbes the servant, Ricketts and Shannon, Berenson, and (at least for a while) Mary Costelloe, by now married to Berenson (185).

[24] The conversion to Catholicism raises another complex set of issues. For solid analyses of this topic, see Cauti, Fraser ("Religious Poetry"), Roden, Snodgrass, and Thain.

is an artfully queer failure: one that, at least to some extent, also anticipates later queer elegiac practices.

Michael Field's earlier elegiac writing, as we have seen, moves toward the resolution of grief. In texts that completely stand on their own, like the ones for Emma Cooper and Robert Browning, the mourning narrative is completed by the end of the poem. In the earlier elegies that occur in a sequence, such as those for James Cooper, the resolution of mourning is achieved by the end of the series. In contrast, *Whym Chow: Flame of Love* articulates inconsolable loss, along with pleas for Chow's return, throughout the collection's thirty poems. To start, the first lyric's title, "I. Requiescat," or "rest in peace," ironically contrasts the desperate tone and actions of the speaker. There is no peace here. Instead, the poem melodramatically begins, "I call along the Halls of Suffering" (WC 9, line 1); and as it unfolds, the grief-stricken survivor releases "reverberated cries / out of deep wounds, out of each fiery spring / Of nerve, or piteous anguish of surprise" (lines 2–4). The speaker frantically paces the house, whose hallways become "grand vaults" in the chow's absence; but the "patter of thy feet" is not forthcoming and thus the empty home becomes hell on earth: "Loud Halls, O Hades of the living" (lines 5, 6, 9). As the opening text of an elegiac sequence, such bathetic proclamations of misery are perhaps not out of place; yet bathos persists even in many of the later poems.

For example, "XXI. Adveni, Creator Spiritus," opens with loss, "My arms, my arms are void" (WC 40, line 1); and each stanza develops a variation, such as "My ears, my ears are still" (line 7) and "Mine eyes, mine eyes are blank" (line 13). However, the speaker's heart is not empty: "My heart, my heart—ah no! / Core of my love there art thou ever hard— / There clasped, there heard, there seen in constant glow" (lines 19–21); and here we see how the mourning process has "failed" because the speaker has not detached from the lost love object. In fact, in a rather heretical request that gestures toward how "failure" is about social expectation rather than feeling, the bereaved implores God to bring Whym Chow back, as proof of the Holy Spirit's power. The well-known hymn to which the title of the poem refers, begins:

| *Veni, Creator Spiritus,* | Come, Holy Spirit, Creator blest, |
| *mentes tuorum visita,* | and in our souls take up Thy rest; |

| *imple superna gratia* | come with Thy grace and heavenly aid |
| *quae tu creasti pectora.* | to fill the hearts which Thou hast made. |

In their version, Michael Field asks to be filled as well; and Chow, elsewhere associated with Christ, here becomes Christ and the Holy Spirit, simultaneously:

> O God, O God, O might
> Of Life Creative, let me hold again
> The ruddy form my arms would lose on tight
> Their cynosure my eyes attain;
> Tingle my ears with every sound they love;
> Oh, re-embody! Be thy Spirit proved. (lines 25–30)

Although, as I discussed in the previous section, Michael Field did experience communion with their dead, phenomenologically, as a "real" event, the commanding, incantatory character of the speaker's plea that the dead return—and, in particular, the sensory focus that he return *as he had been*—render the affect (and effect) of these verses quite different from the elegies in *Underneath the Bough* or *The Longer Allegiance*. In the previous elegies, learning "how love knits me with the loved one now" seems to happen of its own accord; whereas with Whym Chow, the process is far from smooth or automatic. In fact, "XXVI" addresses its eponymous subject with anger: "When others are about me and the lips / Of any other bid me to forget" (WC 53, line 1), "[I] curse these comforters who bring me death" (line 31).

Within the Victorian and Freudian models we have considered thus far, including Michael Field's inventive variations on these models in their earlier elegies, the productive relationship between memory and mourning can be described as hyper-remembering.[25] Through hyper-remembering, "the survivor resuscitates the lost other in the space of the psyche, replacing an actual absence with an imaginary presence" (Clewell 44). This permits the mourner to assess the loss; but eventually, memories of the deceased fall short of the real deceased and the mourner "comes to an objective determination that the lost object no longer exists … The

---

[25] Many thanks to David Orvis for bringing my attention to Clewell's treatment of *The Ego and the Id* and its relevance to my discussion, later on, of Michael Moon's concept of *active mourning*.

Freudian grief work seeks, then, to convert loving remembrances into futureless memory" (Clewell 44). However, unlike Michael Field's other experiences of mourning, with regard to the dog, "Henry" and "Michael" cannot take the high road and claim "Others may drag at memory's fetter." Instead, as if pulling on his leash, Whym Chow literally drags them deeper into their memories, thwarting detachment.

Some of the memories cited in the *Whym Chow* collection relive moments related to his death, such as his still, broken body ("III. Crowned with wine-steeped"; "X. Semper Jam") and his funeral ("IV. O Dionysus"). Other elegies attempt to bring him back through the kind of hyper-remembering described above, especially by invoking strong sense memories of daily activities. To this end, "XXIV. Loved Confessionals there are" develops a rich, charmingly childlike image of sharing secrets with Chow: "down my face was pressed / In thy wondrous fur, enwrought / Of the gilded motes of sun / . . . / There I hid my joys and woes" (WC 47, lines 51–2, 58). Likewise, "XXV. I want you, little Love, not from the skies," expresses desire for little remembered moments including Chow's scowl, his soft quick feet and his "resolute, fine jaw" (WC 50, line 11). The poem also declares:

> I want you, when, to guard our door you rushed
> In whirlwind loyalty; or when you brushed
> Against the knee your little chine with soft
> Claim for caress, ...
> Or when reverberant as echoed shout
> Your face proclaimed the "Yes" of going out. (lines 21–30, *passim*)

Ultimately, the speaker admits that living with Chow *is* different from remembering him; but still, she does not stop desiring her dog "Not far away, as visions may appear / O apple of our eyes, but with us here!" (lines 59–60). It seems that, because their desired outcome is (of course) not possible, the Michaels, rather than detaching, begin to represent their "visions" as real, resulting in numerous eccentric diary passages like the one about the inn that began this chapter.

Hyper-remembering of this ilk—that does *not* become Clewell's "futureless memory" —is, in part, enabled by the kind of thinking that we see in "VI. What is the other name of Love," which recalls with great detail, memories of Chow's behavior in the past that mirrors the speakers' in the present, such as Chow's Bacchic frenzy and "rage of welcome" (*WC* 16, line 7) every time they returned home:

> The state that surged around a daily chance,
> If thy Beloved should enter: in thy Dance
> A worship, in thy light, a universe. (lines 45–7)

Here, it is implied that the Michaels would celebrate with the same frenzied joy, if only Whym Chow could come home to them. Thus in this and many of the *Whym Chow* verses, the texts create a "crossing and interlacing" of subjectivities and of past and present. For instance, in "IX. My loved one is away from me," Bradley is elsewhere and Cooper muses about how she and Chow used to wait together in such moments in the past, when, "For her we loved in absence and together" (*WC* 22, line 11). Now, however, both Bradley *and* Whym Chow are "loved one[s who are] away." Quite similarly, "XII. Absence," memorializes Chow's woeful face behind the windowpane whenever Bradley and Cooper left the house, again taking a precious memory from the past and projecting it upon a parallel meaning in the present. Since they can't let go of these powerful memories, these elegies will not move them toward consolation.

The often-analyzed "V. Trinity" is germane here, as is "XXII. Sleeping Together, Sleep." Both texts employ Aesthetic paradox in order to merge past and present and to further Bradley and Cooper's eroticized narrative of their beloved dog as conduit for queer desire and interwoven subjectivity. As a new puppy in 1898, Bradley prophetically rhapsodized: "Oh I love him! Hennie loves him. He is Michael's own little brimstone soul. Hennie loves him! Amen."[26] Here we see origins both of Bradley's ongoing identification with the dog and the deployment of a transitive logic that establishes a dynamic connection between the three. After the dog's death, Bradley publicly confesses "Nay, thou art my eternal attribute / . . . / The very essence of the thing I am" (*WH* 191, lines 1–3) and Cooper makes clear the dog's function in expressing her love for Bradley when she proclaims:

---

[26] *Works and Days*. MSS Add. 46787, February 3, 1898. (KB). fol. 12v. The British Library.

> I did not love him for myself alone
> I loved him that he loved my dearest love
> O God, no blasphemy
> It is to feel we loved in trinity (WC 15, lines 1–4)

Cooper goes on (some critics would say defensively) to compare their trinity of love to the divine love that comforted Christ on the cross; and thus it is clear that for the Michaels, the gravity of this relationship cannot be underestimated; this is no silly love game. As the lyric concludes, Whym Chow is "O symbol of our perfect union, strange / Unconscious Bearer of Love's interchange" (lines 17–18).

To be sure, Chow's death—like age, disease, and their conversion—challenges and changes Bradley and Cooper's always developing notions of their individual and joined selves, as poets and otherwise. These challenges seemed, to the co-authors, intensely insurmountable at times. Dever identifies, in *Works and Days*, journal entries that document the destruction of Bradley and Cooper's intimacy; she asserts of their (especially Cooper's) trinitarian rhetoric, "[b]ecause Michael Field remains a trinity, his functional form remains intact. This enables Cooper to leave Bradley without actually leaving her. And she does, for the Catholic Church" (Dever 195). I read *Works and Days'* treatment of these shifts in Bradley and Cooper's relationship less literally—more indicative of hyperbolic feeling in the moment. Who has not said or written something in an extravagant fit of passion and then later recanted or modified their position? In analyzing the eight-year arc from Bradley and Cooper's loss of Whym Chow to their own illnesses and deaths (the subject of the next chapter), I see in the events of their joined lives, and in their creative output and ongoing re-visioning of form, not the lessening of their intimacy, but rather an ongoing revision and perhaps even deepening of it. But this required, for Michael Field, creative, indeed strategic and performative, queer orientation toward their trinitarian relationship with the deceased Chow.

In the *Whym Chow* poems, the beloved pet is not merely a metaphorical symbol of their union, as the earlier thyrsus and bramblebough were. Instead, in "XXII. Sleeping together: Sleep" Michael Field develops the themes of "Trinity" by creating a picture of domestic life that is insistently haptic: physical, intimate, and erotic. The aspect of this long poem that most interests me here are repeated references to Whym Chow as witness to physical manifestations of Bradley and Cooper's love and repeated descriptions of how he completes, invigorates, and blesses them. His presence makes their already existing union more palpable. For instance, the first stanza refigures their bedroom as the site of Genesis, "that former deep / of night that was before the world" (WC 42, lines 4–5); and the speaker describes them sleeping "The lull of thy breath on the air / That held the lull of our breath there" (lines 2–3). Whym Chow is both the child and Creator of what "issues thence, / Motion, sigh of heart, caress / Came through sable void to bless" (lines 13–14). As the poem unfolds, the speakers' joined bodies remain the focus: they are together and he greets them in the second stanza; they possess "deeds and dreams" and he "re-illumes" them and "fills" then with "newness." In the third stanza, Whym Chow's presence reinforces a pleasurable awareness of Bradley and Cooper's bodies in relation to one another: in their shared bed, eyes mingled in the sunlight, breath shared on the breeze, they "knew" and "relished well" the "spell of our bodies" (WC 43). The next stanza, on loving, uses euphemisms of eating, flame, and breathing that culminate in "sacred passion blent"; but all euphemism disappears in the penultimate verse, where Chow, associated with ivy and "life's dance" leads them to consider what can only be a Bacchanal, and they are "taught the bliss that must express / Unity of blessedness" (44, lines 69–70). Thus, as Roden and others have noted, recalling memories with the dog becomes a space where Trinitarian rhetoric can bless (or camouflage) Michael Field's love as a couple.[27] In the only gesture toward healing in the entire collection, the elegy closes, much like "Unity," by invoking the power of erotic union, should the couple let go their grief over Whym long enough to take solace in one another:

---

[27] I would argue that critics have made too much over the years, both of assumptions that Bradley and Cooper no longer shared "an active sex life" after Chow's death/the Catholic conversion and of what that fact (if true) might mean. Such assumptions, I would suggest, are first, unable to be proven, and second, not useful. From a feminist, queer, and crip perspectives, there are countless ways to share an intimate relationship, with or without "sex," and equally countless ways to be erotic; and none of these need remain unchanged over the course of time. For more on reclamatory uses of the term "crip" see Chapter 5, note 16.

> Now that thou are dead we meet
> Still together in the sweet
> Company of close-drawn breath,
> If we banish grief from death (WC 54, lines 85–8)

Finally, although many of the Whym Chow lyrics I have addressed thus far, like Michael Field's earlier texts on mourning, refer to quotidian activities and familiar, domestic settings, it cannot be ignored that many more of the Whym Chow poems starkly veer away from the familiar by figuring the dog through extreme Othering, especially using the language of Orientalism. In life as well as death, Michael Field's verse and journals refer to the chow as Dionysus, Bacchus, God, Christ, the Holy Spirit, and a wild Orient Prince bedecked with gemlike, flamelike fur. Upon the puppy's arrival, they write he is:

> a wolf with civilization, softness, an oriental with husky passion-white-rolling eyeballs, the power of inward frenzy-velvet manners and the savagery of eastern armies behind. I suppose our new love of animals is a desire to get into another kingdom. We cannot reach the kingdom of the dead—we can penetrate into the kingdom of animals. Mortals all![28]

Such Orientalist rhetoric becomes common for much of their subsequent writing about Whym Chow. "VIII. Out of the East," for instance, opens with the chow's fur as a treasure chest of exotic gems set in gold:

> Jasper and jacinth, amber and fine gold
> The topaz, ruby, the fire-opal, grey
> And lucent agate covered thee with glory,
> O Eastern Prince from fuming China hoary
> That on thy orient rug celestial lay,
> Thy coat a web of treasure manifold! (WC 20, lines 1–6)

The poem then unfolds with unfortunately stereotypical depictions of the East. The chow, represented as a capricious and somewhat slothful sultan is dubbed, "O Orient Prince, thou Asian

---

[28] *Works and Days*. MSS Add. 46787, [January 28?] 1898. (KB). fol 11. The British Library.

Michael Field and the Elegiac Tradition 201

Bacchant" (20); he has a lustful eye, is slave to passion, indulges in "ancient cruelty," and practices strange rituals of hospitality, which are mentioned, with race and nation, in the context of empire's expansion:

> Thou would'st not break thy trance save at the house
> Of welcome: then the glories of thy race,
> Then dance and sovereign courtesy, elation
> As though would'st heap the substance of a nation
> At feet that had the ritual of thy face,
> And all thy gems in flash, thy gold in shower. (WC 21, lines 37–42)

Repeatedly, Whym Chow's appearance and personality result in exotic description, such as "XIV. Fur for Mandarins," which similarly references rare gems, cruel behavior, and bright tropical colors. Elsewhere, he is "Alert, like strange Anubis, toward the sky" (WC 23, line 44).

Studies of nineteenth-century mourning often note the Victorians' difficulty talking about the unknowable in an increasingly scientific and material age (Wheeler xii). It makes sense, therefore, that Michael Field employ Orientalized imagery when representing, in both death and life, the beloved pet who, as Vanita, Roden, and others have argued, by the turn of the century, functioned as a defensive strategy in the context of heteronormativity, a necessary conduit or proxy for queer desire. We can then read these sublimely over-the-top elegies for Whym as a form of *l'engrenage* that casts the unknown and alienating aspects of death among other things also considered unknowable: female and same-sex desire during the rise of sexology; the far reaches of the colonies in an age of increasing anxiety about the stability of British empire; and even the problem of continuing their literary careers (not to mention their Sapphic relationship), given their recent conversion to Catholicism. In fact, Michael Field's journal entries and published work from these years include increasing references to imperialism that tellingly project their personal investment in controversial or difficult subjects onto to certain kinds of Others.[29] For instance, they marvel, like their fellow Aesthetes, at the strange, compelling beauty of Japanese art; and they worry, with much

---

[29] For a similar treatment of Michael Field's uses of "the East," see Kristin Mahoney, "Michael Field's Eric Gill."

patriotism, about the Boer War's losses, projecting their hope and fears as authors onto England: "Like our Country we shall face the difficulties of Empire building when circumstances are stubborn. I believe both England and Michael Field shall win."[30] When they learn of England's victory, Bradley and Cooper mark empire's mastery by employing parallel mastery over the animal kingdom (which as noted above, they think more penetrable than the kingdom of the dead): they joyfully make their other dog Musico (their English basset, not the untamable Orient Prince) drum out "God Save the Queen" with his paws.[31] In this context, we can better contextualize the Orientalized, inconsolable mourning of Whym Chow that differs so strikingly from the elegiac conventions Michael Field had developed thus far.

I suggest that the function of Bradley and Cooper's interminable grief for Whym Chow (and the related, eccentric elegies) is to strategically preserve the erotic proxy they have, by this point, created to stand in for "Michael Field"—not only Michael Field as lovers but Michael Field as identity—as joint authors and queerly partnered selves. Further, due to increasing social disapprobation of same-sex love at the turn of the century, the precariousness of this proxy—imbued with anxieties about mortal fragility and the would-be marginal status of the secret Michael Field self—is here figured through the rhetoric of imperialism with its anxious tensions of fear and mastery. Put another way, mother, father, and Browning can successfully be mourned in the Freudian sense because Michael Field appropriates Victorian notions of the eternal present, reunion, etc. such that the dead pass on while bolstering Bradley and Cooper's complex, often contested experience of selfhood. Later however, mourning Whym Chow, given the dog's complex, queer relationship to Bradley and Cooper, and their (by now) even more complex, queer relationship to one another, cannot cease—it *must* continue—not as an unconscious impulse, but as a conscious act on their part, if "they" (given their current equation with the dog) are to survive as queer and dual subjects.

At this juncture one might be tempted to state that Whym Chow's death presents, in Freudian terms, a classic instance of

---

[30] *Works and Days*. MSS Add. 46788, December 31, 1899. (EC). fol. 144v. The British Library.

[31] *Works and Days*. MSS Add. 46789, [January] 1900. (EC). fol. 9v. The British Library.

mourning become melancholia, in which the mourner refuses object cathexis; that the poems establish an identification of the ego with the abandoned object, to whom a strong fixation already existed. Most likely, Michael Field's exasperated friends would agree with such a "diagnosis," along with its narcissistic implications. Their neighbor and close friend, fellow Aesthete Charles Ricketts puts it bluntly in this letter dated April 16, 1906:

> My dear Michael. It is now two months that you have bored and distressed me by references to the death of your dog. Not only do I dislike this degradation of the majesty of grief, but in the event of this so preying on your mind it should be your duty to try and put order and a little silence in the place of this angry din of regret; this is your duty to yourself and others . . . All this is journalism; it is not charming but pompous journalism . . . I trust your common sense will prove to you that you jar and are out of tune.[32]

However, other characteristics of melancholia do not apply, such as lack of motivation to engage in the symbolic realm by speaking or writing. Nor do the co-authors display the aggression typically associated with melancholy, where anger or ambivalence toward the deceased is turned inward on the self, as in the "melancholic mourning of modernist elegy" that begins to characterize many twentieth-century poems (Clewell 54).

Nevertheless, we should not dismiss *Whym Chow: Flame of Love*'s potential resonances with modernist elegy categorically or too swiftly, given how both depart from the conventions of nineteenth-century elegy and Victorian insistence on mourning's end. In the aftermath of World War I, T. S. Eliot's *Four Quartets* calls "every poem an epitaph" (Canto V, line 12). Such a modernist shift is, of course, congruent with how in his the post-war *The Ego and the Id* (1923), Freud refigures his previously strict binary between mourning and melancholia and instead posits that an elegiac ego is formed during an endless and inherently melancholic mourning process. Accordingly, Jahan Ramazani notes how the modernist elegies of poets like Eliot, Pound, Hardy, Stevens, and Plath "rebel against generic norms but reclaim through rebellion" and "focus on the psychological structures and literary devices specific to the elegy" (2, 3). Such observations about modernist

---

[32] Ricketts to Bradley. Add. 61723 (1906). fol. 11. The British Library.

misgivings about the redemptive power of mourning recall Marion Thain's important assertions that Michael Field be considered, not just as late Victorians, but in the context of modernism, something I, too, have been suggesting throughout this book. All this said, Michael Field's elegies for Whym Chow also exhibit resonances with what Rebecca Mitchell identifies as the resistances –and pleasures—in late Victorian women's shifting practices toward mourning dress. Despite the pain the poems document—indeed, perform—*Whym Chow* also enacts Michael Field's characteristically Dionysian engagement with sublime feeling. Their *Whym Chow* elegies become, in all their resistance and remaking of the form, a site in which to wallow in Paterian impression.

Using these ideas (and their shortcomings) as a jumping-off point, I would like to propose as a useful model for understanding the elegiac writing about Whym Chow what queer critic Michael Moon terms *active mourning*: a kind of fetishism rescued from Freud's definition of fetishism as an unconscious act of identification with the maternal phallus, castration, Oedipalization, and homosexual panic. Active mourning, which refuses discretion, renunciation of the lost loved one, and mourning's cessation, according to Moon, is a "*conscious* means of extending our homoerotic relations, even with the dead" (235). And, as Moon demonstrates in examples ranging from Walt Whitman to AIDS activism, active mourning can give rise to new and different elegiac forms that are particularly useful for queer elegy. This kind of active mourning is useful because those deemed outside sexual norms may find traditional prescriptions for mourning "fundamentally normalizing and consequently ... may seem to diminish the process and to foreclose its possible meanings instead of making it more accessible to understanding" (Moon 235). It acknowledges that, contra Victorian (and later) progress narratives of mourning, there is no *telos* of mourning, only traversal; and that those who are already queerly oriented in the world perhaps may feel this more keenly than others.

Thus, I think Moon's concept is a useful frame from which to interpret Bradley and Cooper's prolonged and dramatic mourning of Whym Chow. Despite the disapprobation of even their closest friends, the Michael Fields refuse to contain and repress their urgent needs and feelings of bereavement. Instead, their active mourning results, among other things, in fetishizing, by Orientalizing and eroticizing, the body of Whym Chow, which, by

1906, has also become their collective (both dual and Trinitarian) body and identity. Thus, as Michael Moon urges AIDS mourners to do a century later, Michael Field "actively cultivates the erotic component of grief and sorrow," and focuses on "bodily abundance and supplementarity" despite the fact that others, then and now, consider such acts, in their excess and eroticism, to be inappropriate and scandalous (Moon 235). In the case of Michael Field and Whym Chow, such active mourning manifests in elegies that, as we have seen, unabashedly plead for the departed's return and cultivate, through erotic, sensory language, their trinity—an elegiac (triple) ego formed by "taking the lost other into the structure of one's own identity, a form of preserving the lost object in and as the self" (Clewell 61). Entries from the joint diary can be read as active mourning as well: both those passages that express endless grief, anger, or other tumultuous thoughts, and those that insist that Chow still accompanies them, in body as well as spirit.

In this chapter, I have focused on Michael Field's elegies for their personal dead, texts that depart from the elegiac tradition whereby the (male) poet sings in honor of his predecessor's passing and thereby becomes his successor. Future work would do well to examine Michael Field's numerous elegies for public figures with whom they were less personally involved—Christina Rossetti, Matthew Arnold, Oscar Wilde, among others—and to assess whether these participate in or depart from classic, Victorian, and women's elegiac traditions, as well as how they compare to the personal elegies I have considered in this project. As for the texts we have examined here, steeped, as they are, in the languages of Nature, myth, religion, and Orientalism, and pressing the limits of time and space, Michael Field's varied expressions of mourning share discursive characteristics, if not material practices, with the many Victorians who, through Christian mourning, Spiritualism, and/or Imperialism, found themselves contemplating the boundaries of their immediate world and everyday experience. Michael Field's later, queer erotics of mourning Whym Chow, like their earlier elegiac texts and rituals, reside within this tradition; but their revisionary poetics also move beyond it through active mourning strategies that attempt to gear into and negotiate the unknowable (death), the unspeakable (queer desire), and the unthinkable (separation from one another).

After Chow's death, Bradley and Cooper retreat to one of their favorite places, Rottingdean, and ponder moving their home permanently away from Paragon. Cooper records in the journal, "Michael is now like a Queen without a crown, a goddess without her attribute: we live shorn days and desolate is all before us. We must leave if [Michael is to get better.] We must make all things new."[33] This is not the first time, of course, that the Michaels have made this proclamation; and here, as before, we see a glimmer of what we might term queer hope: they know their mourning for Whym Chow will traverse unconventional ground; and although they don't know where it will lead, they take steps, albeit antinormative and queerly excessive ones, toward a vague and new future vision. As it turns out, they don't move house from Paragon. Thus through their return to Rottingdean, and their subsequent return to Paragon, Bradley and Cooper anticipate the complex and conflicted vicissitudes of queer hope, queer identity, and queer relationship as they have before in so many ways: with a "backward glance that enacts a future vision" (Muñoz, *Cruising Utopia* 4).

---

[33] This journal entry reproduces a letter Cooper sent to Marie Sturge Moore. *Works and Days*. MSS Add. 46795, [January] 1906. (EC). folio 20v. The British Library.

5

Becoming Catholic, Desiring Disability: Michael Field's Devotional Verse

"You never attained to Him?" "If to attain
    Be to abide, then that may be."
"Endless the way, followed with how much pain!"
    "The way was He."
        —Alice Meynell, "Via, et Veritas, et Via" (1902)

    Lady of silences
    Calm and distressed
    Torn and most whole
    Rose of memory
    Rose of forgetfulness
    Exhausted and life-giving
    Worried reposeful
    The single Rose
    Is now the Garden
    Where all loves end
        —T. S. Eliot, from *Ash Wednesday* (1930)

"He detests religious poetry ... and he breaks into a frenzy about the psalms, Verlaine's 'Catholic work,' and *Poems of Adoration*. He Wd not know I had written it. [He says] there is nothing in it like me."[1] Thus, with unfiltered bitterness, writes Edith Cooper on 8 May 1912, after a visit from Michael Field's close friend and fellow aesthete, Charles Ricketts. Indeed, for many students and literary scholars, a first encounter with Michael Field's Catholic

---

[1] *Works and Days*. MSS Add. MS 46802, May 8, 1912. (EC). fol. 48r. The British Library.

poems engenders much the same response as Ricketts's. Readers tend not to like the Catholic poems, and (in my experience) their negativity is often articulated in a tone of disappointment, exasperation, and even betrayal. At least on a surface reading, *Poems of Adoration* (1912), written largely by Cooper, and *Mystic Trees* (1913), written largely by Bradley, seem to lack many of the elements—sexy sapphics, playful fauns, witty commentary on art, love poems filled with longing—that have long drawn literary critics and other readers to Michael Field's earlier verse. Their Catholic poems do not seem to touch modern readers in the way that the devotional verse of Christina Rossetti or Gerard Manley Hopkins continues to do. Perhaps it should not be a surprise that *Poems of Adoration* and *Mystic Trees* have remained relatively unstudied compared to other Michael Field texts.[2]

This chapter begins by asserting that Michael Field's devotional verses should not, in fact, be so quickly categorized as anomalies. Here, I build upon the observations of Hilary Fraser and Marion Thain, who each argue that *Poems of Adoration* and *Mystic Trees* possess many elements also found in Michael Field's earlier poetry—that they represent a shift, rather than a radical departure, from Michael Field's other writing. My work in this chapter considers *Poems of Adoration* and *Mystic Trees* in context of the other revisionary experiments in genre and form that this book has addressed thus far: the creative anachronisms of Michael Field's closet drama: *Long Ago*'s creative engagement with Sapphic verse; the innovative picture-poems of *Sight and Song*; *Underneath the Bough*'s adaptation of Renaissance songbooks; and the two verse collections that experiment with elegy: *Wild Honey* and *Whym Chow, Flame of Love*. Broadly speaking, my findings about Michael Field's devotional lyrics are consistent with F. Elizabeth Gray's assertions about one of Bradley and Cooper's female, Catholic contemporaries who was also a prominent poet: Alice Meynell. Gray

---

[2] Hilary Fraser and Marion Thain have long provided the most extensive foundational treatment of *Mystic Trees* and *Poems of Adoration*, with Leire Barerra Medrano and LeeAnne Richardson making valuable recent contributions. Many Michael Field scholars mention biographical aspects of the co-authors' Catholic conversion, but most literary analyses of Michael Field's Catholic writing tend to focus more on selections from *Whym Chow, Flame of Love* and the posthumous collection, *The Wattlefold*, than upon the two collections that are the subject of my essay here. See also Kersh, Vanita, Roden, Cauti, and LaMonaca.

finds no incompatibility in Alice Meynell's Catholic poems and her other writing: "Style, faith, and politics were not incompatible elements to Meynell, indeed quite the reverse" ("Making Christ" 160).

Beyond defense or apologia, however, my aim in this chapter is to advance three claims. First, through close readings of selected verse from *Poems of Adoration* and *Mystic Trees*, I demonstrate how Michael Field sought to become *Catholic* poets by appropriating the formal, including metric, conventions of devotional poetics while also maintaining many of the queer characteristics of their earlier work; in terms of meter, these queer characteristics manifest themselves in shifting, ambiguous metrics that resonate with today's thinking about queer temporality. Second, by drawing upon recent insights from disability studies,[3] as well as my own previous claims that characterize Michael Field's ongoing revisionary projects as possessing qualities we today call both queer and feminist, I argue that Michael Field's Catholic verses engage the ineffable and the unknown as they articulate spiritual and homoerotic love and desire specifically in context of being, seeing, and desiring an embodied (female) subject in pain. Throughout, my approach to *Poems of Adoration and Mystic Trees* is *not* to categorize them as post-conversion texts posited against pre-conversion texts. Instead, I argue here that a more useful and interesting shift can be observed among the poems before and after Edith's diagnosis of bowel cancer in February 1911, when devotional poetry becomes a new way to navigate pain, desire, and disability.

Becoming "Catholic," remaining "Michael Field"

Studies of *Poems of Adoration* and *Mystic Trees* do not fail to note that, unlike Michael Field's other work, the co-authors were quite frank about the fact that Cooper wrote most of *Poems of Adoration* and Bradley wrote most of *Mystic Trees*.[4] Therefore,

---

[3] Cf. McRuer and Wilkerson, "Introduction" to *Desiring Disability*.
[4] In *The Michael Field Catalogue*, Ivor Treby conjectures that Bradley's contributions to *Poems of Adoration* may include the following: "The Blessed Sacrament," composed September 1908, "The Blessed Sacrament," composed July 1910, "Marcinus against Trees," composed April 1912, "The Flower Fadeth," composed March 1908, and "Recognition," composed 1908. He also asserts that Cooper's contributions to *Mystic Trees* are "The Homage of Death," composed in January 1911, "Qui Renovat Juventutem Meam," composed in September 1912, and "Moss," composed in 1913.

some foundational remarks on the authorship and organization of these two volumes perhaps are warranted before proceeding. First, as critics have often argued, Michael Field's claims to likeness, joint authorship, and shared subjectivity were always to a certain extent strategic, and by early critics, overemphasized and romanticized.[5] Bradley and Cooper wrote in separate rooms and then edited one another's work, sometimes delegating to each other responsibility for different characters or scenes. This process was not radically altered for these two devotional collections. Primary sources make clear that the books were written individually, yet Bradley and Cooper edited and ordered them collaboratively, and each felt more than a small degree of joint responsibility for both. For instance, on March 8, 1913, Cooper wrote to Father John Gray about "Bradley's" book: "I am getting anxious about 'Mystic Trees'—for lately there has been reconsiderence of my malady and much pain; and I always grow yearning and desirous for the work to be over."[6] Although Cooper is ill and technically not the author of *Mystic Trees*, "the work" belongs to Michael Field and thus is a matter demanding Cooper's attention as well as Bradley's.

As with all their books of verse, the poems in each of the two Catholic collections are not ordered by date of composition and the organizational structure of each volume is complex. *Poems of Adoration* is a series of verse meditations on the embodied experience of celebrating several of the Catholic Sacraments, including devotional reflection in anticipation of Mass, contemplation of saints and religious doctrines after receiving the Eucharist, and meditations after receiving Last Rites. As for *Mystic Trees*, its first two divisions ("Hyssop" and "Cedar") correspond to the volume's epigraph, and name Mary and Christ as the two mystic trees:

Hic Virgo Puerpera,	This Virgin mother
Hic Crux salutifera:	This saving Cross
Ambo ligna mystica	Both mystic trees
Haec hyssopus humilis	This humble hyssop
Illa cedrus nobilis	The noble cedar
Utraque vivifica.	Both quicken [revive]

---

[5] See, among others, Prins, "Sappho Doubled"; and Ehnenn, "Our Brains."
[6] Edith Cooper to John Gray, National Library of Scotland. Dept. 372 #16, fol. 7, 8 (March 8, 1913).

Notably, a sequential reading of the people and trees alluded to in the epigraph (Virgin, Cross; hyssop, cedar) misleadingly suggests that "Hyssop" (an aromatic plant used for various medicinal purposes) will be a section dedicated to Mary; and that "Cedar" (as in the wood of the cross) will be about Christ. Only when meticulous readers work through the volume do they gradually realize that the identity of the mystic trees is foreshadowed in the chiasmatic relation between the epigraph's lines 1–2 and 4–5. The first section of *Mystic Trees*, "Hyssop," is not about the Virgin Mary; instead, "Hyssop" presents a roughly chronological biography of Christ, calling to mind Christ's saving grace via Psalm 51: "Thou shalt purge me with hyssop and I shall be clean." The "Cedar" section then provides a similarly chronological account of the Virgin Mary's life, and especially resonates with her contemplations of Christ on the wooden cross. After "Cedar," the third section of *Mystic Trees* is titled "Sward," which means a stretch of grassy turf. "Sward" is, with some exception, a collection of verses contemplating nature, various saints' lives and other devotional topics inspiring the pleasant sensation of religious solace, perhaps like walking on grass. The poems in the brief, final section, "A Little While," illustrate that the faithful devotee of the two mystic trees (presumably the ailing Cooper) will, like Christ and Mary themselves, vanquish Death.

The poems composed prior to Cooper's cancer diagnosis can firmly be described as efforts and experiments in how to be devotional poets, writing about Catholic topics. Typical of Bradley and Cooper's obsessive tendencies when working on new subjects, especially historical events and people, in *Poems of Adoration* and *Mystic Trees* we observe the co-authors attempting to master a genre by meticulously depicting events (sacraments) and characters: Christ, the Virgin Mary, and Mary Magdalene in both collections; St. John the Divine, St. Clement, and Simeon among others in *Poems of Adoration*; and Joachim and Anna, St. Agnes, and Fr. Vincent McNabb among others in *Mystic Trees*. In the remainder of this section I examine how Michael Field experiment with Catholic topics within and against nineteenth-century prescriptions about devotional poetics but also alongside various formal and stylistic techniques familiar to readers of their earlier queer, feminist, aesthetic work. As the second half of this study shows, it is not until Cooper's cancer diagnosis in 1911 that we see Michael Field's devotional verse shifting from the worship of

Catholic figures to identifying with them—a shift in relationship and orientation nuanced by the poets' personal experiences with disability, illness, and pain.[7]

Victorian devotional verse, according to F. Elizabeth Gray, often portrays one's reflections on personal religious sentiment through tropes of confession, petition, praise, and meditation. From early nineteenth-century verse collections (such as John Keble's extraordinarily popular *The Christian Year* [1827]), through to the end of the century, Tractarian poetics emphasized feeling and perception, favoring characteristics such as poetic orthodoxy, correctness, and "Reserve," which can be defined as proper reverence for sacred matters that involved suggestion yet restraint in representing religious knowledge and the mysteries of faith (Mason 196). As Gray observes "[a]ppropriate subject matter, according to Keble, was to be found in the moral lessons taught by Nature (through the process Keble called Analogy) and

---

[7] While illness narratives, including cancer narratives, have long been a staple of literary disability studies, some theorists within critical disability studies today fiercely debate what constitutes a disability, including to what extent illnesses like cancer should be considered a disability. Strong proponents of the social model argue there is a difference between a disease and an impairment (which may result in a non-normate body yet a perfectly healthy one); such thinking might also invite making a distinction between the lived experience of the "healthy vs. unhealthy" disabled, chronic vs. acute illnesses, etc. On the other hand, critics of the social model would deem such thinking to depend too much on the concept of diagnosis and to erase the lived realities of pain irrespective of the social politics of built environment. In referring, in this essay, to Edith's cancer as a disability, I align my thinking with Alison Kafer in *Feminist, Queer, Crip*, whose work is self-described as a "friendly departure" from the social model and seeks to "pluralize the way we understand bodily instability" while still critiquing the "social exclusions based on and social meanings attributed to impairment" (7). I find Kafer's focus on lived experience, including the experiences of pain, social and political relationships, and thinking of the future, to be particularly helpful for addressing subjects whose historically contingent concepts of identity, embodiment, diagnosis, cure, etc. may be different from ours, today. For varied thinking on these debates, see, among many others, Susan Wendell, "Unhealthy Disabled, Treating Chronic Illnesses as Disabilities," *Hypatia* 16, no. 4 (Autumn 2001): 17–33; Tom Shakespeare, "The Social Model of Disability," *Research in Social Science and Disability* 2 (2002): 9–28; Emilia Nielsen, "Chronically Ill, Critically Crip?: Poetry, Poetics and Dissonant Disabilities," *Disability Studies Quarterly* 36, no. 4 (2016), n.p.; and Nirmala Erevelles, "Introduction" to *Disability and Difference in Global Contexts: Enabling a Transformative Body Politic* (Basingstoke: Palgrave Macmillan, 2011), 1–23.

in the emotional responses of the religious and sincere heart" ("Syren" 62). Perhaps rather surprisingly, there does not appear to be evidence in Britain of a nineteenth-century (Roman) Catholic poetics that differs significantly from Anglo-Catholic, Tractarian poetics. As Kirstie Blair writes, "Anglo-Catholicism and Roman Catholicism may have had significant theological and doctrinal differences, but on the general question of forms they were united" (199). Devotional styles differ significantly, of course (Hopkins from Rossetti, Field from Patmore, etc.), but these differences are due to individual temperament rather than to a generalized poetic sensibility informed by theology.[8] Thus Tractarian instruction for how to create Anglo-Catholic devotional verse is also apropos to nineteenth-century (Roman) Catholics writing devotional verse.[9] And indeed, although Michael Field's Dionysian proclivities might seem categorically opposed to Tractarian reserve, many other characteristics of Tractarian devotional poetry, especially depicting nature for the greater purpose of Keble's Analogy, can be found in Michael Field's exercises in writing Catholic verse.

For instance, in "Thou Comest Down to Die," composed in 1910, human spiritual joy finds its analogue in the beauty and spontaneity of natural animal actions:

Each day another girds
And binds Thee to the Wood.
I sing as singing birds,
The glory of Thy mood. (*MT* 44, lines 9–12)

Similarly, "O Lovely Host," also composed in 1910, draws a comparison between Christ and the desert rose:

I
O lovely Host
Thou art the Rose
That on us from the desert glows!

---

[8] For a non-Tractarian devotional provenance, cf. Barrera-Medrano who traces Michael Field's debt to Spanish mystic theology.
[9] Many thanks to Michael Hurley and Joshua King for their advice on this topic.

II
Thou art the Flower
Beloved so
Beyond all other flowers that blow. (*MT* 45, lines 1–6)

Such worshipful interaction with the natural world and finding spiritual/philosophical insight in the environment is not, as we know, new to Michael Field. For example, the images and allusions in "A Cette Heure Où J'ecris," [At this time where I write] create an apt example of Analogy in a manner that also resonates with well-known themes from their earlier work:

On the other side the road
Facing this our little parlour, glowed
Over by a murderous sun,
Is a hedge of holly deep, stone-dun:
And this hedge is as a leathern targe
Reared between us, and the open, large
Fields of mustered sunshine on the plain. (*MT* 139, lines 1–7)

Here, in the first half of a modified sonnet composed in 1911, we see a struggle wherein a stalwart neighborhood holly bush protects a domestic space—Bradley and Cooper's "little parlour"—from the "murderous sun." Using a typically Michaelian archaism, the hedge is described as a leather "targe" or target, but it also "rears up" like a horse in battle against the troops "mustered" on the other side and ready to attack. As the second half of this modified Italian sonnet concludes, the stakes become higher as the battle between the natural elements calls to mind for the Michaels the ongoing battle between the Trinity and the Devil:

Holy Trinity, against the strain
Of the Devil, and his demon spite
Twinkling on the fainted anchorite,
Thou the holy Office dost provide—
Buckler of impenetrable hide:
Faithful in its shadow we abide,
And of God, our God, are sanctified. (*MT* 139, lines 8–14)

In this poem's second half, the archaism of the "targe" continues its work. The holly hedge is shown to be both holy and hole-y, as it performs the sacred labor of protecting the "fainted anchorite" (presumably Cooper) from the demonic efforts of the "spite[ful]" sun, which the chinks in the hedge reduce to mere "twinkling." The word "anchorite" also has the effect of rendering the embowered, modern, Aesthetic space of the Field's parlor now a different kind of enclosure: one for abiding faithfully in the shadows, perhaps more prayerfully and less pridefully than before. Notably, by the poem's end the solitary anchorite has become the familiar doubled "we" of Michael Field. Meanwhile, the hedge's stone-dun "Buckler of impenetrable hide" calls to mind a more modest and retiring version, for these two holy virgins, of how Arnold's "Sea of Faith / . . . at the full, and round earth's shore / Lay like the folds of a bright girdle furled" in "Dover Beach" (lines 22–3). This buckler is more enduring, however, than Arnold's girdle; and thus their observations about the holly bush that shields their home from the sun becomes a meditation on how, for Bradley and Cooper (if not for Arnold), God protects the faithful from all evil. Granted, Michael Field's *oeuvre* frequently represents themselves as sanctified, set apart, such as the oath to dwell "Indifferent to heaven and hell" in "It was deep April" (*UTB* 79) and how "The Poet" is "a work of some strange passion / Life has conceived apart from Times harsh drill // . . . / Holy and foolish, ever set apart" (*WH* 58). Yet, here in "A Cette Heure Où J'ecris," what motivates Michael Field's quiet seclusion is not the world's disapproval but their faith: "of God, our God, we are sanctified" (*MT* 139, line 14).

Each of the above examples is typical of devotional verse that sets forth a poetic meditation on a natural scene. The point, for Tractarian doctrine as described by Joshua King, is that analogies to spiritual mysteries can be glimpsed everywhere in the world. In other words, in devotional verse, literary deployment of metaphor and simile take on added weight, just as Nature, by Analogy, teaches the Christian with an open heart.

In addition to the depiction of Nature in the service of Analogy, Keble praised the effect of metrically composed language, which functions as a mode of Reserve by "regulating, and thereby mitigating, the expression of feeling" (qtd in Blair 37). He advocated that meter could provide some clue to "guide [poets] amid a thousand paths to take the right, and this clue, as everyone can see, scansion and measure, simply in themselves, are well able to supply" (Keble 22). Like for Bradley and Cooper, who over the years frequently described their creative ideas as "coming to them" as if from outside themselves, for Keble, "poets do not choose metrical form, they are 'naturally' directed to it; but since nature is a form of divinity, the ultimate arbiter of form is always God's will" (Blair 39). In keeping with tenets of Anglo-Catholic poetics, much of Michael Field's devotional verse features metrical virtuosity that sediments their theological engagement with the natural world and their newly discovered religious thoughts and feelings.

Take for example, the 1908 "Fregit" [He broke] from *Poems of Adoration*, where Christ breaking the Host is brought to mind by observing familiar phenomena like picking fresh blooms, dropping a vase, and the strike of lightning, which are conveyed in "Fregit" through these natural images and also via meter:

> On the night of dedication
> Of Thyself as our oblation
> Christ, Belovèd, Thou didst take
> In Thy very hands and break. . . .
> O Christ there is a hiss of doom
> When new-glowing flowers are snapt in bloom
> When shivered, as a little thunder cloud
> A vase splits on the floor its brilliance loud;
> Or lightning strikes a willow-tree with a gash
> Cloven for death in a resounded crash. (*POA* 6, lines 1–10)

Here, the trochaic tetrameter's regularity in the first four lines conveys the inevitability of Christ's sacrifice, while the catalexis of lines 3 and 4 portends that something momentous is about to occur. In contrast, the jaw-breaking extra syllables of the next lines combine with the alliterative emphasis of the "snap," "shiver," "split," and "strike" of each of the broken items. These breakages, as the poem unfolds and returns to trochaic tetrameter catalectic, call to mind both Judas's break of trust, and Christ's (symbolic and real) broken body:

> Thou, betrayed, Thyself did break
> Thy own body for our sake:
> Thy own body Thou didst take
> In Thy holy hands—and break. (*POA* 6, lines 23–6)

Meanwhile, where meter, aural sensation, and vibrant imagery convey how shocking it can be even when relatively common things break, the repetition in the final four lines of "Thy" and "Thou" emphasize the divine mystery and tremendous self-sacrifice of Christ's breaking of transubstantiated bread and his subsequent Passion. The emphasis, here on Christ's human pain in divine self-sacrifice calls to mind St. Gregory's letter to Cledonius: "That which is not assumed cannot be redeemed." This will become an important theme in Michael Field's later devotional verses that, directly, or indirectly, resonate with Edith's suffering, as we will see.

In addition to Analogy and strict attention of meter, Victorian devotional poetry is also characterized by paradox and contradictory positions; and, of course, much has been made of Michael Field's Aesthetic use of paradox throughout their career, beginning with the paradox of their dual identity and their logos of the early bramblebough and the later pagan/Christian thyrsus interlaced with rings. In 1886, Cooper emphasizes paradox in explaining to Robert Browning how Bradley composed a poem about:

the bramble-bough the emblem of our united life . . .:

> My poet-bride, sweet songmate do I doom
> Thy youth to age's dull society?
> On the same bramblebough the pale-cheeked bloom
> Fondling by purple berry loves to lie;
> Fed by one September sunshine, there is room
> For fruit and flower in living unity.

When we adopted this as our symbol, [Cooper writes to Browning] my father carved the berried and flowery sprays over our mantelshelf and we have them on our study-chair also.[10]

As I mentioned in the introduction, the bramblebough symbol transforms Bradley and Cooper's age difference into an Aesthetic woodcarving that comes to adorn both their home and several of their publications.[11] The bramblebough's bloom and berry are grown on the same vine, under the same sun. In this brief poem,

---

[10] Michael Field to Robert Browning, Add. 46866, 1886. The British Library.
[11] Kate Thomas also writes about the bramblebough, specifically the bramblebough carving, in "Vegetable Love."

it is the aesthetic contrast and paradoxical coexistence of the "pale-cheeked bloom" and "purple berry" that justifies the song-mates' intellectual, emotional, and erotic attraction to one another. The similarly paradoxical "Stream and Pool" from the American version of *Underneath the Bough* (1898) likewise advances an erotics of difference-within-union.

> Mine is the eddying foam and the broken current
> Thine the serene-flowing tide, the unscattered rhythm
> Light touches me on the surface with glints of sunshine
> Dives in thy bosom, disclosing a mystic river
> . . .
> What is my song but the tumult of chafing forces
> What is thy silence, Beloved, but enchanted music? (*UTB* 1898, 53)

Here Michael Field portrays the play of light upon a river, exploring impossible, paradoxical questions: Is there a real difference between foam and current? Where does the glint of light end and the water begin?[12]

Marion Thain finds comparable contradictions and paradoxes in Michael Field's religious poetry: "the fluidity of a poetic identity that interlaces past and present, as well as self and lover, to create a personal mythology" ("Damnable Aestheticism" 332). As Hilary Fraser also observes, Aesthetic paradox, especially of Christian and pagan intertextuality, provides just one of many continuities between the Catholic poems and Michael Field's earlier work. For example, the aforementioned "Thou comest down to die" (composed 1910) from *Mystic Trees* juxtaposes Christ with a classical figure:

> How beautiful Thy feet
> Even as Hermes' are
> That Thou shouldst run so fleet
> To Golgotha! (*MT* 44, lines 5–8)

"White Passion-Flower," from *Mystic Trees*, first composed in 1909, provides another striking devotional experiment in Aesthetic paradox. Here an all-white passion flower inspires the speaker's

---

[12] For an expanded discussion of these two poems in the context of erotic difference, see Ehnenn, "Our brains."

meditation on the absence and presence of color, which leads to contemplation of Christ's Passion:

I
White exceeding is the passion-flower,
When it rayeth and extendeth white.
   Where is the purple thorn,
    Or the robe that He hath worn?
Where are the Wounds? From the waxen flower
The virulence is drawn, the power.

II
Dark exceeding is the passion-flower,
When it rayeth and extendeth, dark,
   The passion intricate
    Of a God in man's debate:
We beheld the Wounds, the Blood is red,
And the dark Blood gathers round His head.

III
Lovely, waxen flower, I am content
With your whiteness of the firmament:
   Even as in the Host
    The Precious Blood is lost,
On your unblooded disk I see
How the Lord is dying on Calvary. (*MT* 43)

In this poem, the speaker admires the white cultivar while simultaneously thinking of the more common species with the purple ring and the religious symbols generally associated with it. Paradoxically, although the contrast between white and purple is great, and although light and dark generally symbolize quite different things in literature, here both the white (present) and purple (absent) flowers create the same effect: they "rayeth and extendeth," touching the devout heart and inviting the religious mind to contemplate Christ's wounds at the moment of his death.

    Here, the white flower precedes the purple one, as the first stanza seems to ask, "O death, where is thy sting" (1 Cor. 15: 55). Only after holding up the purity of the resurrected Christ (taking away the sting of death in the purity of salvation) does the second verse contemplate the physical suffering that salvation required.

This structure reverses the Stations of the Cross;[13] here Michael Field first feels the glorious embrace of salvation, and then turns to the pain of torn flesh.

The white passion flower seems to help the speaker apprehend that, seen or unseen, Christ is always present, always sacrificing, always dying for the faithful believer. As the third stanza moves from the white flower to the white altar host, the paradoxical play of a string of absences and presences intensifies: the poem's flower becomes the Host; for Catholics, Christ is present in the Host as bread becomes body; in the holy Body of the Host there is no blood ("The Precious Blood is lost") yet at the same time the Host serves to remind the faithful how "the Precious Blood [was] lost" for their sake (Do this in remembrance of me). And finally, in a Hegelian sublation of the first two verses, the last lines of the poem return to the pure white of both the flower and the Host and the poem's overarching message is reiterated: the body of Christ need not be present in order to experience his presence, just as the speaker claims, "on the unblooded disk I see / How the Lord is dying on Calvary."

Adoration of the crucified Christ, of course, is an enduring and often eroticized feature of devotional poetry; and many critics have made similar arguments about the homoerotics of *Sight and Song*'s representations of St. Sebastian, especially in context of the many homoerotically inclined men in Michael Field's circle of Aesthetes.[14] Such observations take on a particularly lesbian connotation in "A Crucifix," an ekphrastic poem written in 1909 about a crucifix that Bradley gave to Cooper.

I
Thee such loveliness adorns
On Thy Cross, O my Desire—
As a lily Thou art among thorns,
As a rose lies back against his briar.

II
Thou art as a fair, green shoot,
That along the wall doth run;

---

[13] Thanks to M. Gail Hamner for these observations.
[14] Cf. Ehnenn, *Women's Literary Collaboration* 92–6; Martha Vicinus, "The Adolescent Boy"; and Richard Kaye, "Saint Sebastian and the Victorian Discourse of Decadence."

Thou art as a welcoming open fruit,
Stretched forth to the glory of the sun.

III
Thou art still as one in sleep,
As the blood that Thou dost shed;
Thou art as a precious coral-reef
That scarce lifteth himself from his bed.

IV
Thy limbs are so fine, so long,
'Mid the cords and nails that bind,
Thy body maketh a solemn song,
As a stream in a gorge confined. (*MT* 36)

Devotional and homoerotic desire become intertwined in this poem, with contrasting images in the first stanza that perhaps recall the earlier Michaelian bramblebough. Reclining floral images give way to the more vulvular conceit of the "welcoming opening fruit" in the second stanza; meanwhile, the movement of the second stanza contrasts the stillness of the first and third. Cooper's willowy form seems to haunt Bradley's admiration of Christ's feminine limbs, "so fine, so long" in the final stanza, especially as the speaker declares that "Thy body maketh a solemn song" in the streaming and feminine genital gorge—a speaker, one remembers, who often referred to her fellow Poet-Lover as her songmate.

But let us return to Michael Field's prowess with metrics, for there is much more to say about the queer sounds of this song, or poem, confined in the gorge. As in their earlier verse queering ekphrasis and elegy, in this devotional poem (among others) we see how innovative Michael Field's experimentations with form can be. Just as Bradley and Cooper eagerly sought to learn Catholic ritual while also arguing with their confessors and bending the rules,[15] we see in "A Crucifix" how Michael Field eschews Keble's prescription about divinely inspired strict meter. As talented metrists, they indubitably attend to their metrics in *Poems of Adoration* and *Mystic Trees*; but in "A Crucifix" instead of self-constraint and

---

[15] Here I am thinking particularly of how Bradley and Cooper continued to hold fast to their private beliefs about Whym Chow and what Frederik Roden terms their lesbian Trinitarianism.

Reserve they employ restless, shifting, and downright ambiguous verse forms. Are the first two seven-syllable lines of each stanza primarily trochaic? Or are they mixed anapests and iambs? If trochees, the mood is heavier and plodding, and emphasizes each stanza's initial Thee, Thous, and Thys (lines 1, 5, 9, and 13) and thereby the person (Christ/Cooper) who is the object of the gaze. If anapests and iambs, the mood is much lighter, emphasizing the particular aesthetic and/or sensual embodied qualities that the speaker finds worthy of adoration, and thereby privileging the natural, feminine imagery of the fair green shoot and the stream in the gorge over the blood, cord, and nails:

Trochaic reading of the first two lines of each stanza (stress in bold):	Iambic reading of the first two lines of each stanza (stress in bold):
Thee such **love** li **ness** a **dorns** **On** Thy **Cross**, O my **De** sire—	Thee **such** love **li** ness **a** dorns On **Thy** Cross, **O** my **De** sire—(lines 1–2)
Thou art **as** a **fair**, green **shoot**, **That** a **long** the **wall** doth **run**;	Thou **art** as a **fair**, green **shoot**, That a **long** the **wall** doth **run**; (lines 5–6)
Thou art **still** as **one** in **sleep**, **As** the **blood** that **Thou** dost **shed**;	Thou **art** still as **one** in **sleep**, As the **blood** that **Thou** dost **shed**; (ll. 9–10)
Thy limbs **are** so **fine**, so **long**, '**Mid** the **cords** and **nails** that **bind**,	Thy **limbs** are so **fine**, so **long**, 'Mid the **cords** and **nails** that **bind**, (ll.13–4)

Either way, the last two lines of stanzas one and three necessitate a certain awkwardness and inventiveness in reading aloud their beautiful natural images that so strikingly contrast the lines about the cross and blood that they follow. It is very difficult to pin down the meter of "As a lily Thou art among thorns, / As a rose lies back against his briar" (lines 3–4) and "Thou art as a precious coral-reef / That scarce lifteth himself from his bed" (lines 11–12). It is only the last two lines of stanzas two and four—the ones most suggestive of lesbian erotics—that most easily and unambiguously trip off the tongue in this poem inspired by a gift from one songmate to another.

Thou **art** as a **wel** com ing **o** pen **fruit**,
Stretched **forth** to the **glo** ry of the **sun**. (lines 7–8)

Thy **bo** dy ma **keth** a **so** lemn **song**,
As a **stream** in a **gorge** con **fined**. (lines 15–16)

The metrical phenomenon I identify here shares some features with what Herbert Tucker refers to as di-versification: poems "that stage a psychic potential energy that may be kinetically realized ... in more than one way" (108). Tucker argues, for example, that Augusta Webster's dramatic monologues wield a technique of "rhythmic variance" as a way to perform how the speaker "pits received wisdom against personal witness" and that illustrates a "character's own consciousness of inward schism" (114). While the embodied effect and context of antinormativity are similar, I see in Michael Field's asymptotic wobble the potential for a queer code to be read, or rather felt, only by those also "in the know." Meanwhile, if the metrical shifts and pauses and ambiguities in these verses reveal the homoeroticism otherwise concealed within; they also provide yet another way to think about what Kate Thomas terms "Michael Field's queer temporalities." In addition to her arguments about their intergenerational relationship, their obsession with historical figures, and the fact that they believed they have always been and always will be "out of time," the asymptotic wobble in the metrics of Michael Field's Catholic poems offers another example of "that queer sense of being out of sync" (Thomas, "What Time We Kiss" 330). It also provides another example of their *l'engrenage*: here, their gearing into the unknowns of the past and of desire, and the counterhegemonic potential in both.

In sum, in this section I have argued that the devotional poems written before 1911 illustrate Bradley and Cooper's formal efforts to become Catholic poets not only in their choice of subject matter but also in their use of Analogy, paradox, particular emphasis on the crucified body of Christ, and attention to meter. Yet, in deploying the formal characteristics of devotional poetics, Michael Field's religious verse also reveals their long-standing poetic engagement with nature and Aestheticism, homoeroticism and queer temporality. Thus they revise and transform religious texts with their aesthetics, gearing modern religious and sexual sensibilities into the sedimented matter of the past in ways that come to foreground "the body" (of Christ, of believer) as a body imminently available to pain and deformation. As the next section will show, the poets' task of becoming-Catholic becomes markedly more complicated when their negotiations of nature, art, and religion, body, spirit, and time, also become negotiations with their own disabled embodiment and pain.

Desiring disability

Although Cooper, much more so than hearty Bradley, was no stranger to illness, and in fact had often been ill over their years together, her diagnosis of bowel cancer in early February 1911 brought many changes to their intersubjective relationship as well as their relationship to the physical body, to spirituality, and to writing. A phenomenological approach provides an apt lens for analyzing these changes, especially the work of Sara Ahmed who, following Merleau-Ponty, locates subjectivity not in the mind but in the body as it is oriented in space. Phenomenology helps us recognize that experience is the embodied engagement of subjects with their world, including the sedimentation in the body of paths or habits that others have already established. Thus, phenomenology helps us understand subjectivity as located in the body as it is oriented to other subjects and objects in the world.

As Nirmala Erevelles asserts, "the phenomenological argument—that the body is not just an objective, exterior, institutionalized body ... but is rather a living, animated, experiencing body ... is especially useful in the representation of the embodied experiences of people diagnosed with cancer" (8). Michael Field's life writing and poetry in their final years depicts a new kind of intimate boundary crossing for the Poet-Lovers, a relational corporeality focused upon Cooper's body—always the beloved subject of Bradley's gaze, always luminous and frail, but now increasingly a conduit for theological considerations, now struggling to walk to church, and ultimately confined to writing in bed. The shifting role of Cooper's body provides an example of how "all bodies are in a constant state of renewal and adjustment in changing physical and environmental contexts, making the body intensely aware, not just of its be-ing but also of its becoming-in-the-world" (Erevelles 36). These ideas, combined with Ahmed's assertions about of the importance of bodily orientation, guide the work of the remainder of this chapter. In this section I will explore how Michael Field's devotional verse and related diaries and letters demonstrate how Bradley and Cooper shift from being embodied queer subjects oriented toward "becoming Catholic" to being embodied queer subjects in physical pain and emotional distress, oriented toward both Cooper's chronic and ultimately fatal illness and God.

In *Fictions of Affliction: Physical Disability in Victorian Culture* (2004), Martha Stoddard Holmes identifies, in the nineteenth century, a melodramatic mode of representing disability; one popular trope is the ailing woman whose physical weakness begets increased spiritual insight, such as *Jane Eyre*'s Helen Burns on her deathbed. To a certain extent, this mode characterizes many of the journal and epistolary representations of Cooper as she suffers the ravages of her cancer. But the Catholic poems composed during and after 1911 differ from this melodramatic mode. In the devotional poetry from Cooper's cancer years, Michael Field's engagement with disability blends those homoerotic elements so familiar to readers of their earlier works with qualities that, "out of time," anticipate current discussions in disability studies about desiring disability and queer, crip futures.[16]

In their critiques of both compulsory heterosexuality and compulsory able-bodiedness, Robert McRuer, Abby Wilkerson, and Alison Kafer each contemplate the place of queerness and disability in thinking about the future, and, contra seeing queerness and disability as "no future," posit a crip futurity where queerness and disability is seen as valuable, integral, and desirable.[17] Contrary to the medical/individual model, where disability is a problem to be solved, and also contrary to the social model, where disability "is seen less as an objective fact of the body or mind than a product of social relation," Kafer posits a "hybrid political/relational mode of disability that does not erase the lived realities of impairment, and that acknowledges how disability is not experienced in isolation; but in and through relationships" (6). This model is quite useful for thinking about Michael Field's devotional poetry after 1911, in which one can observe their shift from largely technical experiments about Christian figures and themes to much more personal identification with Christ and Mary.

After the initial grief and shock of the news of her cancer, Cooper writes in *Works and Days* and also to Father John Gray:

---

[16] Here I use "crip" as a reclamatory term that refers to non-normate bodies and identities. Crip theory is influenced by queer theory's critique of the naturalization and normalization of bodies and encourages a troubling of the boundaries that establish given ontologies. Accordingly, a crip reading will be critical of how medical models define and stigmatize disability.

[17] For foundational arguments about heternormative time and the idea that queer theory instead should approach time from the perspective of "no future," see Edelman *No Future*; Halberstam *In a Queer Time and Place* and *The Queer Art of Failure*. For recent queer critiques of the anti-futurity movement see, in addition to Kafer, Hall "No Failure"; Thomas, "Vegetable Love."

"*Fiat, voluntas tua* [thy will be done]."[18] At this time, both Bradley and Cooper can be seen to identify, through their Catholic verse, with Christ, who through his passion, also said those words. Although Cooper's pain is certainly a problem and they both pray for its respite, and although they both want to prolong her life because they don't wish to part, neither desires a miraculous "cure" for Cooper; neither wishes for her to return to a normate body. Instead, Cooper perceives her suffering as martyrdom and as a way to become closer to God. Identifying with the suffering Christ and other suffering male saints is a way to gear into the past, aestheticize her pain, and do so within a homoerotic context. Take, for example, Cooper's erotic, embodied praise of the "Holy Cross" written in 1912 and published in *Poems of Adoration*:

> Mysterious sway of mortal blood,
> That urges me upon Thy wood!—
> O Holy Cross, but I must tell
> My love; how all my forces dwell
> Upon Thee and around Thee day and night!
> I love the Feet upon thy beam,
> As a wild lover loves his dream;
> My eyes can only fix upon that sight.
>
> O Tree, my arms are strong and sore
> To clasp Thee, as when we adore
> The body of our dearest in our arms!
> Each pang I suffer hath for aim
> Thy wood—its comfort is the same—
> A taint, an odour from inveterate balms.
>
> My clasp is filled, my sight receives
> The compass of its power; pain grieves
> About each sense but as a languid hum:
> And, out of weariness, at length,
> My day rejoices in its strength,
> My night that innocence of strife is come. (*POA* 31)

---

[18] *Works and Days*. MSS Add. 46801, February 6, 1911. (EC). fol. 21v. The British Library; ALS Cooper to Gray, National Library of Scotland, Dept. 372 #16, February 1911. fol. 2.

Here, with passion that eschews the doctrine of Reserve, the speaker both beholds and *is* the suffering body. As the speaker worships the crucifix, identifies with Christ's pain, imagines embracing the body of Christ-the-lover, and aspires to share his fate, multiple senses are activated: there is a comforting aroma of "inveterate balms," and the "languid hum" of constant physical pain paradoxically blurs the boundary between touch and sound. Although vision is mentioned, the poem does not dwell clearly on what is seen, which reiterates Cooper's physical and spiritual identification with the suffering Christ, but also reflects the practical reality that while in a close embrace it is difficult to see "The body of our dearest in our arms."

In contrast to "Holy Cross" is Bradley's much more insistently visual 1913 "The Captain Jewel" from *Mystic Trees*. According to *Works and Days*, these two are companion pieces:[19]

> We love Thy ruddy Wounds,
> We love them pout by pout:
> It is as when the stars come out,
>   One after one—
>   We are
>   As watchers for the Morning Star.
>
> The jewels of Thy Feet,
> The jewels of Thy Hands! . . .
> Lo, a Centurion stands,
>   Openeth Thy Side: Water and Blood there beat
>   In fountain sweet:
>   Our Master-jewel now we dote upon! (*MT* 34)

---

[19] *Works and Days*. MSS Add. 46803, May 6, 1913. (EC). fol. 39. The British Library. "A sense of the old Michaelian life comes on us. The little black leather strap, that is to bind our Catholic book 'Adoration' and 'Mystic Trees' together, arrives . . . at night we read from the enchained books dual poems on the same subjects." The companion poems are then listed in pairs in the diary: Cooper's "Real Presence" (1912, *POA*) and Bradley's [blank]; Cooper's "Virgo Potens" (1910, *POA*) and Bradley's "Midsummer Night's Dream" (1913, *MT*); Cooper's "Columba Mea" (1911, *POA*) and Bradley's "Nondum errant abyssi" (1913, *MT*); Cooper's "Purgatory" (1907, *POA*) and Bradley's "In Die Obitus" (1908, *MT*); Cooper's "Holy Cross" (1912, *POA*) and Bradley's "Captain Jewel" (1913, *MT*); Cooper's "Qui Renovat Jevuntitem Meam" (1912, *MT*) and Bradley's "Gather Gather" (The Blessed Sacrament I) (1908, *POA*); and Cooper's "To Notre Dame de Boulonge" (Pax Vobiscum) (1910, *POA*) and Bradley's "Praises" (1908, *MT*).

Here, in a more strongly erotic and Aestheticized conceit of pouting wounds as jewels, Bradley, who writes often of watching Cooper's body in pain, also compares this act of looking to watching for the morning star or Venus, goddess of love. In both "Holy Cross" and "Captain Jewel," the disabled, eroticized Christ is passionately desired, not in spite of but *because of* his physical state, both in his own right and as a stand-in for Cooper.[20] In both of these examples Michael Field creates a kind of queer disability poetics that uses their embodied experience with cancer to identify with Christ and love him more deeply, while it also uses Christianity to articulate their love and desire for one another—for "loving . . . wounds."

Both Cooper and Bradley also write Annunciation poems in which they identify with the Virgin Mary, who famously agreed to bear the burden thrust upon her. As Ruth Vanita and others have observed, Michael Field's praise of Sapphic beauty easily shifts to Marian praise in their devotional verse. Thus, consider the first stanza of Cooper's 1911 "Hour of Need":

> O Mother of my Lord,
> Beautiful Mary, aid!
> He, whom thy will adored,
> When thy body was afraid,
> Is coming in my flesh to dwell—
> Pray for me, Mary . . . and white Gabriel! (*POA* 103, lines 1–6)

Here, embodied fear is acknowledged for both Mary and the speaker (Cooper) who identifies with Mary. Christ simultaneously inhabits Mary's body as the child, the speaker's body as the Eucharist, and Cooper's body as God's will (in this case, cancer). Once again, Mary, (and by extension, Cooper) adores "thy will," in other words, desires her embodiment. She does not wish to escape, deny, or minimize it.

A similar, if more pathos-filled poem is Bradley's "Pondering," composed in 1913:

> I see a Garden, my little son,
> Thou art praying there God's will be done:

---

[20] For foundational insights about the disabled Christ from a disability studies perspective, see Nancy Eiesland, *The Disabled God*.

The ground is wet
With bloody sweat . . .
Yea, and fulfilled His Will shall be
In Thee and me!

Thou art bound, art bleeding in a hall . . .
There is wrath at my breast . . . The scourges fall;
And the swimming eyes of Thine agony
Have no part in me.
Lo, Thine hour is come!
My Bud, my Rose, I am distant, dumb!

Belovèd, I can see a road;
They spur Thee along it as with a goad;
I hear Thy Voice "Ye must not weep" . . .
Babe, Babe, but my sobs will break Thy sleep!

To a Cross Thou art nailed by cruel men—
But I see myself and beside Thee then,
At the foot of that Cross—and it is His Will!
My little One, we will both lie still,
In one peace together, loving His Will! (*MT* 65, ellipses in original)

A meditation on Mary and Christ as well as vision of impending suffering and death apropos to Cooper's illness, "Pondering" is another example among many in these poems of how Michael Field indulges in creative asynchrony making the here and now gear into (*engrener*) the orientations of the historical there and then. "Pondering" also portrays what Kafer describes as crip time, or those strange temporalities peculiar to how disability orients one to time. Thinking about waiting, anticipatory time, Kafer points out how queer and crip time trouble the future in refusing (like Mary and Christ, like Bradley and Cooper) to privilege longevity at all cost. In the opening stanza the speaker (Mary/Bradley) sees her boy's imminent death on the cross and echoes Christ's/Cooper's *Fiat, voluntas tua*: "fulfilled His will shall be / In Thee and Me." In the second and third stanza Mary/Bradley acknowledges Christ's/Edith's physical pain and her own intense emotional suffering; but in the final stanza we see the speaker not merely accepting their lot but "loving" God's will.

In February 1911, motivated by realities of Cooper's illness, Bradley and Cooper decide to take vows to become Dominican Sisters of the Penance, to "have new nuptials of love within the Church."[21] This act brings new weight to their devotional writings' standard trope of Christ as Bridegroom. On December 31, 1911, Cooper writes, "we are here together, hoping together to take the Vow that gives us wholly to our Bridegroom Christ—hoping to love each other in Him ... and beloved Michael, growing so patient, showing me such loveable fruits out of the pain, bitterer than mine she has to bear."[22] Looking forward to the rings that will join them, and in language that recalls the Trinity that she and Bradley formed with Whym Chow, Cooper writes, "we shall be in Thee together and not alone—forever Thine and Thy Twain in thee."[23] As I noted in the previous chapter, in this queer marriage, Christ as Bridegroom, like Whym Chow, becomes another erotic proxy for the Michaels. Thus, in this future-oriented journal entry, Cooper records how she and her beloved approach a new threshold in their relationship. The account provides a sense of Bradley's awareness of Cooper's suffering body, but also Cooper's awareness of Bradley's pain, which she deems more severe than her own. Both experience pain in their own way, but through their love for one another and for Christ, they articulate desire for their new life together, not in a spirit of resignation, but actively embracing "Thy will be done."

Less than six months later, Charles Ricketts would state how alienated he felt by Michael Field's religious verse and would voice the scathing critique with which I opened this chapter. Indeed, as Martin Lockerd's *Decadent Catholicism and the Remaking of Modernism* reminds us, many *fin de siècle* and modernist converts, including T. S. Eliot, faced similar criticism. Yet, as I hope I have demonstrated, with its Aesthetic pouts, wounds, jewels, and flowers; with paradox and asynchrony; with experimental approaches to form; and animated by both masculine and feminine homoerotic tropes, *Poems of Adoration* and *Mystic Trees* are *very much* like Michael Field's earlier poems—like the poems

---

[21] *Works and Days*. MSS Add. 46801, February 9, 1911. (EC). fol. 26v. The British Library.

[22] *Works and Days*. MSS Add. 46801, December 31, 1911. (EC). fol. 161r. The British Library.

[23] *Works and Days*. MSS Add. 46801, December 31, 1911. (EC). fol. 166r. The British Library.

Charles Ricketts prefers over the Catholic verse he claims that he does not recognize. Explorations in how and why one might desire disability—both Christ's and one's own—these devotional poems expand our understanding of what it meant for Bradley and Cooper to become Catholic Poets while remaining Michael Field.

Writing a Life:
A Conclusion and a Provocation

> I came too soon.
> —George Egerton, "A Keynote to *Keynotes*" (1932)

> I am well aware that I have never written anything but fictions.
> —Michel Foucault, Interview with Lucette Finas (1977)

This book has been concerned with how to understand Michael Field's re-visions of forms and narratives as they pursued their greatest hope—for great recognition and acclaim—a hope that famously prompted Robert Browning to caution, "Wait fifty years."[1] In seeking such understanding, I have asked how experimentation with literary form and genre helps Michael Field navigate the paradox of looking backward in order to "Be contemporaneous";[2] and, "to make all things new."[3] I have also considered how the co-authors' anachronisms and formal literary innovations function in the context of being homoerotically inclined, female authors and aesthetes, and in context of their conflicted attitudes toward late Victorian modernity in general and decadence in particular. Throughout this project I have asserted that Michael Field's *oeuvre* can and should be read as a series of ambitious experiments with literary traditions and forms; that their revisionary poetics are shaped by a Dionysian eros and queer-feminist sensibility that complicate their otherwise

---

[1] *Works and Days*. MSS Add. 46777, 1888–9. (KB). fol. 5r. The British Library.
[2] *Works and Days*. MSS Add. 46781, July 12, 1893. (KB). fol. 47v. The British Library.
[3] See Introduction, note 6.

Paterian aesthetics and Hegelian view of history; and that we can observe, in their varied formal and historical experiments, an affective orientation toward and phenomenological engagement with the unknowable and unutterable that, among other things, reflects their status as embodied female, homoerotically inclined *fin de siècle* subjects. In many ways, as we have seen, Bradley and Cooper celebrate their femininity, queer desires, and queer friends, but they also felt keenly disadvantaged by what we today would call heteronormativity, as well as the sexism and male entitlement they experienced while, as Sara Ahmed would put it, "traveling under the sign, woman" (*Living a Feminist Life* 14). Navigating health and spiritual change, cultural developments ranging from wars to omnibuses to telephones, and personal and professional successes and tragedies, Bradley and Cooper's life and work, as Michael Field, provide consistent examples of "the vital role art can play in developing self-determining queer identities" and how queerness can be an advantage that makes possible intellectual and creative freedom (Friedman 6–7).

In examining these issues I have been influenced, directly and indirectly, by Adrienne Rich's ideas about writing as re-vision, Heather Love's notion of feeling backward, and José Esteban Muñoz's thinking about the utopian potential of negative affect for "enacting a mode of critical possibility"—the notion of queer hope as "a backward glance that enacts a future vision" (Muñoz, *Cruising Utopia* 4). And I have attempted to respond to my core research questions with historical and textual accuracy, of course, but also in ways that are relevant to us, reading Michael Field now, so much later than fifty years on. Thus while *Michael Field's Revisionary Poetics* situates Michael Field in conversation with their contemporaries—the late Victorians and decadent Moderns with whom they bridge the nineteenth and twentieth centuries—it also places Bradley and Cooper and their work in conversation with our own theories, thoughts, and concerns.

Reading Michael Field in this way would not be complete without acknowledging that, in addition to verse drama, short prose, ekphrases, and amatory, elegiac, devotional and other forms of lyric poetry, Bradley and Cooper left twenty-nine years of joint diaries, which they titled *Works and Days*. The oversized cream-colored foolscap notebooks that Bradley and Cooper referred to as the "White Book" were published in a highly excerpted version edited by T. Sturge Moore in 1933, providing early enthusiasts and scholars with insight into Michael Field's life and literary circle. Bowdlerized as it was, that edition invited interpretation of Michael Field's life and work that often essentialized and sanitized their complicated identities and relationship, especially with regard to sex, gender roles, and sexuality. After the 9,500-page collaborative journal, written in both Bradley and Cooper's hands, became fully available for study at the British Library, subsequent scholars discovered how very complex, queer, and performative "The Michaels" were. Literary critics and historians continue to mine Bradley and Cooper's rich legacy for insights both about the co-authors' life and works and about the decades in which the Victorians adopted the more modernist sensibilities of the early twentieth century.[4] The joint diary is currently being digitally transcribed by an international team of researchers.[5]

What do these diaries tell us about the co-authors' hopes? What kind of future vision do these diaries enact? These questions are much too large for a short conclusion! Fortunately, Carolyn Dever's *Chains of Love and Beauty: The Diary of Michael Field*, just published as I edit this conclusion, is solely dedicated to the diaries and has begun to address some of the issues I have flagged. In what follows I will contribute a few thoughts to Dever's innovative reading of *Works and Days* as "the great unknown novel of the nineteenth century" (4), as a record of a rapidly changing world, and as an "extended dialogue internal to a pair of writers engaging in sensitive questions of beauty, desire and fame" (2). Yet ultimately, in this conclusion I am interested a bit less in what the diaries mean for Michael Field's life, and a bit more in what they might mean and do for us, now. In other words, inspired by their own methodology, I want to meditate upon Michael Field's *Works and Days* with a backward glance in order to think about its effect on the present and to enact a future vision.

---

[4] In addition to Carolyn Dever's recent book, which is the only full-length study of *Works and Days*, much of the foundational scholarship on Michael Field analyzes the unique doubleness of the diaries as providing important insights into Bradley and Cooper's construction of "Michael Field" as a joint author and joined selves. See, among many others, Lillian Faderman, Angela Leighton, Virginia Blain, Holly Laird, and Marion Thain.

[5] See <https://michaelfielddiary.dartmouth.edu/home>

Works and Days: a diary

In keeping with my project's interest in Michael Field's creative making and remaking of existing forms and narratives through their verse and drama, it seems we should begin with a nod to the original *Works and Days* by Hesiod (c. 700 BCE). This first *Works and Days* is a didactic address by Hesiod to his brother Perses, whom he bids to live a just life and to work hard in order to reap reward. Framed by the stories of Prometheus and Pandora, the Myth of the Ages, and the fable of the nightingale and the hawk, Hesiod's message is that although Zeus has control of the fates, individuals nevertheless have an active role to play in the making of the self and one's life. In addition to instruction through story, Hesiod's *Works and Days* is part almanac and part ethical instruction; for instance, it advises when to plant, how to dress, how to establish a household, when to sail, and admonishes: "He does mischief to himself who does mischief to another, and evil planned harms the plotter most" (23). Hesiod also advocates self-reflection: "That man is altogether best who considers all things himself and marks what will be better afterwards and at the end" (25); and promises that living as he describes will have great results: "Through work men grow rich in flocks and substance, and working they are much better loved by the immortals" (25–6). In Michael Field's allusion to Hesiod (rather than eighteenth- and nineteenth-century women's conduct books, which also advocate self-reflective practices), the title of their diary announces that, from the beginning, they perceive their journal both as an account on par with the classical poets who wrote lasting epics, and as an account of their creation, or self-fashioning, of themselves, over time, for the future.

Michael Field heeds Hesiod's instruction to take up forms of constant observation and self-reflection, yet their content makes many things new. Their *Works and Days* marries Hesiod with Pater's advice to live philosophically, "The service of philosophy, of speculative culture, toward the human spirit, is to rouse, to startle it to a life of constant and eager observation"; and aesthetically, "Not the fruit of experience, but experience itself is the end ... To burn always with this hard gemlike flame, to maintain this ecstasy, is success in life" (*Renaissance* 236). Consequently, as an epic account of Michael Field the Poet and Dramatist, *Works and Days*' self-told story of Bradley and Cooper, combined with the impressions they leave inwoven in their verse and drama, use the past passionately and bravely to transform many of the late nineteenth-century assumptions of what a woman is supposed to do. Who and how she is supposed to love. What it means to read history, look at art, experience the natural world, mourn, and worship. What and how one is supposed to write. Indeed, what a diary is.

Shifting now from Hesiod's *Works and Days* to Michael Field's, I must confess that my knee-jerk response has been (at least until recently) that in both form and content, Michael Field's *Works and Days* is a very unusual diary. Lo-o-o-ong. Unusually frank, even "juicy," for a nineteenth-century diary. Written by two people, not one, in two sets of handwriting, not one (see Fig. 6.1). With the added complication of dictation, ongoing collaborative conversation, and revision, the writer's hand is often not a reliable indicator that the documented thoughts or poems "belong" to the person who has put ink to paper. Sometimes the entries in different hands can be read as a way for Bradley and Cooper to communicate something to one another. (Sometimes this feels passive aggressive.) Strange stuff for a diary, right?

With more research and thinking, however, I've come to the realization that *Works and Days*, while a remarkable, historically valuable diary, is *not* really an unusual one. It might be unusual that we have a completely preserved example of such a long diary from this period; but to keep a diary for most of one's adult life is not an unusual nineteenth-century practice. Many nineteenth-century diaries seem quite dry and uninteresting compared to *Works and Days* but there are plenty that are equally full of personal disclosure. We bring assumptions of privacy to the words "diary" and "journaling;" but nineteenth-century diaries were often read aloud and even published, a fact I'll return to, below. So these assumptions of privacy, perhaps, project onto Michael Field's *Works and Days* our own experiences of diaries with little locks and keys that we might buy today (or for the more technically oriented, password-protected laptops) and of tweens and teens stomping and screaming, "Don't touch my things!" Such assumptions of privacy also conveniently ignore the fact of diaries/calendars shared electronically in the workplace, or sharing journals (handwritten or typed) with teachers or classmates in a typical low-stakes writing assignment. Such assumptions of privacy also overlook the ways in which people who might have documented

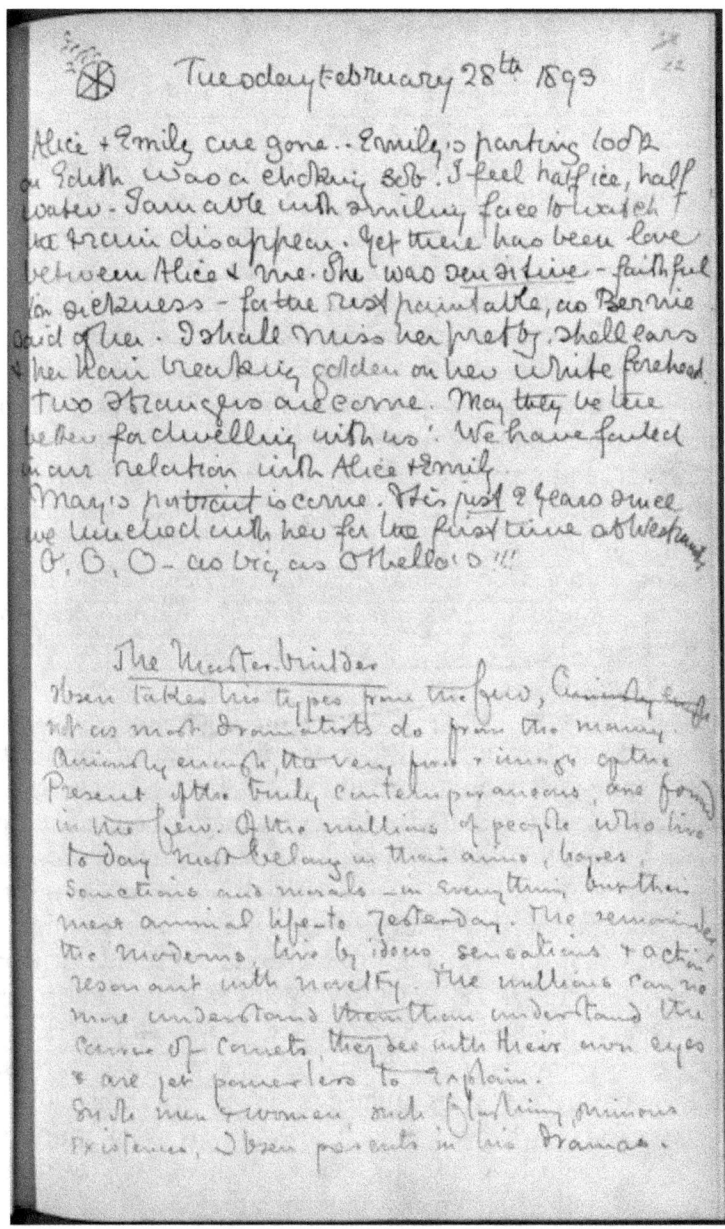

Fig. 6.1 Works and Days: The Diary of Michael Field. Journal entry dated February 28, 1893. Hand of Katharine Bradley (top) and Edith Cooper (bottom). Courtesy of the British Library, London. MSS Add. 46781. folio 22r.

their lives in diaries are now doing so in the public arenas of blogs, vlogs, and social media.

But that is now; what of then? What is a nineteenth-century diary supposed to be and do? Because most scholars agree that an important characteristic of the diary is its fluidity and its mixing of genres, this turns out to be a difficult question without a single answer. This is especially the case for women's diaries, which, according to Mary Jane Moffat, were seen as analogous to women's lives: "emotional, fragmented, interrupted, modest, not be taken seriously, trivial, formless, concerned with the self, and as endless as their 'tasks'" (5). Michael Field's *Works and Days*, gesturing as its title does at an epic rather than a trivial life, nevertheless is emotional, fluid, fragmented, interrupted, concerned with the self, and mixes genres. As we have seen throughout this and other studies of the co-authors, it combines personal and scholarly reflection, lecture and gallery notes, creative non-fiction, poetry and snippets of drama, lists, letters, newspaper cuttings, invitations, mourning cards, pressed flowers, and the occasional drawing. Like other diaries, it "expose[s] the complicated relationship between life and its narrative" with its "nonlinearity, interruption, lack of closure," and documents an "open, improvised self" (Cottam 268–9). To this end, Rita Felski notes that an approach to autobiography—including journal writing—emerges as a form in the eighteenth century out of practices of religious confession and self-analysis; and this new approach is grounded in the "possibility and legitimacy of self-knowledge" (87). Felski makes a connection between such autobiographical writing and bourgeois subjectivity: the idea that self-examination will yield a "source of truth" and expose a core self (89). Thus, in ways that are important in thinking about what a diary is and does, *Works and Days* is not so strange. Meditating on these matters is a welcome exercise if we are to consider how this archive (perhaps any archive) can be useful to us today, why we feel such an archive is usual or unusual, and why we might be drawn to such an archive. Why we bother looking (and feeling) backwards into such texts at all.

If these are some of the characteristics of nineteenth-century diaries (and diaries in general) how might reflecting on the affordances of form help us consider Michael Field's *Works and Days*? How does form *form* what a diary does and can be—for its author(s) and for those, like ourselves, who encounter it as part of a historical archive? How does the diary, as form, organize experience; what is its pattern/shape/arrangement? What are the latent potentialities in the diary as genre/form? How is Michael Field's joint diary formed by such affordances and/or how does it revise them? Here, I'll touch upon four affordances that seem particularly relevant to thinking about Michael Field's journals—and the extent to which we may or may not consider them experimental, revisionary engagements with the diary as form.

First, the form of the diary creates the illusion that one is touching and/or managing time. As Margo Culley notes, "the diary is always in process, always in some sense a fragment ... their shapes derive from time passing (courtship diary, travel diary) and are structured by specific kinds of events" (220). As in *Works and Days*, "The calendar year provides the structural rhythms of many diaries, frequently, diarists mark the end of each year with repeated rituals" such as a list of persons who died, books read, reflections, resolutions, etc. (Culley 220). This management of time is also a practice predicated upon the ways that the form of the diary creates a horizon of expectation that one will be writing again. All the White Books match, necessitating purchase ahead of time, for the eventuality that one will need a new one when space runs out, or when the new year turns. And we know that Bradley and Cooper took the current White Book with them when they traveled. Much like taking a vacation with one's laptop because one anticipates there will be an opportunity to work (whether this actually happens or not), *Works and Days* capitalizes on the affordance of the diaries' ability to manage time: both past and future. Perhaps something epic will happen to Michael and Henry that will warrant making a note of it while they are away from home; once written in the diary they can reflect back upon it later, in the future, for the further future. This potential for managing time, latent in the diary's form, is also related to the next two affordances I'll discuss: potentials for rereading and for self-fashioning.

Culley observes that "evidence abounds in all periods that women read and reread their diaries" (219). As Bradley and Cooper sometimes do, commenting upon, adding and striking out words, and removing pages, is common among diarists. In this way, "The pages of the diary might be thought of as a kind of mirror before which the diarist stands assuming this posture or that. One might even draw analogies between the process of psychoanalysis" (Culley 219). Therefore, as the form of the diary manages time, it also creates the potential—even an expectation—that one will read over one's writing again in the future.

Rooted as it is in the practice of the confessional, the diary also affords the potential for self-fashioning; historically, this was to learn to manage one's time better, and to reflect upon one's thoughts and actions in the spirit of self-improvement. Felicity Nussbaum writes of autobiographical texts, "many specifically resist a self-made whole by human ideology, Cartesian philosophy, or Christian ideology" (162). Put more strongly, Culley states that a diary creates a self that "is some degree of fiction, a construction" (218). In fact, Cecily's made-up diary in Oscar Wilde's *The Importance of Being Earnest* indicates that, by the 1890s, the notion that diaries involved a certain degree of self-fashioning was common enough to satirize. Certainly, as this and other studies have shown, Bradley and Cooper capitalize upon this third affordance of the diary. As a space for reflection and rationalization, for goal setting, for dreaming, for self-criticism, and for affirmation, the diary is a tool whose form enables Bradley and Cooper to practice their conviction that "We are Michael Field." The diary's form potentially invites continual revision of what "We are Michael Field" means, and it shapes what such a conviction means for others in the present and in the future, despite the ultimate futility of engaging such an unknown.

Finally, we should think about the affordance of the diary's potential for audience. As I mentioned above in my discussion of privacy, it's not historically accurate to think that a nineteenth-century diarist would necessarily have assumptions about their diary's privacy. As Martin Hewitt writes:

> Although diary keeping had a long history, there is no doubt that its emergence in the early nineteenth century as a widely practiced and even more widely constructed literary genre meant that [as early as the] 1830s it was impossible for a diarist to write without a degree of self-conscious positioning within a published tradition, and without being fully aware of the ambiguous state of the diary's claim to privacy. (25)

Martin Danahay and others note how many nineteenth-century writers, especially men of note, anticipate publication, modeling their journal on the published life writing of famous men (115). Since so many kinds of life writing were published in the nineteenth century, this blurs the boundary between public and private in ways that are relevant to how we consider *Works and Days*, its reference to Hesiod's epic, its obvious self-fashioning, and its equally obvious sense of an audience. Culley argues:

> The importance of the audience, real or implied, conscious or unconscious, of what is usually thought of as a private genre cannot be overstated. The presence of a sense of audience, in this form of writing as in all others, has a crucial influence over what is said and how it is said. Friend, lover, mother, God, a future self—whatever role the audience assumes for the writer—that presence becomes a powerful "thou" to the "I" of the diarist. It shapes the selection and the arrangement of detail within the journal and determines more than anything else the kind of self-construction the diarist presents. (218)

If in Bradley and Cooper's day women's private lives were perhaps not considered important enough to be of public interest, recasting their lives as the story of a developing artist—in the context of an era when autobiographies of famous men were valued—increases the importance of both their lives and their writing. In the context of a time when reading "The Life of" this or that famous man was a worthy goal, having a record of Michael Field's life makes it worthy of recording. Thus Michael Field write *Works and Days* as something that might be mined for publication of extracts, or that might be read in its entirety by future generations. It is a tangible artifact of their hope for recognition and acclaim: they provide a backward glance on their own dual, queer self in order to contribute to a future when that self is acknowledged in ways that they currently are not. In these ways, the affordances of the diary are such that, among all the forms with which Michael Field experiment, the diary is the one that perhaps needs the *least* revision. The diary is a form quite suited to explaining how Katharine Bradley and Edith Cooper became Michael Field.

Works and Days: a fiction, an archive, and a provocation

While it is useful to consider the specific affordances of the diary and how Michael Field's diary takes advantage of those affordances, it's also useful to remember, as Danahay cautions, that "the formal distinctions between autobiography, biography and fiction obscure the cultural assumptions about identity that inform them" (88). Such considerations are particularly apropos to *fin de siècle* contexts, as Margaret Stetz illustrates in her essay on genre-bending, gender, and the inclusive category belles-lettres, which offered encouragement for authors, publishers, and readers to transcend boundaries of genre, especially poetry and prose. On this topic, Richard Gallienne famously proclaimed that "one should no more classify a book, based merely on its appearance, than one should categorize the gender of a body: 'To ask the sex of a beautiful person is as absurd as it would be to ask a publisher the sex of a beautiful book'" (in Stetz, "Ballads" 619). Genre-crossing experimentation, Stetz demonstrates, proved particularly beneficial to female (and Irish) authors; yet such genre-bending could not hold in the wake of the gender and sex-panic of the Oscar Wilde trials. The term belles-lettres with its more inclusive ideals about both genre and gender emerged . . . then disappeared.

Since the capaciousness—and caprices—and constructedness of identity in the context of the *fin de siècle* are crucial to thinking about Michael Field (as homoerotically inclined, as female, as authors, aesthetes, collaborators, etc.) I think it's useful to further contemplate the entanglement of writing and identity by considering Michael Field's *Works and Days* in such a genre-bending context. What happens when we think of *Works and Days* not only in tradition of the journal (no matter how apt a journal it is) but in the tradition of a Hesiod "made new" by crossing it with the more contemporaneous form of nineteenth-century fictional autobiography, which also functions as an archive of a life? Granted, Bradley and Cooper were not enthusiasts of the novel, and their diaries and letters indicate that their taste ran to Tolstoy and Flaubert rather than to English novelists. Nonetheless, considering Michael Field's self-fashioning as a fiction, in the context of actual fiction, might be instructive.[6]

Like Hesiod's *Works and Days*, the fictional autobiography is about the creation of the self (everyman as hero) in the epic endeavor of having a life. As a *Bildungsroman*, the fictional autobiography, like Hesiod, has pedagogical underpinnings; and as a

---

[6] Reading *Works and Days* as a novel is the goal of Dever's *Chains of Love and Beauty*. My brief consideration here differs from hers insofar as I am thinking quite strictly about philosophical resonances with the specific self-fashioning project of the fictional autobiography, which is not a genre engaged in Dever's project.

realist endeavor, the fictional autobiography, like the diary and memoir, makes truth claims about the selves and events represented therein. Heidi L. Pennington persuasively argues that getting to know the protagonist of a fictional autobiography (David Copperfield, Jane Eyre, Lucy Snowe, Esther Summerson, *The Lifted Veil*'s Latimer, etc.) involves many of the same elements as getting to know a real person, thus "fictional autobiography calls attention to the process of identity creation," including the role of others (here, readers) in identity creation (4). Even as fictional autobiographies present identities that readers experience as real, such texts notoriously invite active reader participation to fill in gaps and perhaps reorder a narrative, to judge reliability, and more.[7] Following Lejeune—who proposes that the only real difference between autobiography and fiction is how the reader perceives the author's relationship to the text—to consider such matters is to question whether our subject is a reliable narrator, along with more philosophical questions about what we mean by "reliable narrator." The reader of a fictional autobiography, like the reader of a diary, must think about the narrator's self-fashioning. To be such a reader one must engage an archive of a life that they then must piece together and interpret. For Pennington, fictional autobiography reveals how the "processes of fiction, as they are enacted within and beyond the literary text" shape lived experience into a sense of the self (10). Pennington further argues that readers who engage in such practices of reading may become more attuned to how such mechanisms of subject creation occurs in all contexts, not just fictional ones (4). The implications for understanding Michael Field's self-fashioning in *Works and Days*, and how we engage their self-fashioning, now, are vast.

In *Senses of the Subject*, Judith Butler considers the beginning of *David Copperfield* in order to illustrate the complexity of subject formation: how subjects are produced by norms, through language/discourse, and via the recognition of others; and how such dynamics are always "continuous and repeated" and always dependent on a belated narrativizing. David documents the story of his life thusly:

---

[7] Of course all novels—all texts—do this to a certain extent, especially from a reader-response perspective. But Pennington, and others, demonstrate that novels like *David Copperfield*, *Jane Eyre*, etc. do this in a different way, and to a greater extent.

> Whether I shall turn out to be the hero of my own life, or whether that station will be held by anybody else, these pages must show. To begin my life with the beginning of my life, I record that I was born (as I have been informed and believe) on a Friday, at twelve o'clock at night. It was remarked that the clock began to strike, and I began to cry, simultaneously. (Dickens 13)

"Will this narrator be authored, or will he author himself?" Butler asks (3), then moves to Merleau-Ponty to emphasize that subject formation is always interdependent, and/yet is confounded by the unknowns inherent in the transitivity of interaction.[8] For Butler, the emergence of the subject is an ongoing series of tales (and disavowals) of crafting and being crafted; Butler asserts, "we require forms of fiction to arrive at self-understanding" (16). Or as Pennington asserts of fictional autobiography's resonances with real life interactions, "you and I and everyone we know are fictions" (5).

In this vein, although we often venture to the archive seeking truth in diaries, letters, images, and ephemera, the archive is just as slippery as any other text. In fact, Derrida describes the archive as "retrospective science fiction" (17), and warns of the inherent contradictions of "archive fever": the way it's driven by nostalgia, a kind of homesickness, and desire for origins; and how, like all histories, it never culminates in truth-telling but is instead a project of knowledge about the past that is shaped by how it is curated, ordered, stored, and accessed (57). Again, consider David Copperfield, who (like Michael Field), "exposes the process of self-creation in his attempts to control the production and consumption of his image" (Pennington 73). We must ask in what ways the story presented by the diary/archive is reliable, much as we might ask if the narrator of a novel, especially a fictional autobiography, is a reliable narrator.

When we read *Works and Days*, do we think Bradley and Cooper are reliable narrators? *Does it matter if they are not?* What are we looking for, what are our aims as readers of the archive? Maybe these questions about ourselves are just as important as those we pose about our "subjects". Heather Love provocatively notes that the turn to affective history urges us to [stop] asking "were there

---

[8] This is Butler glossing Merleau-Ponty's "The Intertwining" from *The Visible and the Invisible*; it is also an example of gearing into the unknown (*l'engrenage*)."

gay people in the past . . . and [focus on] questions such as why do we care so much if there were gay people in the past" (31). How and why do we (especially feminist, queer readers) read/teach Michael Field or any other queer figure from the past?[9] These are important things to know about oneself, and for our students to know about themselves.

Bradley and Cooper's life and work can be understood as an example of how one might look backward in order to look forward—how to use one's encounters with the uncertainty and unknowability of the Other as a zone of possibility, critical intervention, imagination, and queer-feminist resistance. Michael Field's passion is palpable as they gear into (*engrener*) those uncertainties, viewing themselves—like Sappho, Tiresias, Callirrhoë, and Canute the Great—as radical figures who venture into unknown territory. Indeed, Holly Laird says, "Field . . . anticipates the feminist, historicizing scholar, the scholar who seeks representation of women and gender in the fracturing mirror of the past in order to put the fragments together in her own documents" ("Contradictory" 112). Bradley and Cooper's writing about their collaboration in *Works and Days* also documents their efforts to negotiate both positive and negative responses from others—and their own sometimes significant personal differences—as they sought to find their way in the very uncertain terrain of an intimate life and writing partnership for which they had few role models.

Living, loving, and writing as Michael Field, Bradley and Cooper's central concern was Art: writing it, living among it, understanding it, talking about it. While not all readers of Michael Field today will share that central concern, there are still many questions we can bring to their archive: What might reading Michael Field help us understand about our struggles to live authentically in less than ideal conditions, and about consuming artistic and other cultural artifacts in ways that acknowledge the epistemic tensions between the subjective and the objective? How might Michael Field help us think about navigating the entanglements and intra-actions between self and other in the larger context of a natural environment that causes us to ponder, simultaneously, both simple and sublime natural beauty, the inevitability of environmental destruction, and the imminence of decay? What might Bradley and Cooper help us understand about the

---

[9] I consider this topic at length in "From 'We Other Victorians.'"

multiple things that cause one to experience grief and the multiple ways to mourn? Multiple ways to explore spirituality and the multiple ways that faith and hope can be shaken? What might we learn about desire, disease, having (or not having) community, and facing death?

Here I pause to channel Virginia Woolf in the first paragraph of *A Room of One's Own*, and to inform the reader that I am not going to be able to fulfill the duty of a conclusion and hand you a nugget of pure truth to wrap up between the pages of your notebooks and keep on the mantelpiece forever. But in order to make some amends I am going to do what I can to show you how I arrived at the opinion that I should end with a provocation, which is that we can better explore our questions about Michael Field and their revisionary poetics if we acknowledge our own role, not just as consumers, but as co-creators of *Works and Days*—or indeed, as co-creators of any archive. In saying this, I am influenced by Lynne Huffer's analysis of Foucault's dialectical interactions with the alterity of archives both past and present, which first requires one to recognize one's own self-understanding, one's own time, as an archive. Huffer writes: "[Foucault] comes to know the present through contact with the past in an experience of strangeness that renders the familiar unintelligible: the archive makes him feel the startlingly unfamiliar edges of our own time" (82).

My provocation has its origins in a lesson I learned when, early in my career, I first ventured into the Michael Field archive. I had worked briefly in archives before, but not in London; it was too expensive, and too far away. So I had not had the opportunity to work in the archives of the subjects with whom I was obsessed: Michael Field. In the summer after my first year of full-time employment, and with my fifteen-month-old doctoral degree still feeling fresh and shiny, I took myself to the British Library, determined to find answers and to have an intellectually transformative experience. On the transatlantic flight, I resolved to take up daily journaling, something I had not done in years. And so every morning I met Michael Field in the pages of the White Book in the British Library's manuscript reading room, every evening I emailed friends back in the States about what "Katharine and Edith had done that day," and later that night I penned copious thoughts and feelings in the pages of a journal I had purchased in the British Library gift shop. About two weeks into my four-week stay, I reread everything I had written in that journal.

And I thought: "Jill, you are so full of crap!" And then I thought if some of what I had penned in my diary was, at least to some extent, a fiction, it was likely that at least some of the truths I was discovering in the archive were probably fictions, too. And indeed, it was an intellectually transformative experience. And it's a story I've been telling my students for years, as a way to explain the epistemological slipperiness and interpretive multitudes inherent in all texts, even the ones that are supposed to be the most authoritative. And even as I retell it now, I'm actually not sure it's a retelling of what really happened, or of what I really thought.

I close with Michael Field's poem "A Palimpsest" from *Wild Honey*, which can be read as just such a study of the self, one that acknowledges the lure of the archive—and a testimony to how the lure of the archive necessitates the study of the self. They write:

>   ... The rest
> Of our life must be a palimpsest-
> The old writing there the best.
>
> In the parchment hoary
> Lies a golden story,
> As 'mid secret feathers of a dove
> As 'mid moonbeams shifted through a cloud:
>
> Let us write it over
> O my lover,
> For the far Time to Discover,
> As 'mid secret feathers of a dove,
> As 'mid moonbeams shifted through a cloud! (180)

This is a backward glance that enacts a future vision of the self, for both the self and the beloved. It invites a future reader to parse through the faint shadows of what's been previously written and discover a hidden truth—the golden story—while also acknowledging that that truth (like Bradley and Cooper's study of history and art history) is always going to be subjective, perhaps to the point of being a fiction, always gearing into the unknown, and always in progress. Here Michael Field write themselves into their equally unknown future selves, making, creating, revising what their poem performs, and in so doing become the subject of their own *poiesis*.

Bibliography

Manuscript sources

Archive of "Michael Field." Oxford, Bodleian Libraries.
Correspondence from Michael Field to John "Dorian" Gray. The National Library of Scotland.
Michael Field. *Works and Days*, 1868–1914. Unpublished MSS Add. 46776–46804. The British Library, London.

Printed sources

Ahmed, Sara. *Living a Feminist Life*. Duke UP, 2017.
—. *Queer Phenomenology: Objects, Orientations, Others*. Duke UP, 2006.
Alaimo, Stacy. *Bodily Natures: Science, Environment, and the Material Self*. Indiana UP, 2010.
Andrews, Kit. "Walter Pater as Oxford Hegelian: *Plato and Platonism* and T. H. Green's *Prolegomena to Ethics*," *Journal of the History of Ideas* 72, no. 3 (2011): 437–59.
Anon. "Michael Field's New Plays." Rev. of *Canute the Great; A Cup of Water*. *The Spectator* (November 12, 1886), pp. 1536–8.
Archer, William. "A Pre-Shakespearean Playwright." Rev of *The Father's Tragedy, William Rufus, Loyalty or Love*. *Pall Mall Budget* (August 27, 1885), p. 20.
Armstrong, Isobel. "D. G. Rossetti and Christina Rossetti as Sonnet Writers." *Victorian Poetry* 48, no. 4 (December 2010): 461.
—. *Victorian Poetry: Poetry, Poetics and Politics*. Routledge, 1993.
Armstrong, Kit. "Byrd's Counterpoint," January 6, 2018. Web. <https://www.youtube.com/watch?v=7axwDzY21Qw>

Arnold, Matthew. *Matthew Arnold: Selected Writings*. Ed. Seamus Perry. Oxford UP, 2020.

Bashant, Wendy. "Aesthetes and Queens: Michael Field, John Ruskin, and *Bellerophôn*," *Journal of Pre-Raphaelite Studies* 15 (March 2006): 74–94.

Bashford, Christina. "Historiography and Invisible Musics: Domestic Chamber Music in Nineteenth-Century Britain," *Journal of the American Musicological Society* 63, no. 2 (Summer 2010): 291–360.

Beers, Henry A. "Retrospects of the Drama," *The North American Review* 185, no. 619 (1907): 623–34.

Benjamin, Walter. "The Task of the Translator." *The Translation Studies Reader*. Ed. Lawrence Venuti. Routledge, 1997, pp. 75–83.

Bennet, Jane. *Influx and Efflux: Writing Up with Walt Whitman*. Duke UP, 2020.

—. *Vibrant Matter*. Duke UP, 2020.

Berenson, Bernard. *The Florentine Painters of the Renaissance: With an Index to Their Works*. G. P. Putnam's Sons, 1898.

Bickle, Sharon. *The Fowl and the Pussycat: Love Letters of Michael Field, 1876–1909*. U Virginia P, 2008.

—. "Living 'Willfully': The Same-Sex Marriage Ceremony of 'Michael Field' by the Smutt River," *Hecate: A Woman's Interdisciplinary Journal* 41, no. 1/2 (2016).

—. "Victorian Mænads: On Michael Field's *Callirrhoë* and Being Driven Mad," *The Michaelian* 2 (December 2010). Web.

Blain, Virginia. "'Michael Field, the Two-Headed Nightingale': Lesbian Text as Palimpsest," *Women's History Review* 5, no. 2 (1996): 239–57.

Blair, Kirstie. *Form and Faith in Victorian Poetry and Religion*. Oxford UP, 2012.

Booth, Michael. *Prefaces to English Nineteenth-Century Theatre*. Manchester UP, 1980.

Bourget, Paul. "Essai de psychologie contemporaine: Charles Baudelaire," *La Nouvelle Revue* 13 (1881): 398–417.

Bristow, Joseph. "Michael Field's Lyrical Aestheticisim: *Underneath the Bough*," in *Michael Field and Their World*. Ed. Margaret Stetz and Cheryl Wilson. Rivendale Press, 2007.

—. "Michael Field in Their Time and Ours," *Tulsa Studies in Women's Literature* 29, no. 1 (2010): 159–79.

Bronfen, Elisabeth. *Over Her Dead Body: Death, Femininity, and the Aesthetic*. Routledge, 1992.

Browning, Elizabeth Barrett. *Aurora Leigh (and other poems)* (1856). Ed. John Bolton and Julia Bolton Holloway. Penguin, 1996.

Bullen, A. H. (ed.) *Lyrics from the Song-Books of the Elizabethan Age*. Nimmo, 1887.
Burroughs, Catherine (ed.) *Closet Drama: History, Theory, Form*. Routledge, 2018.
Butler, Judith, *Senses of the Subject*. Fordham UP, 2015.
Byrd, William. *Songs of Sundrie Natures (1589)*. Ed. David Mateer. Stainer & Bell, c. 2004. (The Byrd Edition, 13.)
Campion, Thomas. *The Works of Dr. Thomas Campion*. Ed. A. H. Bullen. Chiswick Press, 1889.
Capgrave, John. *The Life of Saint Katherine of Alexandria*. Trans. Karen Winstead. U Notre Dame P, 2011.
Castle, Terry. *The Apparitional Lesbian: Female Homosexuality and Modern Culture*. Columbia UP, 1993.
Cauti, Camille. "Michael Field's Pagan Catholicism," in *Michael Field and their World*. Ed. Margaret D. Stetz and Cheryl A. Wilson. Rivendale Press, 2007. pp 181–9.
Clewell, Tammy. "Mourning Beyond Melancholia: Freud's Psychoanalysis of Loss," *Journal of the American Psychoanalytic Association* 52, no. 1 (2004): 43–67.
Codell, Julie. "The Aura of Mechanical Reproduction: Victorian Art and the Press," *Victorian Periodicals Review* 24, no. 1 (Spring 1993): 4–10.
Codell, Julie F., and Linda K. Hughes. *Replication in the Long Nineteenth Century: Re-Makings and Reproductions*. Edinburgh UP, 2018.
Cohen, William A. *Embodied: Victorian Literature and the Senses*. U Minnesota P, 2009.
Cottam, Rachel. "Diaries and Journals," in *Encyclopedia of Life Writing: Autobiographical and Biographical Forms*. Ed. Margaretta Jolly. Routledge, 2013.
Crary, Jonathan. *Techniques of the Observer: On Vision and Modernity in the Nineteenth Century*. MIT P, 1992.
Culley, Margo. "Introduction to *A Day at Time: Diary Literature of American Women, from 1764 to 1985*," in *Women, Autobiography, Theory: A Reader*. Ed. Sidonie Smith and Julia Watson. U Wisconsin P, 1998.
Danahay, Martin A. "Male Masochism: A Model of Victorian Masculine Identity Formation," in *Life Writing and Victorian Culture*. Ed. David Amigoni. Ashgate, 2006.
Davis, Lennard J. *Enforcing Normalcy: Disability, Deafness, and the Body*. Verso Books, 1995.

Dellamora, Richard. *Masculine Desire: The Sexual Politics of Victorian Aestheticism*. North Carolina UP, 1990.
Denisoff, Dennis. *Decadent Ecology in British Literature and Art, 1869–1910: Decay, Desire, and the Pagan Revival*. Cambridge UP, 2021.
—. "The Dissipating Nature of Paganism," *Modernism/modernity* 15, no. 3 (September 2008): 431–46.
—. "The Lie of the Land: Decadent Ecology and Arboreal Communications," *Victorian Literature and Culture* 49, no. 4 (2021): 621–64.
—. "Natural Environments in Victorian Culture," *Victorian Review* 36, no. 2 (Fall 2010): 7–10.
—. "The Queer Ecology of Vernon Lee's Transient Affections," *Feminist Modernist Studies* 3, no. 2 (2020): 148–61.
Derrida, Jacques. "Archive Fever: A Freudian Impression," *diacritics* 25, no. 2: 9–63.
Dever, Carolyn. *Chains of Love and Beauty: The Diary of Michael Field*. Princeton UP, 2022.
Dickens, Charles. *David Copperfield*. Ed. Jeremy Tambling. Penguin, 2004.
Donoghue, Emma. *We are Michael Field*. Absolute Press, 1998.
Doty, Alexander. *Making Things Perfectly Queer: Interpreting Mass Culture*. U of Minnesota P, 1993.
Dowling, Linda. *Hellenism & Homosexuality in Victorian Oxford*. Cornell UP, 1994.
Drury, Annmarie. "Accident, Orientalism, and Edward FitzGerald as Translator," *Victorian Poetry* 46, no. 1 (Spring 2008): 37–53.
Edelman, Lee. *Homographesis: Essays in Gay Literary and Cultural Theory*. Routledge, 1994.
—. *No Future: Queer Theory and the Death Drive*. Duke UP, 2004.
Egerton, George. "A Keynote to *Keynotes*," in *The Late-Victorian Marriage Question: A Collection of Key New Woman Texts*. Ed. Ann Heilmann. Routledge, 1998.
Ehnenn, Jill R. "From 'We Other Victorians' to 'Pussy Grabs Back': Thinking Gender, Thinking Sex, and Feminist Methodological Futures in Victorian Studies Today," *Victorian Literature and Culture* 47, no.1 (Spring 2019): 35–62.
—. "Haptic Ekphrasis," *Victorian Studies* 64, no. 1 (2021): 88–114.
—. "Looking Strategically: Feminist and Queer Aesthetics in Michael Field's *Sight and Song*," *Victorian Poetry* 42, no. 3 (2004): 213–59.
—. "'Our Brains Struck Fire Each from Each': Disidentification, Difference, and Desire in the Collaborative Aesthetics of Michael

Field," *Economies of Desire at the Victorian Fin de Siècle: Libidinal Lives*. Ed. Jane Ford et al. Routledge, 2016, pp. 180–204.
—. *Women's Literary Collaboration, Queerness, and Late-Victorian Culture*. Ashgate, 2008/Routledge, 2017.
Eiesland, Nancy. *The Disabled God: Toward a Liberatory Theology of Disability*. Abingdon Press, 1994.
Eliot, T. S. *Ash Wednesday*. Faber & Faber, 1930.
—. *Four Quartets*. <http://www.davidgorman.com/4quartets>
—. *The Sacred Wood: Essays on Poetry and Criticism*. Methuen and Co., 1920.
Ellis, Havelock. "Introduction" to *Au Rebours* by Joris-Karl Huysman (1884). Dover, 1969. Web. <http://www.ibiblio.org/eldritch/jkh/rebours.html>
Erevelles, Nirmala. *Disability and Difference in Global Contexts. Enabling a Transformative Body Politic*. Palgrave Macmillan, 2011.
Evangelista, Stefano-Maria. *British Aestheticism and Ancient Greece: Hellenism, Reception, Gods in Exile*. Palgrave Macmillan, 2009.
—. "Greek Textual Archaeology and Erotic Epigraphy in Simeon Solomon and Michael Field," *Cahiers Victoriens et Edouardiens: Revue Du Centre d'Etudes et de Recherches Victoriennes et Edouardiennes de l'Université Paul Valéry, Montpellier* 78 (2013). Web.
Faderman, Lillian. *Surpassing the Love of Men: Romantic Friendship from the Renaissance to the Present*. William Morrow, 1981.
Fehrle, Johannes, and Mark Schmitt. "Adaptation as Cultural Translation," *Komparatistik Online* (2018), pp. 1–86.
Felski, Rita. "On Confession," in *Women, Autobiography, Theory: A Reader*. Ed. Sidonie Smith and Julia Watson. U Wisconsin P, 1998.
Field, Michael. *Callirrhoë. Fair Rosamund*. George Bell & Sons, 1884.
—. *Canute the Great. The Cup of Water*. George Bell & Sons, 1887.
—. "Effigies," *Art Review*. (March 3, 1890), pp. 89–91.
—. *The Father's Tragedy. William Rufus. Loyalty or Love?* George Bell & Sons, 1885.
—. *Long Ago*. George Bell & Sons, 1889.
—. "Mid-Age," *The Contemporary Review*. (September 1889), pp. 431–2.
—. *Music and Silence: The Gamut of Michael Field*. Ed. Ivor Treby. De Blackland Press, 2000.
—. *Mystic Trees*. Everleigh Nash, 1913.
—. *Poems of Adoration*. Sands & Co., 1912.
—. *A Question of Memory*. Matthews and Lane, 1893.

—. *A Shorter Shīrazād: 101 Poems of Michael Field*. Ed. Ivor Treby. De Backland Press, 1999.
—. *Sight and Song*. Elkin Mathews and John Lane, 1892.
—. *The Tragic Mary*. George Bell & Sons, 1890.
—. *Uncertain Rain: Sundry Spells of Michael Field*. Ed. Ivor Treby. De Blackland Press, 2002.
—. *Underneath the Bough*. George Bell & Sons, 1893.
—. *Underneath the Bough*. T. Mosher, 1898.
—. *Whym Chow: Flame of Love*. Eragny Press, 1914.
—. *Wild Honey from Various Thyme*. T. Fisher Unwin, 1908.
—. *Works and Days: From the Journal of Michael Field*. Ed. T. and D. C. Sturge Moore. John Murray, 1933.
FitzGerald, Edward. *The Rubáiyát of Omar Khayyám*, A Critical Edition. Ed. Christopher Decker. U Virginia P, 2008.
Fletcher. Robert. "I Leave a Page Half-Writ," in *Women's Poetry, Late Romantic to Late Victorian*. Ed. Isobel Armstrong and Virginia Blain. Palgrave Macmillan, 1999, pp. 164–82.
Flint, Kate. *The Victorians and the Visual Imagination*. Cambridge UP, 2000.
Fothergill, Robert. "19th century diaries," in *Encyclopedia of Life Writing: Autobiographical and Biographical Forms*. Ed. Margaretta Jolly. Routledge, 2001.
Foucault, Michel. "Interview with Lucette Finas." Trans. P. Foss and M. Morris, in *Michel Foucault: Power, Truth, Strategy*. Ed. M. Morris and P. Patton. Prometheus Books, 1979.
—. "What is an Author?" in *Textual Strategies: Perspectives on Post-Structuralist Criticism*. Ed. Josue Harari. Cornell UP, 1979, pp. 141–60.
Fraser, Hilary. "The Religious Poetry of Michael Field," in *Athena's Shuttle: Myth Religion Ideology from Romanticism to Modernism*. Ed. Franco Marucci and Emma Sdegno. Cisalpino, 2000, pp. 127–42.
—. "A Visual Field: Michael Field and the Gaze," *Victorian Literature and Culture* 34, no. 2 (2006): 553–71.
—. *Women Writing Art History in the Nineteenth Century: Looking Like a Woman*. Cambridge UP, 2014.
Freedgood, Elaine. *Worlds Enough: The Invention of Realism in the Victorian Novel*. Princeton UP, 2019.
Freeman, Elizabeth. *Beside You in Time: Sense Methods and Queer Sociabilities in the American Nineteenth Century*. Duke UP, 2019.
—. *Time Binds: Queer Temporalities, Queer Histories*. Duke UP, 2010.
Freud, Sigmund. *The Ego and the Id* (1923). Trans. Joan Riviere. Rev. and ed. James Strachey. Norton, 1962.

—. "Mourning and Melancholia" (1917), in *Sigmund Freud, Collected Papers* Vol. IV. Trans. Joan Riviere. Basic, 1959.

Friedman, Dustin. *Before Queer Theory: Victorian Aestheticism and the Self*. The Johns Hopkins UP, 2019.

Frye, Northrop. *Anatomy of Criticism: Four Essays* (1957). Ed. Michael Dolzani. U Toronto P, 2006.

Fuchs, Thomas. "Presence in absence: The ambiguous phenomenology of grief," *Phenomenology and the Cognitive Sciences* 17 (2018): 43–63.

Garofalo, Devin. "The Victorian Lyric in the Anthropocene," *Victorian Literature and Culture* 47, no. 4 (November 2019): 753–83.

Gates, Barbara. *Kindred Nature: Victorian and Edwardian Women Embrace the Living World*. U Chicago P, 1999.

Gazzaniga, Andrea, "Collaborative Space and the Poetics of Enclosure in Michael Field's *Underneath the Bough*," *Victorians Institute Journal* 42, no. 1 (December 2014): 144–78.

Genette, Gérard. *Narrative Discourse*. Trans. Jane E. Lewin. Blackwell, 1980.

Gilbert, Sandra, and Susan Gubar. *The Madwoman in the Attic: The Woman Writer and the Nineteenth-Century Literary Imagination*. Yale UP, 1979.

Gilmore, Jonathan. "Between Philosophy and Art," *The Cambridge Companion to Merleau-Ponty*. Ed. Taylor Carman and Mark B. N. Hansen. Cambridge UP, 2005, pp. 291–317.

Glavey, Brian. *The Wallflower Avante-garde: Modernism, Sexuality, and Queer Ekphrasis*. Oxford UP, 2016.

Glavin, John. *After Dickens: Reading, Adaptation, Performance*. Cambridge UP, 1999.

Gold, Barry. *ThermoPoetics, Energy in Victorian Literature and Science*. MIT Press, 2010.

Gorman, Francis. "Michael Field and Sapphic Fame: My Dark-Leaved Laurels Will Endure," *Victorian Literature and Culture* 34, no. 2 (2006): 649–61.

Gracia, Dominique. "'The One Question Is Not What You Mean but What You Do': Michael Field's Ekphrastic Verse," *Victorian Poetry* 57, no. 3 (2019): 345–64.

Gray, F. Elizabeth. "Making Christ: Alice Meynell, Poetry, and the Eucharist," *Christianity and Literature* 52, no. 2 (Winter 2003): 159–79.

—. "Syren Strains. Victorian Women's Devotional Poetry and John Keble's *The Christian Year*," *Victorian Poetry* 44, no. 1 (Spring 2006): 61–76.

Green-Lewis, Jennifer. *Framing the Victorians: Photography and the Culture of Realism*. Cornell UP, 1996.
—. *Victorian Photography, Literature and the Invention of Modern Memory: Already the Past*. Bloomsbury Academic, 2017.
Gregory of Nazianus. *On God and Christ: The Five Theological Orations and Two Letters to Cledonius*. St. Vladimir's Seminary Press, 2002.
Hagstrum, Jean H. *The Sister Arts; the Tradition of Literary Pictorialism and English Poetry from Dryden to Gray*. U Chicago P, 1958.
Halberstam, Jack. *In a Queer Time and Place*. New York UP, 2005.
—. *The Queer Art of Failure*. Duke UP, 2011.
Hall, Jason David, and Alex Murray. *Decadent Poetics: Literature and Form at the British Fin de Siècle*. Palgrave Macmillan, 2013.
Hall, Kim Q. "No Failure: Climate Change, Radical Hope, and Queer Crip Feminist Eco-Futures," *Radical Philosophy Review* 17 (2014): 203–25.
Harrington, Emily. "Michael Field and the Detachable Lyric," *Victorian Studies* 50, no. 2 (2008): 221–32.
—. *Second Person Singular: Late-Victorian Women Poets and the Bonds of Verse*. U Virginia P, 2014.
Harris-McCormick. "Introduction" *Nineteenth-Century Gender Studies* 7, no. 2 (Summer 2011). Web.
Hedley, Jane, Nick Halpern, and Willard Spiegelman (eds). *In the Frame: Women's Ekphrastic Poetry from Marianne Moore to Susan Wheeler*. U Delaware P, 2009.
Heffernan, James A. W. *Museum of Words: The Poetics of Ekphrasis from Homer to Ashbery*. U Chicago P, 2008.
Hegel, G. W. F. "Die Phänomenologie Des Geistes Das Bewußtsein: The Phenomenology of Spirit Consciousness," *The Berlin Phenomenology/ Die Berliner Phänomenologie*, 2011.
Helsinger, Elizabeth. *Poetry and the Thought of Song in Nineteenth-Century Britain*. U Virginia P, 2015.
Henchman, Anna. "Edward Lear Dismembered: Word Fragments and Body Parts," *Nineteenth-Century Contexts* 35, no. 5 (December 2013): 479–87.
Hensley, Nathan K. *Forms of Empire: The Poetics of Victorian Sovereignty*. 1st edn. Oxford UP, 2016.
Hensley, Nathan K. and Philip Steer. "Introduction: Ecological Formalism; or, Love among the Ruins," *Ecological Form: System and Aesthetics in the Age of Empire*. Fordham UP, 2018.
Herzog, Patricia. "The Condition to which all art aspires: Reflections on

Pater and Music," *The British Journal of Aesthetics* 36, no. 2 (April 1996): 122–34.

Hesiod. *The Homeric Hymns and Homerica, with an English translation by Hugh G. Evelyn-White*. Heinemann, 1914.

Hewitt, Martin. "Diary, Autobiography and the Practice of Life History," in *Life Writing and Victorian Culture*. Ed. David Amigoni. Ashgate, 2006.

Heyes, Cressida. *Anaesthetics of Existence*. Duke UP, 2020.

Hollander, John. *The Gazer's Spirit: Poems Speaking to Silent Works of Art*. U Chicago P, 1995.

Hudson, Benjamin. "The Exquisite Amateur: FitzGerald, the *Rubáiyát*, and Queer Dilettantism," *Victorian Poetry* 54, no. 2 (Summer 2016): 155–77.

Huffer, Lynne. *Foucault's Strange Eros*. Columbia UP, 2020.

Hughes, Linda K. "Feminizing Decadence: Poems by Graham R. Tomson," *Women and British Aestheticism*. Ed. Talia Schaffer and Kathy Alexis Psomiades. U Virginia P, 1999, pp. 119–38.

Huseby, Amy Kahrmann. "Queer Social Counting and the Generational Transitions of Michael Field," *Women's Writing* 26, no. 2 (May 2019): 199–213.

Hutcheon, Linda. *A Theory of Adaptation*. Routledge, 2006.

Jalland, Patricia. *Death and the Victorian Family*. Oxford UP, 1996.

Joseph, Gerhard, and Herbert Tucker. "Passing On: Death," in *A Companion to Victorian Literature and Culture*. Ed. Herbert Tucker. Blackwell, 1999.

Kafer, Alison. *Feminist, Queer, Crip*. Indiana UP, 2013.

Kaye, Richard. "Saint Sebastian and the Victorian Discourse of Decadence," *Victorian Literature and Culture* 27 (1999): 269–303.

Keble, John. *Lectures on Poetry, 1832–1841 Volume 1*. Clarendon Press, 1912.

Keefe, Anne. "The Ecstatic Embrace of Verbal and Visual: Twenty-First Century Lyric beyond the Ekphrastic Paragone," *Word & Image: A Journal of Verbal/Visual Enquiry* 27, no. 2 (April 2011): 135–47.

Kersh, Sarah. "'Betwixt Us Two': Whym Chow, Metonymy, and the Amatory Sonnet Tradition," in *Michael Field, Decadent Moderns*. Ed. Sarah Parker and Ana Parejo Vadillo. Ohio UP, 2019, pp. 256–75.

Kessler, Jeffrey C. "Vernon Lee's Imaginary Portraits: 'Somewhere in the Borderland between Fact and Fancy,'" *Nineteenth-Century Contexts* 38, no. 5 (December 2016): 377–86.

Kreisel, Deanna. "'Form Against Force': Sustainability and Organicism in the Work of John Ruskin," in *Ecological Form: System and Aesthetics in the Age of Empire*. Eds. Nathan K. Hensley and Phillip Steer. Fordham UP, 2018.

Krieger, Murray. *Ekphrasis: The Illusion of the Natural Sign*. The Johns Hopkins UP, 1986.

Laird, Holly. "The Coauthored Pseudonym: Two Women Named Michael Field," *The Faces of Anonymity: Anonymous and Pseudonymous Publication from the Sixteenth to the Twentieth Century*. Ed. Robert J. Griffin. Palgrave Macmillan, 2003, pp. 193–209.

—. "Contradictory Legacies: Michael Field and Feminist Restoration," *Victorian Poetry* 33, no. 1 (Spring 1995): 111–28.

—. *Women Coauthors*. U Illinois P, 2000.

LaMonaca, Maria. *Masked Atheism: Catholicism and the Victorian Secular Home*. Ohio State UP, 2008.

Landes, Donald, "Translation as *Engrenage*: Between Creating and Repeating *The Phenomenology of Perception*," Keynote Address: Diverse Lineages of Existentialism II. The George Washington University, Washington, DC, June 3, 2019.

Landow, George. "Introduction," *Approaches to Victorian Autobiography*. Ohio UP, 1979.

Lee, Michelle S. "Michael Field's *Stephania*: The Closet Drama as a Space for Female Fortitude and Artistic Agency," *Closet Drama: History, Theory, Form*. Ed. Catherine Burroughs, Routledge, 2019, pp. 127–38.

Leighton, Angela. "Michael Field," in *Victorian Women Poets: Writing Against the Heart*. Harvester, 1992, pp. 202–43.

—. *Victorian Women Poets: A Critical Reader*. Blackwell, 1996.

Leighton, Angela, and Margaret Reynolds, Eds. *Victorian Women Poets: An Anthology*. Wiley-Blackwell, 1995

Leitch, Thomas. "Twelve Fallacies in Contemporary Adaptation Theory," *Criticism: A Quarterly for Literature and the Arts* 45, no. 2 (2003): 149–71.

Lejeune, Phillip. *On Autobiography*. U Minnesota P, 1989.

Lessing, Gotthold Ephraim. *Laocoön: An Essay on the Limits of Painting and Poetry*. The Johns Hopkins UP, 1984.

Levine, Caroline. *Forms: Whole, Rhythm, Hierarchy, Network*. Princeton UP, 2015.

—. "Strategic Formalism: Toward a New Method in Cultural Studies," *Victorian Studies* 48, no. 4 (2006): 625–57.

Lewes, G. H. Rev. of Hegel's *Lectures on Aesthetics*. *The British and Foreign Review*. Vol 13, No. XXV, 1842.

—. "Principles of Success in Literature," *Fortnightly Review* 1 (1865): 707.

Lockerd, Martin. *Decadent Catholicism and the Making of Modernism*. Bloomsbury, 2020.

Loizeaux, Elizabeth Bergmann. *Twentieth-Century Poetry and the Visual Arts*. Cambridge UP, 2008.

Lootens, Tricia. *The Political Poetess: Victorian Femininity, Race, and the Legacy of Separate Spheres*. Princeton UP, 2017.

Love, Heather. *Feeling Backward: Loss and the Politics of Queer History*. Harvard UP, 2007.

Lysack, Krysta. "Aesthetic Consumption and the Cultural Production of Michael Field's *Sight and Song*," *SEL: Studies in English Literature 1500–1900* 45, no 4 (Autumn 2005): 935–60.

MacDuffie, Allen. *Victorian Literature, Energy, and the Ecological Imagination*. Cambridge UP, 2014.

McGrath, F. C. *The Sensible Spirit: Walter Pater and the Modernist Paradigm*. U Florida P, 1986.

Machann, Clinton. *The Genre of Autobiography in Victorian Literature*. U Michigan P, 1994.

McRuer, Robert, and Abby Wilkerson, "Introduction" to *Desiring Disability, Queer Theory Meets Disability Studies* [special issue], *GLQ* 9.1–2 (2003): 1–23.

Madden, Ed. "Penetrating Matthew Arnold," in *Michael Field and Their World*. Ed. Margaret D. Stetz and Cheryl A. Wilson. Rivendale Press, 2007.

Mangum, Teresa. "Animal Angst: Victorians Memorialize their Pets," in *Victorian Animal Dreams: Representations of Animals in Victorian Literature and Culture*. Ed. Deborah Denenholz Morse and Martin A. Danahay. Ashgate, 2007.

Mahoney, Kristin. *Literature and the Politics of Post-Victorian Decadence*. Cambridge UP, 2015.

—. "Michael Field's Eric Gill: Radical Kinship, Cosmopolitanism, and Queer Catholicism," in *Michael Field, Decadent Moderns*. Ed. Sarah Parker and Ana Parejo Vadillo. Ohio UP, 2019, pp. 230–55.

—. "Michael Field and Queer Community at the Fin-de-Siècle," *Victorians Institutes Journal* 41, no. 1 (2015): 35–40.

Manuwald Gesine. "Thomas Campion: A poet between the two worlds of classic and English literature," in *Neo-Latin Poetry in the British Isles*. Ed. L. B. T. Houghton and Gesine Manuwald. Bloomsbury Academic, 2012.

Martin, Meredith. "Prosody," *Cambridge Companion to Victorian Women's Poetry*. Ed. Linda Hughes. Cambridge UP, 2019, pp. 28–44.

Mason, Emma. "Christina Rossetti and the Doctrine of Reserve," *Journal of Victorian Culture* 7, no. 2 (2002).

Matthews, Brander. "The Legitimacy of the Closet-Drama," *The North American Review* 187, no. 627 (1908): 213–23.

Maxwell, Catherine. "Michael Field, Death, and the Effigy," *Word & Image* 34, no. 1 (January 2018): 31–9.

Medrano, Leire Barerra. "St. Theresa, I call on you to help …" in *Michael Field: Decadent Moderns*. Ed. Sarah Parker and Ana Parejo Vadillo. Ohio UP, 2019, pp. 210–29.

Meisel, Martin. *Realizations: Narrative, Pictorial, and Theatrical Arts in Nineteenth-Century England*. Princeton UP, 1983.

Meisel, Perry. *The Absent Father: Virginia Woolf and Walter Pater*. Yale UP, 1980.

—. *The Myth of the Modern: A Study of British Literature and Criticism after 1850*. Yale UP, 1987.

Merleau-Ponty, Maurice. *The Phenomenology of Perception*. Trans. Donald A. Landes. Routledge, 2012.

—. *The Visible and the Invisible: Followed by Working Notes / Maurice Merleau-Ponty*. Ed. Claude Lefort. Trans. Alphonso Lingis. Northwestern UP, 1980.

Meynell, Alice. *Poems*. Burns Oates and Washburn, 1913.

Mill, J. S. "Thoughts on Poetry and Its Varieties," Part I *The Crayon* 7, no. 4 (April 1860): 93–7.

—. "Thoughts on Poetry and Its Varieties," Part II *The Crayon* 7, no. 5 (May 1860): 123–8.

Miller, Elizabeth Carolyn. *Extraction Ecologies and the Literature of the Long Exhaustion*. Princeton UP, 2021.

Miller, Tracy. "Matthew Arnold's Poetics of Place and the Victorian Elegy," *Victorian Poetry* (2012).

Mitchell, Rebecca. "Death Becomes Her: On the Progressive Potential of Victorian Mourning," *Victorian Literature and Culture* 41 (2013): 595–620.

Mitchell, W. J. T. "Ekphrasis and the Other," *The South Atlantic Quarterly* 91, no. 3 (June 1992): 695.

—. *Iconology: Image, Text, Ideology*. U Chicago P, 1986.

—. *Picture Theory*. U Chicago P, 1994.

Moffat, Mary Jane, and Charlotte Painter. *Revelation: Diaries of Women*. Vintage, 1974.

Moine, Fabienne. *Women Poets in the Victorian Era: Cultural Practices and Nature Poetry*. Routledge, 2015.

Moon, Michael. "Memorial Rags," in *Professions of Desire: Lesbian and Gay Studies in Literature*. Ed. George Haggerty and Bonnie Zimmerman. MLA, 1995.

Mortimer-Sandilands, Catriona, and Bruce Erickson (eds). *Queer Ecologies: Sex, Nature, Politics, Desire*. Indiana UP, 2010.

Morton, Timothy. "Queer Ecology," *PMLA* 125, no. 2 (March 2010): 273–82.

Muñoz, José Esteban. *Cruising Utopia: The There and Then of Queer Futurity*. NY UP, 2019.

—. *Disidentification: Queers of Color and the Performance of Politics*. U Minnesota P, 1999.

Murray, Alex. "Michael Field's Wordsworth," *Victorian Poetry* 58, no. 4 (March 2020): 427–50.

Nietzche, Friedrich. *The Birth of Tragedy*. Trans. Wm A. Haussman. Allen & Unwin, 1923.

—. *Untimely Meditations*. Cambridge UP, 1997.

Nussbaum, Felicity. "The Politics of Subjectivity and the Ideology of Genre," in *Women, Autobiography, Theory: A Reader*. Ed. Sidonie Smith and Julia Watson. U Wisconsin P, 1998.

O'Gorman, Francis. "Michael Field and Sapphic Fame: 'My Dark-Leaved Laurels Will Endure,'" *Victorian Literature and Culture* 34, no. 2 (2006): 649–61.

Ohi, Kevin. *Henry James and the Queerness of Style*. U Minnesota P, 2011.

Olverson, T. D. "Libidinous Laureates and Lyrical Maenads: Michael Field, Swinburne and Erotic Hellenism," *Victorian Poetry* 47, no. 4 (2009): 759–76.

—. *Women Writers and the Dark Side of Late-Victorian Hellenism*. Palgrave Macmillan, 2010.

Ovid. *The Amores*. Trans. H. Riley, 1885. Web. <https://www.gutenberg.org/files/47676/47676-h/47676-h.htm>

Parker, Sarah. "Bittersweet: Michael Field's Sapphic Palate," *Decadence and the Senses*. Ed. Jane Desmarais and Alice Condé. Legenda Books, 2017, pp. 121–40.

Parker, Sarah, and Ana Vadillo, Eds. *Michael Field, Decadent Moderns*. Ohio UP, 2019.

Parkins, Wendy. "Edward Carpenter's Queer Ecology of the Everyday," *Interdisciplinary Studies in the Long Nineteenth Century* 19, no. 26 (June 2018): 1–18.

Pater, Walter. *Greek Studies, A Series of Essays*. Macmillan, 1895.
—. *Plato and Platonism: A Series of Lectures*. Macmillan, 1893.
—. *The Renaissance* (1893). Macmillan, 1922.
—. "The School of Giorgione," *The Fortnightly Review* (October 1, 1877), pp. 526–38.
—. *Studies in the History of the Renaissance*. Macmillan, 1873.
—. *Walter Pater: Three Major Texts*. Ed. William E. Buckler. NY UP, 1986.
Patmore, Coventry. "A Farewell," in *Poems* (1877). George Bell & Sons, 1915.
Pausanias. *Description of Greece*. Trans. W. H. S. Jones and H. A. Omerod. Loeb Classical Library Volumes. Harvard UP, 1918. Web. <https://www.theoi.com/Text/Pausanias1A.html>
Pearsall, Cynthia. "Burying the Duke: Victorian Mourning and the Funeral of the Duke of Wellington," *Victorian Literature and Culture* (1999), pp. 365–93.
Pennington, Heidi L. *Creating Identity in the Victorian Fictional Autobiography*. U Missouri P, 2018.
Peterson, Linda. *Victorian Autobiography: The Tradition of Self-Interpretation*. Yale UP, 1986.
Plumwood, Val. *Environmental Culture: The Ecological Crisis of Reason*. Routledge 2001.
—. *The Eye of the Crocodile*. Ed. Lorraine Shannon. Australian National University Press, 2012.
—. "Prey to a Crocodile," *The Aisling Magazine* 30 (2002). Web. <https://www.aislingmagazine.com/aislingmagazine/articles/TAM30/ValPlumwood.html>
Preyer, Robert. "Victorian Wisdom Literature: Fragments and Maxims," *Victorian Studies* 6, no. 3 (March 1963): 245–62.
Prins, Yopie. "Greek Maenads, Victorian Spinsters," *Victorian Sexual Dissidence*. Ed. Richard Dellamora. U Chicago P, 1999, pp. 43–81.
—. *Ladies' Greek: Victorian Translations of Tragedy*. Princeton UP, 2017.
—. "Sappho Doubled: Michael Field," *The Yale Journal of Criticism* 8, no. 1 (1995): 165–86.
—. *Victorian Sappho*. Princeton UP, 1999.
Propertius. *Elegies*. Ed. Vincent Katz. Perseus Digital Library. Web. <https://www.perseus.tufts.edu/hopper/text?doc=Perseus:text:1999.02.0067>
Ramazani, Jahan. *Poetry of Mourning: The Modern Elegy from Hardy to Heaney*. U Chicago P, 1994.

Ratcliffe, Matthew. "Toward a Phenomenology of Grief: Insights from Merleau-Ponty," *European Journal of Philosophy* (2019): 1–13.

Rich, Adrienne. "When We Dead Awaken: Writing as Re-Vision," *College English* 34 (October 1972): 18–30.

Richardson, LeeAnne M. *The Forms of Michael Field*. Palgrave, 2021.

Ritchie, Helen. "The Portrait Jewels of Charles Ricketts," *Jewelry Studies* 3 (2020): 3–18.

Robinson, A. Mary F. Rev. of *Callirrhoë* and *Fair Rosamund*, *The Academy* 25 (June 7, 1884), pp. 395–6.

Roden, Frederick S. *Same-Sex Desire in Victorian Religious Culture*. Palgrave, 2003.

Rothenstein, Sir William. "Introduction" to *Works and Days: from the Journals of Michael Field*. Ed. T. and D. C. Sturge Moore. John Murray, 1933.

Rowlinson, Matthew. "The Victorian Lyric," *Blackwell's Companion Victorian Poetry*. Ed. Richard Cronin, Alison Chapman, Antony H. Harrison. Blackwell Publishing, 2002, pp. 59–79.

Rudy, Jason R. "Embodiment and Touch," *Cambridge Companion to Victorian Women's Poetry*. Ed. Linda K. Hughes, Cambridge UP, 2019, pp. 79–94.

Sacks, Peter M. *The English Elegy: Studies in the Genre from Spenser to Yeats*. The Johns Hopkins UP, 1985.

Sander, Jochen. *Italienische Gemälde im Städel 1300–1500: Oberitalien, die Marken und Rom* (Kataloge der Gemälde im Städelschen Kunstinstitut Frankfurt am Main, 7). Mainz, 2004, pp. 172–86.

Sanders, Julie. *Adaptation and Appropriation*. Routledge, 2006.

Saville, Julia. "Michael Field's Poetic Imaging," *The Fin-de-Siècle Poem: English Literary Culture and the 1890s*. Ed. Joseph Bristow. Ohio UP, 2005, pp.178–206.

Schaffer, Talia. *The Forgotten Female Aesthetes: Literary Culture in Late-Victorian England*. U Virginia P, 2000.

Schaffer, Talia, and Kathy Alexis Psomiades (eds). *Women and British Aestheticism*. U Virginia P, 1999.

Schenck, Celeste M. "Feminism and Deconstruction: Re-Constructing the Elegy," *Tulsa Studies in Women's Literature* 5, no. 1 (Spring 1986): 13–27.

Scott, Heidi. *Chaos and Cosmos: Literary Roots of Modern Ecology in the British Nineteenth Century*. Penn State UP, 2014.

Sdegno, Emma. *Looking at Tintoretto with John Ruskin. A Venetian Anthology*. Marsilio Editore Spa, 2018.

Sherry, Vincent. *Modernism and the Reinvention of Decadence.* Cambridge UP, 2014.
Shuter, William. "History as Palingenesis in Pater and Hegel," *PMLA* 86, no. 3 (May 1971): 411–21.
—. *Rereading Walter Pater.* Cambridge UP, 1997.
Siegel, Jonah. "Among the English Poets: Keats, Arnold, and the Placement of Fragments," *Victorian Poetry* 37, no. 2 (1999): 215–31.
—. *Desire and Excess: The Nineteenth-Century Culture of Art.* Princeton UP, 2000.
Smith, Logan Pearsall. *Reperusals and Re-collections.* Constable, 1928.
Snodgrass, Chris. "Keeping Faith: Consistency and Paradox in the World View of Michael Field," in *Michael Field and Their World.* Ed. Margaret Stez and Cheryl A.Wilson. Rivendale Press, 2007.
Sophocles. *Antigone.* Ed. Mark Griffith. Cambridge UP, 1999.
Spinoza, Baruch. *The Collected Works of Spinoza.* Vol 2. Ed. Edwin Curley. Princeton UP, 2016.
Stam, Robert. "Beyond Fidelity: The Dialogics of Adaptation," *Film Adaptation* (2000), pp. 53–76.
Strange, Julie-Marie. *Death, Grief, and Poverty in Britain, 1870–1914.* Cambridge UP, 2005.
Stetz, Margaret. "'As She Feels a God Within': Michael Field and Inspiration," in *Michael Field, Decadent Moderns.* Ed. Sarah Parker and Ana Parejo Vadillo. Ohio UP, 2019, pp. 47–66.
—. "'Ballads in Prose': Genre-Crossing in Late-Victorian Women's Writing," *Victorian Literature and Culture* 34 (2006): 619–29.
Stetz, Margaret and Cheryl Wilson (eds). *Michael Field and their World.* Rivendale Press, 2007.
Stoddard Holmes, Martha. *Fictions of Affliction: Physical Disability in Victorian Culture.* U Michigan P, 2004.
Stolte, Tyson. "Atoms, Energy and *The Rubiáyát of Omar Khayyám*," *Victorian Studies* 63, no. 3 (Spring 2021): 354–76.
Stone, Carol. "Elegy as Political Expression in Women's Poetry: Akhmatova, Levertov, Forsche," *College Literature* 18, no. 1 (February 1991): 84–95.
Sturgeon, Mary C. *Michael Field.* G. G. Harrap, 1922.
Summa, Michela. "Toward a Transcendental Account of Creativity. Kant and Merleau-Ponty on the Creative Power of Judgment and Creativity as Institution," *Continental Philosophy Review* 50, no. 1 (2017): 105–26.
Symonds, John Addington. *New Italian Sketches.* Bernhard Tauchnitz, 1884.

Symons. Arthur. "The Decadent Movement in Literature" (1893), in *Aesthetes and Decadents of the 1890s, an Anthology of British Poetry and Prose*. Ed. Karl Beckson. Academy Chicago Publishers, 1993, pp. 134–51.
Tagliaferro, Giorgio. "Celebrating the Most Serene Republic," in *Tintoretto, Artist of the Italian Renaissance*. Ed. Robert Echols and Frederick Ilchman. Yale UP in association with the National Gallery of Art, 2018.
Taylor, Jessie Oak. *The Sky of our Manufacture: The London Fog in British Fiction from Dickens to Woolf*. U Virginia P, 2014.
Tennyson, Lord Alfred. *In Memoriam* (1850). Ed. Erik Gray. Norton, 2004.
Teukolsky, Rachel. *The Literate Eye: Victorian Art Writing and Modernist Aesthetics*. Oxford UP, 2009.
Thain, Marion. "'Damnable Aestheticism' and the Turn to Rome: John Gray, Michael Field, and a Poetics of Conversion," in *The Fin-de-Siècle Poem: English Literary Culture and the 1890s*. Ed. Joseph Bristow. Ohio UP, 2005.
—. *The Lyric Poem and Aestheticism: Forms of Modernity*. Edinburgh UP, 2016.
—. *Michael Field and Poetic Identity, with a Biography*. Eighteen Nineties Society, 2000.
—. *'Michael Field': Poetry, Aestheticism and the Fin de Siècle*. Cambridge UP, 2007.
Thain, Marion, and Ana Parejo Vadillo, Eds. *Michael Field, The Poet: Published and Manuscript Materials*. Broadview, 2009.
Thomas, Kate. "'What Time We Kiss': Michael Field's Queer Temporalities," *GLQ: A Journal of Lesbian and Gay Studies* 13, no. 2 (May 2007): 327–51.
—. "Vegetable Love," in *Michael Field: Decadent Moderns*. Ed. Sarah Parker and Ana Parejo Vadillo. Ohio UP, 2019, pp. 25–46.
Treby, Ivor. *The Michael Field Catalogue: A Book of Lists*. De Blackland Press, 1998.
Tucker, Herbert. "Fretted Lines: Di-versification in Augusta Webster's Dramatic Monologues," *Victorian Poetry* 55, no. 1 (Spring 2017): 105–24.
Vadillo, Ana Parejo. "Aestheticism and Decoration: At Home with Michael Field," *Cahiers: Victoriens et Édouardiens* 74 (2011): 17–36.
—. "'This Hot-House of Decadent Chronicle': Michael Field, Nietzsche and the Dance of Modern Poetic Drama," *Women: A Cultural Review* 26, no. 3 (2015): 195–220.

—. "Outmoded Dramas: History and Modernity in Michael Field's Aesthetic Plays," *Michael Field and Their World*. Ed. Margaret D. Stetz and Cheryl A. Wilson. Rivendale Press, 2007.

—. "Poets of Style: Poetries of Asceticism and Excess," *Cambridge Companion to Victorian Women's Poetry*. Ed. Linda K. Hughes. Cambridge UP, 2019, pp. 230–46.

—. "Sculpture, Poetics, Marble Books: Casting Michael Field," in *Michael Field, Decadent Moderns*. Ed. Sarah Parker and Ana Parejo Vadillo. Ohio UP, 2019.

—. "*Sight and Song:* Transparent Translations and a Manifesto for the Observer," *Victorian Poetry* 38, no. 1 (2000): 15–34.

Vanita, Ruth. *Sappho and the Virgin Mary: Same-Sex Love and the English Literary Imagination*. Columbia UP, 1996.

Vicinus, Martha. "The Adolescent Boy: Fin de Siècle Femme Fatale?" *Journal of the History of Sexuality* 5, no. 1 (1994): 90–114.

—. "Faun Love: Michael Field and Bernard Berenson," *Women's History Review* 18, no. 5 (2009): 753–64.

Wang, Shou-ren. *The Theatre of the Mind: A Study of Unacted Drama in Nineteenth-century England*. Palgrave, 1990.

Weir, David. *Decadence and the Making of Modernism*. U Massachusetts P, 1995.

Westrup, J. A. "William Byrd, 1543–1643," *Music and Letters* 24, no. 3 (July 1943): 125–30.

Wharton, H. T. *Sappho, Memoir, Text, Select Renderings and a Literal Translation*. John Lane, 1884.

Wheeler, Michael. *Death and the Future Life in Victorian Literature and Theology*. Cambridge UP, 1990.

White, Chris. "Flesh and Roses: Michael Field's metaphors of pleasure and desire," *Women's Writing* 3, no. 1 (1996): 47–62.

—. "'Poets and Lovers Evermore': Interpreting Female Love in the Poetry and Journals of Michael Field," *Textual Practice* 4, no. 2 (1990): 197–212.

—. "The Tiresian Poet: Michael Field," *Victorian Women Poets: A Critical Reader*. Ed. Angela Leighton. Blackwell Publishing, 1996, pp. 148–61.

Wilde, Oscar. Rev. of Michael Field's *Canute the Great*, *Woman's World* (February 1888).

—. *The Picture of Dorian Gray*. Ed. Norman Page. Broadview Press, 1998.

Williams, Carolyn. *Transfigured World: Walter Pater's Aesthetic Historicism*. Cornell UP, 1989.

Williams, Kelsey. "'Copied without Loss': Michael Field's Poetic Influence on the Work of W.B. Yeats with Appendix: Yeats's Unpublished Draft Review of Field's Plays," *Journal of Modern Literature* 40, no. 1 (December 2016): 128–46.

Wilson, Cheryl A. "Bodily Sensations in the Conversion Poetry of Michael Field," *Victorian Poetry* 54, no. 2 (September 2016): 179–97.

Witcher, Heather Bozant. *Collaborative Writing in the Long Nineteenth-Century: Sympathetic Partnerships and Artistic Creation.* Cambridge UP, 2022.

—. "A Royal Lady [Re]Born: Balladry, Transport, and Transgression in Michael Field's *A Tragic Mary*," *Victorian Poetry* 55, no. 4 (Winter 2017): 495–516.

Woolf, Virginia. *A Room of One's Own* (1929). Ed. Susan Gubar. Harvest/Harcourt, 2005.

Zigarovich, Jolene. *Writing Death and Absence in the Victorian Novel: Engraved Narratives.* Palgrave, 2012.

Index

"A Bacchic Theatre" (MF), 189–90
"A calm in the flitting sky" (MF), 148–9
"A Cette Heure Où J'ecris" (MF), 214–15
"A Crucifix" (MF), 130, 220–3
"A Girl" (MF), 144n, 153, 155, 158, 182
"A Japanese Print" ("Fellowship," or, "Of Meeting") (MF), 122–4, 126–8
"A Miniature" (MF), 124, 126–8
"A Palimpsest" (MF), 33, 247
"A Pen Drawing of Leda and the Swan" (MF), 113–16
"A spring morning by the sea" ("My deare asleep") (MF), 156–8
ableism, 79n; *see also* compulsory ablebodiedness
absence, 66, 179n, 180, 182–3, 194, 197, 219
  and/as presence, 80, 179n, 182, 184–5, 190, 192, 195, 220
  see also presence
"Absence" (MF), 197
adaptation theory, 27–8, 31–4, 35, 55
adaptation, 2, 21n, 27–8, 30, 45, 46, 48, 160, 208
  blurring boundaries, 99, 110
  as *l'engrenage*, 38
  queer-feminist, 76
  as reconceptualizing the self, 30–1
  as revision of history, 30, 50–1, 64, 71, 165
  see also appropriation; replication
"Adveni, Creator Spiritus" (MF), 194–5
Aesthete, 12, 16, 17, 18, 50, 73, 94n, 175, 179, 201
  female, 2, 4, 17, 74, 89, 93, 124, 232, 242
  male, homoerotically-inclined, 30, 46, 162, 171, 220
Aestheticism, 1, 4, 17–19, 23, 24, 65–6, 68, 223
  Aesthetic paradox, 70, 105–6, 177, 197, 218
  as protoqueer forerunner, 30–1, 73, 94n
  see also Decadence
affect, 4, 18, 31, 34–7, 39–40, 51, 58, 72–3, 104, 166, 195, 233, 244
  affective turn, 3

  queer affect 49, 64
affordance, 33, 40, 43–5, 47, 48–9, 58
  of diary form, 238–41
  of ekphrasis, 90–2, 94, 96–9
  of elegy, 173, 186
  of fragment, 77, 79, 81–2
  of lyric, 138–9
agency, 26, 53, 148
  female, 52, 115
  queer-feminist, 94
Ahmed, Sara, 35, 38–9, 88, 224, 233
Alaimo, Stacy, 146n
amateur, 77, 98, 165
"An Invitation" ("Come and sing my room is south") (MF), 153–5, 158–9
anachronism, 28–9, 48–51, 63–4, 82, 89; *see also* history; looking backward
Anglo-Catholicism, 47, 213, 216; *see also* Christian; Tractarian
Antigone (Sophocles), 169, 192
Apollo, 22, 26, 84, 156, 158, 159
appropriation 21, 32–3, 35, 38, 46, 56, 68, 105, 137, 166, 171; *see also* adaptation
archaism, 46, 62–3, 137, 144, 214; *see also* anachronism
Archer, William, 63
archive, 47, 82, 89, 238, 241–7
  archive fever, 81, 244
  queer archive, 66, 74, 85
Ariadne, 108–13, 117
Armstrong, Isobel, 58, 97, 139
Armstrong, Kit, 142–3
Arnold, Matthew, 78, 176n, 205, 215
art history, 8, 45, 93, 110, 113, 120, 247
art, 22, 40, 116, 223, 233, 245, 247
  art for art's sake, 17, 45
  autonomous art object (challenge to), 89, 92, 116, 120
  critics and philosophers of, 2, 8, 28–9, 35, 76, 89, 93–4, 101, 112–13, 135
  domestic objects vs high art, 18, 90, 124–32
  and the female spectator, 45, 89, 90–4, 99, 116, 120

267

art (cont.)
  Japanese, 14, 123-4, 126-7, 201
  life as, 3, 27, 63
  and queer selfhood, 31, 46, 94n, 126-7
  re-visions of, 31, 66, 88, 99-100
  and/as translation, 38, 100
  see also Aestheticism; ekphrasis
audience 33, 88, 127, 138, 149-50, 240-1; see also listener
Aurora Leigh (Barrett Browning), 5, 40
autonomy, 24, 30, 53-4, 74, 89, 92, 116, 120, 168
Aytoun, W. E., 40

Bacchus, 108-13, 117, 200; see also Dionysus
Bal, Mieke, 28, 30
Baudelaire, Charles, 23, 160
beauty, 68, 124, 126, 180, 188, 201, 213, 222, 228, 245
  and/as aesthetic value, 8, 17, 79, 190
  and erotics, 127, 143-4, 147, 157-8
  queer beauty, 93, 104, 149
  of women, 18, 228
Beers, Henry, 75
Bellerophôn (MF), 6, 50
belles-lettres, 242
Benjamin, Walter, 35
Bennett, Jane, 146n
Berenson, Bernard, 2, 8, 10, 12-14, 64, 97-9, 101, 112-13, 145, 193n
Bickle, Sharon, 50, 189n
Blain, Virginia, 33, 184
Blair, Kristie, 213, 215
body, 21, 56, 71, 92, 115, 133, 172-3, 205, 220-3
  disabled, 105, 212n, 216, 223-30
  in motion, 40-3
  in phenomenology, 34, 224
  while thinking/creating, 43, 89
Boer War, 202
Borgia (MF), 13, 170
boundary, 45, 82, 89, 96-7, 100, 122, 147, 175, 205, 225n, 227, 240, 242
  between Aestheticism and Decadence, 24
  gendered, 44, 77, 100, 138
  between bodies/entities, 137, 181, 224
Bourget, Paul, 79, 160, 162
boy (figure of the), 41, 99, 171n, 220n
Bradley, Katharine, 2n, 16, 19-21, 23, 25, 30, 35, 37, 40, 43, 47, 51, 59, 62, 73, 74-5, 77, 79, 89, 94, 100-1, 108, 134, 140-2, 154-6, 180-2, 185-6, 193, 197, 200, 202-6, 228-30, 233, 237, 245
  biography, 4-17
  and Greek, 6, 77
  nicknames, 1n, 5-6, 12, 14, 171
  relationship with Alfred Gérente, 5
  relationship with John Ruskin, 6
  works/first drafts attributed to, 22-3, 123-7, 129, 156-8, 208, 209n, 220-1, 227-8
  on writing, 1-2, 65, 210, 217
  see also Michael Field
bramblebough insignia, 8-9, 198, 217, 221

Bristow, Joseph, 18, 68-9, 134n, 135
Browning, Elizabeth Barrett, 16, 40, 91n
Browning, Robert, 2, 7, 8, 47, 58, 67, 74, 77, 85, 91n, 136, 150, 171n, 183, 185, 202, 217, 232
  elegiac verse for, 172, 177, 182, 192, 194
  historical subjects, 16, 68
Bullen, A.H., 133, 141
Butler, Judith, 31, 243-4
"Butterfly Bright" (MF), 160-3
Byrd, William, 135, 137-140, 166
  counterpoint, 142-3, 145, 159, 162
  Songs of Sundrie Natures, 133, 140

Callirrhoë (MF), 7, 42, 45, 48-58, 63, 66-8, 70-1, 73-4
Campion, Thomas, 133, 135, 137-9, 141, 149-53, 155-8, 165-6
cancer, 15, 209, 211, 212n, 224-5, 228; see also disease
Canute the Great (MF), 7, 48, 69-73, 76, 245
Carlyle, Thomas, 78
carpe diem, 160-1, 164
Castle, Terry, 81
Catholic, Catholicism, 14, 74, 169-71, 198-9, 207-11, 221
  pagan and, 15, 218
  poetics 213, 216
  poets, 47, 208-9, 223-4, 231
  see also Anglo-Catholicism; Christian
Catullus, 155
Cauti, Camille, 193n, 208n
Christ, 56, 128, 198, 210-11, 213-15, 218-21, 223, 225, 230-1
  Chow as, 195, 200
  Cooper as, 222, 228
  identification with, 225-9
Christian, Christianity, 172, 175, 205, 215, 225
  pagan and, 21, 25, 26, 56, 129, 164, 190-1, 192, 217-18
Circe and her lovers in a landscape (Dosso Dossi), 117-20
Clewell, Tammy, 174n, 195-6, 203, 205
closet drama, 4, 13, 15, 48, 55, 68, 75, 78, 82
  affordances of 50, 57-8, 66-7
  prefaces to 49, 51, 54-5, 57, 65, 69, 76, 141
  see also verse drama
co-authorship, 128, 184, 191, 209-10; see also collaboration
Codell, Julie, 28, 30, 55, 116n
Cohen, William A., 36, 48, 97
collaboration, 26, 170, 180, 185, 210, 234, 236, 245
  authorial persona and, 183, 242
  performed in the poem, 153-5, 182
  see also co-authorship; Michael Field
community, 39, 57, 73-4, 83, 85, 164, 192, 246
  queer, 31, 38, 66-7, 77, 162, 165
compulsory ablebodiedness, 225
compulsory heterosexuality, 39, 225
conduct books, 235

convention, 54, 67, 77, 96, 122, 149, 158, 206
　artistic, 17, 47, 98–9, 113, 115, 168, 171–2, 182, 188, 202–3, 209
　marriage, 21–3
　social, 41, 44, 137, 148, 160
conversion
　to Catholicism, 26, 169, 171, 193, 198, 199n, 201, 203, 209
　in Michael Field's works, 49, 50
Cooper, Amy, 5, 13, 15, 128, 177n
Cooper, Edith, 2, 5, 8, 18, 21–2, 24–6, 52, 54, 59, 63–4, 74, 93–4, 100, 104–5, 108, 110n. 111n, 117, 124, 150, 150n, 154, 156, 161, 177n, 180–1, 183, 185, 189, 197–8, 202, 206–7, 215, 217
　biography, 4–17
　bowel cancer, 15, 224–41
　nicknames, 1n, 6, 10, 12, 14, 171, 181n
　relationship with Berenson, 12, 12n, 64n
　works/first drafts attributed to, 7, 15, 117, 128, 133, 133n, 208–10, 227n
　see also Michael Field
Cooper, Emma, 5, 177, 179, 192–4
Cooper, James, 5, 8, 10, 13–15, 169, 185–8, 190, 192
Costelloe, Mary (later Berenson), 10, 12, 14, 193n
counterpoint, 138, 140, 142–5, 146–7, 162–3, 166
"Cowslip Gathering" (MF), 159
creativity, 23, 28, 36–7, 82
　creative process, 35, 63, 65, 92, 97, 116
　see also imagination
Culley, Margo, 239–41

Danahay, Martin, 240–1
dance, 40–3, 63, 70, 130, 133, 159–60, 180, 197, 199, 201
Darwin, Charles; Darwinism, 27, 29, 136
David Copperfield (Dickens), 243–4
death, 24, 26, 46, 69, 135–6, 138, 143, 152, 160, 166–7, 175–6
　of Browning, 150n, 182, 185
　in *Callirrhoë*, 49–50, 56, 63, 70, 74
　and Catholicism, 213, 216, 219
　Edith Cooper's impending, 224–31
　of Emma Cooper, 8, 177–80, 185
　of James Cooper, 186–92
　as liminal space, 23, 174–5
　as unknowable (*l'engrenage*), 160, 176–7, 201
　of Whym Chow, 169–70, 172, 177, 193–206
　see also mourning
Decadence, Decadent, 10, 16–20, 24, 25–6, 73, 97, 120, 126, 159–60
　ecodecadence, 25n, 135–7, 140, 146–7, 190
　style, characteristics and definition, 12, 23–4, 68, 76, 79, 164, 167, 172
　see also Aestheticism
Dedicated (MF), 15
Denisoff, Dennis, 25n, 135, 136n, 146, 166
Derrida, Jacques, 22n, 244
descriptio, 91, 107, 120, 123, 129

desire, 21–4, 52, 54, 70, 90, 104, 110–11, 115, 120, 148, 153–4, 156–7, 163, 171, 200, 223, 228, 230, 244
　for fame, 2, 12, 22, 47, 74, 76, 232, 234, 241
　for historical knowledge, 65
　homoerotic, queer, 18, 31, 47, 50, 81, 83, 116, 124, 129, 140, 158, 165, 184, 190–2, 197, 201, 205, 209, 221, 233
Dever, Carolyn, 3, 4, 12n, 172, 193, 198, 234, 242n
devotional poetry, 2, 15, 26, 39, 47, 74, 87, 120n, 130, 169, 171n, 207–31
dialectic, 30, 52, 65, 92, 94, 116, 145, 185, 190, 246
diary (journal), 3, 5, 16, 39, 42, 64n, 110, 135, 137, 174, 183, 185, 189, 205, 232–47
　affordances of, 47, 239–41
　gendered aspects of, 238, 240–1
　nineteenth-century, 236, 238
　as self-fashioning, 47, 242–3, 247
　see also Works and Days
difference, 20n, 24, 38, 116, 149, 184–5, 192, 212n, 217–18, 243, 245; *see also* paradox
Dionysus (Bacchus), 19, 25–6, 66, 89, 110, 190
　cult of (*Callirrhoë*), 49–50, 57, 70
　thyrsus and, 19–23, 25–7, 63–4, 73, 135
　Whym Chow as, 196, 200
disability, 47, 207, 209, 212, 212n, 224–31
disease, 40, 198, 212, 246; *see also* cancer; disability
disidentification, 21, 23, 26
Dolmetch, Arnold, 141
domestic object (decorative), 18, 90, 124–32
Donoghue, Emma, 4n, 13, 186
Dowden, Edward, 6
drama *see* closet drama
dramatic envoicing *see* prosopopoeia
Drury, Annamarie, 164–5
Dryope, 84

ecodecadence *see* decadence
Edelman, Lee, 81, 164n, 225n
"Effigies" (MF), 94–6, 98
ekphrasis 4, 8, 10, 30, 34, 39–40, 45–6, 88–132, 135, 145, 153, 166, 208, 220–3, 233
　affordances of, 90–101
　as haptic, 40, 45, 90, 97, 109, 110, 113, 115, 123–4
　as metalepsis, 45, 89, 98–100, 108, 110, 116, 122
　see also Sight and Song
elegy, 46, 98, 169, 178, 183, 186, 199, 203–4
　classical, 171, 173, 179n
　feminine, 171, 181
　Victorian, 172–3, 174–6, 184–5
Eliot, T.S., 1, 75–6, 203, 207, 230
Ellis, Havelock, 7, 79, 160, 162, 164, 183
embodied (embodiment), 4, 24, 50, 58, 110, 121, 146, 172, 233
　act of thinking/writing, 35, 41, 58, 130
　and pain, 47, 209, 212, 223–8

embodied (embodiment) (cont.)
  and prosody, 222–3
  phenomenological, 36, 94, 97, 100, 117, 210, 224
emotion, 23, 67, 75–6, 83–4, 107–8, 185, 187, 213, 218, 224, 229
  accurate portrayal of, 55–63, 72, 122–3, 134
  Dionysian passion, 63, 134, 152, 190
  and entanglement, 46, 137, 151
  and women, 18, 51, 58, 104, 238
  and writing/poetry, 43–4, 58, 90, 138, 155, 159
  see also feeling; mourning; thyrsus
empire, 201–2, 205; see also Orientalism
enargeia, 91, 103–4, 109, 120, 123, 129
energy (science), 160, 163–4
ennui, 25–6
entanglement, 46, 73, 136, 148, 158–61, 163–4
  eco-entanglement, 137, 146–7, 166–7, 171–2, 180
environment, 36, 46, 212
  of adaptation, revision, 32, 35, 37
  environmentalist, 136–7, 165–8
  natural environment, 135, 145–9, 158–9, 161–4, 190, 214, 224, 245
  see also nature
epic, 235, 238, 241–2
epistemology, 65, 91, 94–6, 122, 132, 135, 245, 247; see also objectivity, subjectivity
Erevelles, Nirmala, 212n, 224
eros, 4, 49–50, 53–4, 57, 82, 110, 232
erotics, 218
  homoerotics, 8, 66, 116, 140, 172, 174, 220, 222–3
  of mourning, 46, 205
Evangelista, Stefano, 18, 21n, 25, 31, 64, 80, 96
excess, 25, 68, 80, 205
experience, 27, 35, 37, 46, 82, 88, 91, 126, 155, 185, 190–2, 195, 202, 230, 235–6, 239, 243, 246
  embodied, 17, 36–7, 40–1, 154, 210, 212, 224, 228
  female/women's, 158, 233
  of grief/mourning, 173, 175–6, 188, 196
  intersubjective/entangled 38, 146, 159, 180, 225
  queer, 66, 137, 205
  see also lived experience

Faderman, Lillian, 184
Fair Rosamund (MF), 7, 58–9, 61–3, 66–8, 70–4
Fair Rosamund (Burne-Jones), 59–60
"Falling Leaves" (MF), 188
Fane, Violet, 137
faun, 42, 50, 56–7, 63, 70, 93, 160, 208
feeling, 43, 55–8, 61–2, 65, 72–3, 75–6, 78, 89, 92, 103, 110–11, 113, 120, 134, 138, 148, 204
  feeling backward, 31, 49, 65, 74, 233, 238
  feeling vs. content, 55, 63

queer structures of feeling, 31, 67, 100, 164
  see also emotion
Felski, Rita, 238
female aesthetes/aestheticism, 2, 4, 17–18, 74, 89, 93, 124
female authors, 2, 58, 76, 91, 232
feminist, 18, 31–2, 199n, 233, 245
  approaches to art, 45, 88–120
  appropriation of history, 31, 65, 74, 153
  ecofeminism, 167–8
  phenomenology, 38–40, 49, 72, 76
  protofeminist, 8, 67
  queer-feminist, 4, 18–19, 31, 47, 51, 77, 81, 85, 123–4, 209
fictional autobiography, 242–4
fidelity (adaptation theory), 32–5, 55, 165
Field, Michael
  as co-authors, 7, 26, 33, 35, 43, 54, 62, 65, 79, 117, 128, 138–9, 144–5, 153–5, 169, 181–5, 19, 210, 245
  and Decadence, 17–19, 23–6, 46, 68, 76, 79, 96, 35–6, 146–7, 160, 164, 171
  draft/unpublished poems, 111, 117–19, 122–7, 129–32, 156–7
  as female, 4, 13, 18, 21, 44–5, 50–2, 54, 58, 67, 73, 76, 81, 85, 90–1, 93–4, 96, 98–100, 104, 108, 116, 124, 149–50, 158, 171, 181, 233, 236
  and modernism, 3, 17, 19, 73–4, 91, 96–8, 127–8, 145, 203–4, 230, 233
  persona, 1n7, 21–3, 40, 51, 67n, 73, 183–4, 191, 204–5, 209–10, 215, 236, 240–1, 244
  reception, 7, 12–13, 17–18, 47. 62–3, 67–9, 71n, 74, 76–7, 85, 112–13, 139, 143, 207–8
  self-fashioning, 21, 31, 47, 85, 198, 202, 235, 239–43, 247
  Victorian characteristics of, 16, 19, 46–7, 78, 97, 121, 160, 163, 172–7, 201–2, 204–5, 212–13, 215–17, 232–3, 236, 238, 240
  WORKS (are indexed by title); see also Katharine Bradley; Edith Cooper
fin de siècle, 16, 19, 21n, 23, 76, 124, 135, 162, 230, 242
FitzGerald, Edward, 46, 134, 137, 159, 160, 165
  on energy, 161, 163
  queerness and, 164–6
Fitzgibbon, Gerald, 15
Flaubert, Gustave, 155, 242
Fletcher, Robert, 134n, 139–40, 153
flow (state of), 41, 43, 130
form, formalist, 2–4, 24, 39n, 40–5, 48, 57, 67, 232, 242
  and devotional poetry, 208, 216, 221, 230
  and diary, 236, 238–41
  and ekphrasis, 89, 92–3, 95, 97–100, 106, 121
  and elegy, 178, 182, 198, 204
  and fragment, 75–82
  see also affordance
Fortey, Emily, 15

Index 271

Foucault, Michel, 22n, 82, 232, 246
fragment, 4, 49, 81, 89, 140
  affordances of 48, 77, 79–82
  diary and, 238, 239, 245
  l'engrenage and, 39, 82
  nineteenth-century discourse and, 78–9
  Sappho and, 2, 8, 40, 45, 48, 77, 85
Fraser, Hilary, 98n, 193n, 208, 218
Freedgood, Elaine, 98–9
Freeman, Elizabeth, 31, 65n, 164n
"Fregit" (MF), 216
Freud, Sigmund, 173, 182, 193, 195–6, 202–4
Friedman, Dustin, 18, 28, 30–1, 73, 94n
Frye, Northrop, 138–9
"Fur for Mandarins" (MF), 201

Galliene, Richard, 242
Garafalo, Devin, 139
garden, garden poetry, 137, 161, 167, 188
gaze, 115, 127, 148, 157, 222
  female, 158, 224
  revisionary, 99–100
Gazzaniga, Andrea, 161n
Genette, Gérard, 98
genre, 98, 110n, 134n, 135, 138, 208, 211, 232, 238–42
Gérente, Alfred, 5
Gilbert, Sandra, 171
"Good Friday" (MF), 191
Gray, F. Elizabeth, 208, 212
Gray, John (Dorian), 12, 14, 16n, 120, 210, 225
Gray, John Miller, 7, 100, 133, 141–2
Greece (ancient), 16, 23, 25, 49, 50, 83, 104
  drama of, 58, 62, 75–6
Greek (women reading), 5–7, 77–9, 98n, 155
grief *see* mourning
Grimani breviary, 120n
Gubar, Susan, 3

Hagstrum, Jean, 90
Halberstam, Jack, 31, 164n, 165, 193, 225n
haptic, 40, 45, 97, 198
  ekphrasis, 90, 109–10, 113n, 115, 123–4
Hardy, Thomas, 26, 203
Harrington, Emily, 138
Heffernan, James, 90, 97, 104
Hegel, 4, 28–31, 33–4, 36, 49, 51, 55, 58, 73–4, 76, 96, 220, 233
Helsinger, Elizabeth, 139
Hensley, Nathan K., 44, 93, 136
Heraclitus, 29, 33–4, 36, 51, 133, 167
Hesoid, 235–6, 241–2
heteronormativity, 24n, 41, 68, 90, 112, 148, 158, 164, 174, 201, 233
Hewitt, Martin, 240
history
  and adaptation theory, 31–4
  aesthetic historicism, 65, 76–7, 82, 85
  Field's approach to revisions of, 48–76
  philosophies of, 28–31, 36–7, 51–74, 76
  presentism, 3, 39, 64, 66
  see also anachronism; looking backward

Hollander, John, 90
Holmes, Martha Stoddard, 224
"Holy Cross" (MF), 226–8
homoerotically-inclined, 2, 4, 17–18, 30, 46, 65, 93, 123, 127, 162, 172, 220–1, 232–3, 242; *see also* queer
homoeroticism; 8, 47, 49–50, 53, 66–7, 71, 77, 83, 99, 116, 140, 153, 174, 181, 190, 192, 204, 209, 223, 225–6, 230; *see also* queer desire
hope, 25, 76, 85, 91, 174, 232, 241, 246
  queer hope, 31, 206, 233
Hopkins, G.M., 142n, 208, 213
Horne, Herbert, 8, 141
"Hour of Need" (MF), 228
Howitt, Mary, 137
Hudson, Benjamin, 165
Huffer, Lynne, 31, 81n, 82, 246
Hughes, Linda K., 24, 28, 30, 55, 116n
human
  and animal, 41, 84, 116, 147–8, 162
  and nature, 136, 140, 146, 148–9, 167–8, 188, 213
  see also non-human
Hutcheon, Linda, 27, 32, 165
hyper-remembering, 195–6

"I want you, Little Love, not from the skies" (MF), 196
identity, 30, 136, 139, 185, 202, 205–6, 217, 218, 241, 242–3; *see also* subject formation
"Image and Superscription" (MF), 130–2
Image, Selwyn, 8, 19–20
imaginary portrait, 121
imagination, 65, 76, 88–9, 130–2, 245; *see also* creativity
impression (Pater), 17, 23, 25, 37, 46, 63, 92, 104, 107, 145, 147, 149, 162, 164, 192, 204, 236
"In the moony brake" (MF), 146
Independent Theatre, 12
influence, 19, 57, 116, 163, 225, 233, 240–1
  on Michael Field, 3, 5, 8, 15, 62, 68, 77, 79, 85, 120, 133, 135, 139, 142, 144–5, 150, 155, 160–1, 166
inspiration, 2, 22, 39, 50, 56–7, 74, 78, 127, 186, 211, 221–2
  Bacchic library, 66, 154
  for ekphrasis, 41, 93, 120, 128
  of nature, 147, 161, 180, 218
  of philosophy, 28, 89
  of Sappho, 77, 80, 85
  for *Underneath the Bough*, 12, 46, 143
interdependent, interdependence
  contrapuntal, 142, 144–5
  for Merleau-Ponty, 35, 244
  in nineteenth-century ecological understanding, 136, 146–7
intersubjectivity, intersubjective knowledge, 28, 30, 33, 38, 55, 191, 224
  species intersubjectivity, 135, 159
  see also entanglement; merging

intertextuality, 32–3, 100, 184, 218
"Invocation" (MF), 159
"Irises" (MF), 144–5
"It was deep April" (MF), 22–3, 192, 215

Jalland, Patricia, 174n, 175
Jane Eyre (C. Bronte), 225, 243
jewelry 13, 90, 123–7, 189, 230
Joseph, Gerhard, 174n, 185n
journal *see* diary
Jowett, Benjamin, 29
Jude the Obscure (Hardy), 26

Kafer, Alison, 212n, 225, 229
Keats, John, 10, 66, 93
Keble, John, 212–13, 215–16, 221
Kersh, Sarah, 172, 208n
Kessler, Jeffrey, 121
Khayyám, Omar, 12, 46, 134–9, 159–60, 162–3, 164–6
"King Apollo" (MF), 156–8
King, Joshua, 213n
knowing *see* epistemology
Krieger, Murray, 91, 116

l'engrenage, 39–40, 45, 49, 138, 223, 240, 245
  eco-entanglement as, 137
  and ekphrasis, 89, 94, 100
  and death, 177, 201
  and the fragment, 82
  and history, 57, 73, 141, 151, 165, 229
  Merleau-Ponty's use of, 35–8
  see also unknown; unutterable
L'Indifferent (Watteau), 141
"L'Indifferent" (MF), 40–3, 130
La Gioconda (daVinci), 2, 93, 120
Laird, Holly, 14n, 234n, 245
language, 68, 71, 91, 113, 151, 205, 215, 230, 243
  archaic, 46, 76, 137, 144
  experiments with, 40–1, 68
  and sense experience, 36–7, 41
  see also translation
Leda, 84–5, 113–16
Lee, Vernon (Violet Paget), 8, 121, 166
Leigh, Arran, 6, 16, 50n
Leigh, Isla, 6, 16, 50n
Leighton, Angela, 234n
Leitch, Thomas, 31–2
Lejeune, Phillipe, 243
Leppington, Dora, 62
lesbian *see* homoerotically-inclined
lesbian trinitarianism, 172, 221n
Levine, Caroline, 43–4, 91
Lewes, G.H., 28–9
life writing *see* autobiography; diary
lived experience, 34–5, 37–8, 65, 73, 88–9, 94, 97, 117, 132, 158–9, 186, 212n, 243
  of dramatic characters/poetic speaker, 61, 69, 72, 77, 144, 150, 152
  see also experience
Lockerd, Martin, 230
Loizeaux, Elizabeth, 91, 93, 96, 110n, 127

Long Ago (MF), 8, 86, 89, 93, 108, 114, 138, 153, 155
  fragment, 4, 40, 45, 48, 77, 80–2, 85
  theme of transformation, 82–5
looking backward, 2, 48, 66, 232; *see also* history
Love, Heather, 31, 65–6, 233, 244
"Loved confessionals there are" (MF), 196
Lucretius, 163
lyric, 12, 46, 80, 98n, 99, 133–68, 184–5, 208

McNabb, Vincent, 15, 128, 211
McRuer, Robert, 209n, 225
maenad, 25, 50, 51, 93
  Bradley and Cooper as, 12n, 16, 21, 74
  in *Callirrhoë*, 49, 52–3, 56, 63, 66, 68, 70
Mahoney, Kristin, 162, 165, 201n
Manuwald, Gesine, 153
marriage, 62, 83, 108, 110–13
  to Christ, 103, 230
  queer, 21–3, 71, 159, 189n
Marriage of Bacchus and Ariadne (Tintoretto), 108, 110
Marshall, Mary Paley, 5
Martin, Meredith, 44, 149
Mary Magdalene, 113, 211
Mary, Queen of Scots, 2, 8, 51, 65, 141
Mary, Virgin, 210–11, 228–9
Matthews, Brander, 75
Maxwell, Catherine, 95
medieval, medievalism, 16, 52, 59, 133
Medrano, Leire, 208n, 213n
memory, 69, 71, 122, 165, 180; *see also* mourning
Meredith, George, 7
merging, 146, 181, 183–4, 190, 197; *see also* entanglement; tropes of likeness
Merleau-Ponty, Maurice, 34–8, 49, 57, 90, 94, 97, 176, 224, 244; *see also* l'engrenage
metalepsis, metaleptic leap, 45, 89, 98–100, 108, 110, 116, 122
meter, 19, 44, 98, 110, 122, 144–5, 154, 215–17
  and queer ambiguity, 47, 209, 221–3
metonym, 19, 21n, 33, 68, 81, 172
Meynell, Alice, 208–9
"Mid-Age" (MF), 160
Mill, J.S., 58, 138–9, 143, 166
Miller, Elizabeth Carolyn, 136
Mitchell, Rebecca, 204
Mitchell, W. J. T., 90, 91n
modern, modernity, 1–3, 48, 69, 73–5, 93, 137, 143–4, 164, 166, 223, 232
modernism, modernist, 17, 16, 46–7, 73–4, 90–1, 97–8, 132, 145, 203–4, 230, 233–4
Moffat, Mary Jane, 238
Moine, Fabienne, 137, 161n
Moon, Michael, 204–5
Moore, George, 10, 26
Moore, Marianne, 96
Moore, Marie Sturge, 14, 193n
Moore, Thomas Sturge, 14, 16, 233
Morris, William, 6, 8

motion, movement, 29, 41–3, 107, 109, 112, 115, 126, 143, 145, 179, 189, 221
Moulton, Louise Chandler, 10
mourning, 14, 46–7 83, 169–206, 238; see also elegy
Muñoz, José Esteban, 21n, 31, 165, 206, 233
museum label, 101, 113, 116
music, 133, 141–9; 150, 154–5, 160, 163; see also counterpoint; song
Musical Antiquarian Society, 140
'My loved one is away from me" (MF), 197
Mystic Trees, 15, 47, 120n, 128, 130, 207–31
 companion poems in *Poems of Adoration*, 227

Narcissus at the Fountain (Altobello Meloni), 101–2; see also Saint Katharine of Alexandria
nature, 19, 29, 46, 59, 61–2, 72, 115, 120, 135–8, 145–9, 159–68, 180–1, 186–90, 205, 211–16
 and women, 18, 59–61, 137
 see also entanglement; environment
Nesbitt, Edith, 137
Nietzsche, Friedrich, 21n, 28, 30, 33–4, 36–7, 51, 63–4, 74, 89
"No beauty born of pride my lady hath" (MF), 143–4, 147, 153
non-human, 36, 136, 139, 146, 148, 159, 161–3, 167–8; see also human
norm, 81, 88, 147, 171, 173, 192, 203, 243
 anti-heteronormative, 30, 90, 201, 204, 206, 223
 heteronormative, 24n, 41, 46, 68, 112, 148, 158, 164, 174, 233
 normate, 79n, 212n, 225n, 226
Nussbaum, Felicity, 240

"O Lovely Host" (MF), 213–14
objectivity, 27, 46, 58, 65–6, 76, 89, 92–9, 103–8, 120–8, 132, 137, 145, 159, 165–6, 195, 224, 245; see also epistemology; reliable narrator
Olverson, T. D., 25, 50, 63, 70
"On a portrait by Tintoret" (MF), 121–2
"On Dosso Dossi's Circe" (MF), 117–20
Orientalism, 165, 200–2, 204–5
orientation, 55, 61, 73, 158, 167, 212, 229–30, 233
 phenomenological, 35, 38–40, 88, 224
 queer-feminist, 4, 45, 49, 67, 72, 76, 81, 86, 94, 149, 158, 164, 177, 198, 204: toward art object, 89, 95, 100–27, 128–9
original (context of revision), 32–5, 38, 40, 100–1, 113, 115n, 117
Other, Otherness, 38, 183, 200–1, 245
"Others may drag at memory's fetter" (MF), 182–3, 187, 196
"Out of the East" (MF), 200
Ovid, 157

pagan, 135–7, 146, 156, 159, 166, 169, 172, 177, 180
 Christian and, 15, 21, 25–6, 56, 129, 164, 190–1, 217–18
pain, 47, 95, 174, 187, 204
 Edith Cooper's cancer, 15–16, 209–12, 224, 226, 228–30
 of heterosexual love, 10, 13, 53, 83, 108–12, 152–3
 of modernity, 70, 74
 and spiritual growth, 40, 105–6, 217, 220, 223, 226–7
palimpsest, 32–3, 159, 247
paradox, 3, 37, 39, 46, 71, 170, 177, 217–20, 227, 230
 aesthetic, 70, 105–6, 129, 175–6, 182–6, 190, 192, 196, 223, 232
 temporal, 2, 48, 106, 143
paragonal, *paragone*, 89–91
Parker, Sarah, 3, 73, 96
Pater, Walter, 1, 4, 6, 10, 18, 50, 98, 121, 131, 141, 235
 aesthetics, Paterian, 17, 25, 27, 30, 37, 63, 191–2, 204, 233
 Decadent ecopaganism and, 135, 166
 on Hegel, 28–30, 33–5, 49, 51, 55, 76
 queerness and, 65–7, 99, 104
Patmore, Coventry, 175, 213
patriarchy (critique of), 18, 68, 233
Pausanias, 52–7
Pegasus pendant (Ricketts), 124–6
Pen drawing of Leda (da Vinci), 113–16
Pennington, Heidi, 243–4
perception, 35–7, 95n, 97, 99, 166, 168, 212
 subjective nature of, 65, 122, 127
 see also Merleau-Ponty
performativity, 39, 43, 198, 234
perspective (point of view), 27, 37–8, 72–3, 94, 143, 145, 148–9, 182, 190, 228, 243n
 gendered, 32, 45, 54, 62, 88, 93, 96, 99, 104, 111, 120, 153, 199
 see also subjective
phenomenology, 24, 34–8, 43, 49, 55, 57, 73, 77, 82, 90, 99, 137, 176, 185, 192, 195, 224, 233
 feminist and queer, 38–40, 88n
 see also Sara Ahmed, Maurice Merleau-Ponty
philosophy, 6, 18, 41, 95, 141, 176, 182, 214, 235
 carpe diem, 160–1, 164
 Dionysian, 4, 25, 27, 30, 37, 49, 63–6, 73, 89, 160, 171, 191, 204, 232
 of mourning, 182–7, 192
 phenomenological method, 34–40
 Spinozan, 78–9
 of working with historical subjects 28–31, 51–74, 76
photograph/photography, 90, 108n, 124, 128–9
picture-poem *see* ekphrasis
pleasure, 17, 50–1, 92, 115, 126, 144, 154–5, 157, 159, 171, 204
Plumwood, Val, 133, 167–8
poiein, 19, 44, 51, 76, 82, 89, 158, 247

Poems of Adoration, 15, 47, 120n, 207–31
  poems paired with *Mystic Trees*, 227n
poetess, 18, 51, 58, 104, 149–50
poetics, 17, 19
  decadent, 17–27
  devotional, 209, 211–13, 216, 223
  ecopoetics, 145–9, 158–61, 166–8, 177–80, 186–92
  of elegy, 171
  and *l'engrenage*, 35–40, 45, 49, 77, 205
  queer, 24, 81, 88, 94, 228
  and transformation, 27, 33, 34–5, 39–40, 44, 51, 64, 82, 85, 101–22, 156–9
poetry, 24, 51, 58, 67–8, 78, 90, 98, 113, 138, 150, 184, 220, 242
  modernist poetry, 17, 19, 46–7, 90–1, 97–8, 203, 230
  poems about poetry, 33, 85, 141–2, 144n, 147, 153–5, 158, 182, 218, 247
  Victorian poetry, 16–17, 19, 24, 58, 79, 104, 138, 212–13, 217
  see also devotional poetry; ekphrasis; elegy; lyric; verse drama
point of view *see* perspective
"Pondering" (MF), 228–9
Portrait of Composer Adrian Willaert at the Spinet (Tintoretto), 121–2
"Possession" (MF), 187
possibility, 65, 81, 184, 238
  queer, 31, 116, 233, 245
postmodern, 27, 31, 33
presence, 80, 241
  in lyric, 138–45
  of the dead, 170, 178–86, 192, 195, 199
  see also absence
presentism, perverse presentism, 3, 49, 64, 66
Prins, Yopie, 18n, 50, 58n, 77n, 78, 84n, 98n, 138, 184, 210n
progress narrative, 173, 186, 204
Propertius, 155, 157–8
prosody, 19
prosopopoeia, 91, 95–6, 104, 120–1
pseudonym, 6

queer
  queer desire, 18, 31, 47, 50, 81, 83, 116, 124, 129, 140, 158, 165, 184, 190–2, 197, 201, 205, 209, 221, 233; *see also* homoerotically-inclined
  queer ecology, 3, 135–7, 146–7, 166–7, 190
  queer failure, 66, 165, 194
  queer-feminist, 4, 31–2, 47, 69, 72–4, 76–8, 81, 85, 88–9, 93–4, 100, 116, 135, 153, 232, 245
  queer hope, 31, 206, 233
  queer poetics, 24, 24n
  queer reading, 116, 165
  queer subjectivity, 3, 17–18, 37–8, 89, 165, 224
  queer temporality, 3, 31, 47, 49, 164, 209, 223

Raffalovich, Marc André, 7, 67
Ramazani, John, 203
reader, 43, 49, 55, 57, 61, 99, 110, 242
  author/text's effect upon, 43, 54, 66–7, 72, 93–4, 104, 106, 126, 208
  future, 47, 232, 244–5
  role in identity creation, 243–7
  and understanding the author, 38, 41–2
referent, 48, 108
  ekphrastic, 88–9, 91–2, 99–101, 113, 117, 123n, 130, 166
reliable narrator, 236, 243, 244
religion, 29, 55, 176, 206, 223; *see also* Catholic; Christian; pagan
Renaissance, 16, 50, 97, 158, 166
  art, 94–6, 101–22
  music, 12, 46, 133, 140–3, 150
  Pater's writings about, 17, 29–30, 63, 191, 235
  see also archaism
renunciation, 105, 204
repetition, 32, 38, 83, 178, 188, 192, 217
replication, 25, 27–9, 32, 55, 116; *see also* adaptation
representational friction, 100–1, 104, 106–8, 112–13
reproductive futurism, 136, 164
"Requiescat" (MF), 194
Rich, Adrienne, 31, 100
Richardson, LeeAnne, 39n, 134n, 208n
Ricketts, Charles, 15, 124–5, 129–32, 203, 207–8, 230–1
  and Shannon, Charles, 10, 12, 14, 16, 18, 123n, 193
ritual, 15, 25, 46, 53, 174, 180–2, 186, 189–92, 201, 205, 221, 239
Robinson, A. Mary F., 7, 74, 137
Roden, Frederick, 171n, 172, 193, 199, 201, 208n, 221n
role model, 66, 88, 137, 245
Romantic, 50, 150, 166, 186
Ross, Robert, 68
Rossetti, Christina, 177n, 205, 208, 213
Rossetti, D. G., 6, 91, 136, 159, 176
Rossetti, W. M., 8
Rottingdean, 14, 205–6
Rubáiyát of Omar Khayyám (FitzGerald), 46, 134, 159–66
Rudy, Jason, 110
Ruskin, John, 6, 59, 98, 122n, 166
Ryan, John, 15

Sacks, Peter, 171, 173–4, 179n
sacrifice, 49–50, 53–7, 108, 172, 190, 216–17, 220
"Saint Katharine of Alexandria" (MF), 101–8
Sanders, Julie, 32–4
Sappho 2, 8, 30, 40, 45, 48, 76–87, 155, 158, 245
Saville, Julia, 18, 51, 58n, 104, 115n
"Say if a gallant rose my bower doth scale" (MF), 147–8
Schenck, Celeste, 171, 181

Schlegel, Karl Wilhelm, 58
sculpture, 13–14, 79n, 95, 128
self, 30, 36, 51, 65, 70, 94, 97, 104, 135, 202–5, 217, 221
  autonomy, 24, 30, 53–4, 74, 108, 168
  as a fiction, 242–7
  and other, 43, 136, 138, 166, 192
  self-fashioning, 18n, 23, 31, 36, 47, 73, 77, 82, 115, 176, 192, 218, 233, 235–47
  see also subjective; subjectivity
Semele, 190
sensation, 23–5, 36, 41, 92, 113, 151, 216
sexism, 245
sexology, 213
Shakespeare, William, 49, 62, 66–7, 75, 88–9, 92, 127, 134, 150n, 172, 177, 180–1
Shannon, Charles see Ricketts, Charles
sight see vision
Sight and Song (MF), 4, 8–10, 30, 34, 34n, 40–1, 45–6, 83n, 89–90, 92–4, 101–17, 120, 220
silence, 119–20, 126, 139, 146, 179–80, 203, 218
  silenced voices, 91, 96
"Sleeping together, sleep" (MF), 197–200
Smith, Logan Pearsall, 74
Snodgrass, Chris, 183, 193n
song, songbook, 46, 77, 110, 112, 133, 139–50, 153–63, 217–18, 221–2; see also lyric
sonnet, 98, 101, 103, 106–8, 114–15, 122–4, 129, 159, 172, 186, 188–9, 214
source text, 32, 34, 50, 52, 155, 157–8; see also referent
space, 85, 109, 164, 174, 214–15
  between binaries, 159, 161, 175, 181
  orientation in, 38–9, 224
  and time, 37, 88, 90, 96, 175–9, 184, 205
spectator, 41, 92, 94, 97, 103–4, 107–8, 115, 126–7, 130, 132, 163
  female, 45, 116
  objective vs subjective spectatorship, 92
  queer, 94, 116–17, 123, 156
  universal, 89, 120, 158
  see also audience
Spencer, Herbert, 8
Spinoza, Baruch, 78–9, 181
St. Catherine of Alexandria (da Sesto), 101
Stedman, Edward, 16
Stein, Gertrude, 96
Stephania (MF), 10, 12, 26n
Stetz, Margaret, 3, 84n, 242
Stolte, Tyson, 163
"Stream and Pool" (MF), 218
Sturgeon, Mary, 4n, 6, 184
subject formation, 94, 243–4; see also identity
subjective, subjectivity, 29, 36, 46, 65–6, 72, 76, 145, 165–7, 184, 197, 210, 224, 238, 245, 247
  and Aestheticism, 17, 37
  and drama, 58
  looking at art, 89, 92–6, 99, 103–7, 120–2, 128

queer, 17–18, 135, 137, 158–9
  see also epistemology; intersubjectivity; objectivity
"Suggested by a Picture" (MF), 128–9
Swannick, Anna, 7
Swinburne, Algernon Charles, 6–7, 25, 59, 67, 134, 177n
symbiosis, 162; see also entanglement; merging
Symonds, J.A., 7, 18, 77, 122n, 150
Symons, Arthur, 7, 23–4
synaesthesia, 33, 96, 110, 120, 227
synecdoche, 77, 81, 85

teleology, teleological, 29, 164–5, 174
temporal, 38, 192
  paradox, 3, 106, 175–6
  queer temporality, 3, 24n, 31, 47, 49, 148, 164–5, 209, 223
  see also time
Tennyson, Lord Alfred, 2, 16, 59, 134, 139
  In Memoriam, 169, 174
Thain, Marion, 3–6, 70, 80, 91n, 106, 150, 158, 171, 176, 183–5, 193n, 204, 208, 218, 234n
"The Captain Jewel" (MF), 227–8
The Father's Tragedy (MF), 7, 55, 63, 67
"The Forest" (MF), 188
"The Heavenly Love" (MF), 189
The Longer Allegiance (MF), 15, 46, 172, 177, 186–93
"The Marriage of Bacchus and Ariadne" (MF), 108–13
The New Minnesinger (MF), 6
"The Poet" (MF), 215
The Question of Memory (MF), 12–13
"The salt cellar sonnet" (MF), 129
"The Torrent" (MF), 186–9
The Tragic Mary (MF), 8, 10, 65, 68, 140–1
The Well of Loneliness (Hall), 116
The Yellow Book, 23, 26
thermodynamics, 163
Theseus, 108, 111–12
Thomas, Kate, 8n, 106n, 146, 148, 217n, 223, 225n
"Thou Comest Down to Die" (MF), 213, 218
thyrsus, 19–23, 25–7, 63–4, 73, 135, 198, 217
time, 37, 39, 43, 65n, 66, 70, 136, 138, 164, 190, 235, 239–40, 246
  crip, 223, 225, 229
  and mourning, 173–8, 192, 205
  queer, 31, 160, 164, 223, 225n
  and space, 88, 90, 96–8, 100, 106n, 181
  see also temporality
Tiresias, 84, 245
"To Pearls on a Net" (MF), 127
"To the field where now the forests fail" (MF), 147
Tolstoy, Leo, 242
Tomson, Graham R. (Rosamund Marriott Watson), 24, 96, 104n
Tractarian, 175, 21, 212–13
  analogy, 212–15, 217, 223
  reserve, 212–13, 222, 227

Index   275

tragedy, 13, 26, 45, 48, 64–5, 69
transcorporeality, 146n, 167, 181
transformation
  of energy, 163
  personal, 30, 61
  poiesis 76, 158
  theme in *Long Ago*, 48, 77, 82–7, 89
translation, 27, 63n, 78, 134, 142, 160, 164–5
  adaptation and, 33–5
  ekphrasis and, 41, 98, 100, 112, 120
  and *l'engrenage*, 37–8, 82
  of Sappho, 8, 77
  by women, 7, 78
traveling concept, 28, 30, 55
Treby, Ivor, 16, 117, 128, 130n, 191n, 209n
trinity, 171–2, 205, 214, 230
"Trinity" (MF), 197–8
tropes of likeness, 181, 183; *see also* merging
Tucker, Herbert, 174n, 185n, 223
"Turning Homeward" (MF), 188
type, 29–30, 39

Underneath the Bough (MF), 12, 19–20, 22, 25, 42, 46, 114n, 133–68, 177, 179–83, 192, 195, 218
unity, 37, 79–82, 91, 181, 184–5, 190, 217
"Unity" (MF), 190–1, 199
universal, universalist, 29, 30, 37, 46, 49, 73, 135, 137, 155, 158, 161, 166, 190
  spectator, 89, 92–3, 116, 120, 158
unknown; 35, 38–9, 45, 47, 49, 57, 73, 77, 82, 85, 87, 89, 94, 100, 137, 151, 177, 201, 209, 223, 240, 244–5, 247; *see also l'engrenage*; unutterable
untimeliness 30, 34, 37
unutterable 4, 58, 132 233; *see also l'engrenage*; unknown

Vadillo, Ana Parejo 3, 34n, 40, 45, 50, 63, 68, 74, 78, 79n
Vanita, Ruth, 171, 181, 201, 208n, 228
Veneto, Bartolomeo, *St. Catherine of Alexandria*, 101–2
Venus, 92–3, 108–12, 116, 228
Venus and Mars (Botticelli), 92
Verlaine, Paul, 23–4, 142, 155, 207
verse drama; 7, 12–13, 45, 48–9, 58, 63, 70, 74, 170
  T. S. Eliot on, 75–6
  Michael Field's theories of, 51–2, 57, 62, 65, 73
  see also closet drama
verse *see* poetry

Vicinus, Martha, 12n, 171n, 220n
violence, 45, 48, 66, 70, 104, 115
vision (imagination), 27, 35, 65, 68, 110–11, 141, 229, 233
  future vision, 31, 165, 206, 233–4, 147
vision (sight), 41, 90, 92, 96–7, 99–100, 109, 116, 145, 147, 209, 227
vital materialism, 146n, 167

Ward, A. W., 8
Webster, Augusta, 139, 143, 149, 223
Westrup, J. A., 140
Wharton, H. T., 8, 77
"What is the other name of Love" (MF), 196
Wheeler, Michael, 174n, 175, 186
"White Passion Flower" (MF), 218–20
Whym Chow, 2n, 14–15, 46, 81n, 116, 169–72, 177, 190, 193–206
Whym Chow, Flame of Love (MF), 15, 46, 193–206, 208n
Whymper, Edward, 13–14
Wild Honey from Various Thyme (MF), 15, 33, 46, 121, 169, 172, 176, 186–93, 247
Wilde, Oscar, 10, 18, 26, 48, 68–9, 116, 121, 205, 240, 242
Wilkerson, Abby, 209n, 225
William Rufus (MF), 7, 51, 54–5, 57, 63
Williams, Carolyn, 29, 65
Wilson, Cheryl, 3, 105
Winckelmann, Johann Joachim, 29, 96
Woolf, Virginia, 246
Wordsworth, William, 61, 135n, 150
Works and Days (Hesiod), 236, 241
Works and Days (MF), 5, 12, 15–16, 47, 133, 140, 150, 198, 225–6
  gallery notes, 92–4, 105, 110
  on paired poems, 227, 227n, 232–47
  unpublished drafts, 111–12, 117–19, 123–7, 129–31
World War I, 16, 203
writing
  act of (process of), 12, 35, 43, 63, 73, 140–1, 155, 192, 239–41
  experiments with, 15, 39–40, 44, 82, 91, 172, 233
  and self-formation, 47, 98, 174, 184–6, 192, 211, 213, 238, 241–2, 245–7
  women, 4, 17, 96, 127, 137

Yeats, W. B., 14

Zeus, 25, 84, 113, 115–16, 235
Zola, Émile, 23

EU representative:
Easy Access System Europe
Mustamäe tee 50, 10621 Tallinn, Estonia
Gpsr.requests@easproject.com

www.ingramcontent.com/pod-product-compliance
Lightning Source LLC
Chambersburg PA
CBHW050210240426
43671CB00013B/2282